For Alan

Shakespeare on the Radio

Shakespeare on the Radio

A Century of BBC Plays

Andrea Smith

EDINBURGH
University Press

Edinburgh University Press is one of the leading university presses in the UK. We publish academic books and journals in our selected subject areas across the humanities and social sciences, combining cutting-edge scholarship with high editorial and production values to produce academic works of lasting importance. For more information visit our website: edinburghuniversitypress.com

Edinburgh University Press Ltd
13 Infirmary Street
Edinburgh EH1 1LT

Typeset in 11/13pt Adobe Sabon by
Cheshire Typesetting Ltd, Cuddington, Cheshire

A CIP record for this book is available from the British Library

ISBN 978 1 3995 4726 0 (hardback)
ISBN 978 1 3995 4728 4 (paperback)
ISBN 978 1 3995 4729 1 (webready PDF)
ISBN 978 1 3995 4727 7 (epub)

Contents

Appendix : Shakespeare Plays on BBC Radio
https://edinburghuniversitypress.com/book-shakespeare-on-
the-radio.html

Figures

Acknowledgements

I have had a long-held love of both Shakespeare and radio drama, but it was my PhD at the University of East Anglia that enabled me to bring these two things together. Matthew Woodcock was instrumental in shaping my research from a very early stage as well as playing a key role in supervising the first half of my doctoral studies. I would also like to thank his fellow supervisors Richard Hand and Sophie Butler, particularly for coping so well with the difficulties of working through a screen rather than in person during Covid. In addition, I am grateful for the support of the CHASE Doctoral Training Partnership during my PhD.

This research could not have been carried out without the support of the BBC, particularly Mark Macey, who arranged the digitisation of archive material that had not previously been converted as well as making both the plays discussed and other audio readily available. His colleagues at the BBC Written Archives Centre also helped me delve through scores of pages of microfiche. Similarly, the Shakespeare Collection team at the Library of Birmingham were hugely supportive, although possibly a little surprised by my over-excitement at seeing dozens of bound copies of early radio scripts. The Box of Broadcasts website, hosted by Learning on Screen, has also been an invaluable repository of audio.

Several past and present BBC producers have given up their time to discuss their work for my research, which has been greatly appreciated. In particular, Jeremy Mortimer and Emma Harding have not only been kind enough to help me on more than one occasion but have also championed my research. Alison Hindell, Kate Rowland, Roger Elsgood, Gaynor Macfarlane and Clive Brill all spoke to me via Zoom, while Martin Jenkins and Nigel Bryant corresponded via email. Sound designer David Thomas and composers Ilona Sekacz, Vic Gammon and Timothy X Atack were also kind enough to share information about their working processes and memories of productions. Sadly, during the course of my research, two influential producers died. I was lucky enough to talk to John Tydeman but unfortunately not to Marc Beeby. Marc in particular has received little recognition for his work; I hope this book goes a small way towards rectifying that.

My students at the University of Suffolk are a constant source of inspiration. Their ability to come up with the trickiest of questions always pushes me to think more deeply. My colleagues, both within the English department and outside, have been wonderfully supportive. In addition, the British Shakespeare Association has been a great source of both academic wisdom and friendship. I'd also like to thank Tim Crook for his unwavering belief that this book was more than worthy of publication.

Finally, the team at Edinburgh University Press. As a first-time author, I've had a lot of questions and queries, but they've always been patient, helpful and encouraging. In particular I'd like to thank Fiona Conn, Cathy Falconer, Heather Ramsay and Carla Hepburn, but most of all Emily Sharp and Elizabeth Fraser, who've shepherded this book from idea to completion. I am extremely grateful for their enthusiasm and support.

Glossary of Broadcasting Terms

¼-INCH TAPE   For many years this was the primary recording method. The tape itself was not unlike that found in a domestic audio cassette, but on larger, open reels. It could be edited by making a diagonal cut with a razor blade and, after the portion to be removed was taken out, the two ends were stuck back together with specialist tape.

ACOUSTIC   Characteristic sound of a space, e.g. large hall, outside, confined space, etc.

ACTUALITY   Sounds that are genuinely produced, e.g. recording the sound of birdsong on location. Also used to describe clips in news bulletins from interviews or news conferences. 'Fake' actuality such as this is occasionally used in Shakespeare productions when recreating news bulletins.

BINAURAL   A form of stereo recording that gives a spatial effect when listened to on headphones. In most cases, a dummy head with a microphone in each ear is used to record sound in a way that mimics how we hear. When reproduced, it should give the listener the sense of being in the same position as the original head. Also referred to by the German name *Kunstkopf*, literally meaning 'artificial head'.

CLOSE MIC   Speaking very close to the microphone, creating a more intimate effect.

DAB   Digital Audio Broadcasting, an interference-free system without hiss, crackle, fading or station overlap, unlike AM or FM radio, giving a clear, high-quality sound. DAB can also transmit text with the audio signal, which can be read on a small screen on the receiving radio.

DISTORT	Deliberate distortion of a sound (usually a voice) for effect, e.g. to simulate a phone call.
DRAMATIC CONTROL PANEL	The first form of MIXING DESK. In either case it is a desk or console that enables a producer or studio manager to combine all the sources being used in the production from a variety of studios and/or microphones.
DUBBING	Copying audio from one source to another.
EDITING/ CUTTING	Generally used to refer to the cutting/mixing of audio, rather than the cutting of the text. For analogue editing, see ¼-INCH TAPE. For digital editing, see MULTI-TRACK.
EDITOR	Usually refers to an audio editor, rather than a production editor or an editor of the text. Similarly, the EDIT usually refers to the audio edit of the production, rather than the textual one.
FADING	Either bringing audio up to full level from nothing, or vice versa (fading in or fading out). CROSS FADING is the mixing between fading one piece of audio out and fading another in.
FM	Frequency Modulation. Associated with VHF, a method of transmission enabling stereo broadcasts and suffering from less interference than MEDIUM WAVE.
FX	Abbreviation for 'sound effects'. See also SPOT EFFECTS.
GRAMS	Short for 'Gramophone' to indicate pre-recorded music in a script. Continued to be used into the twenty-first century, even after all music was on CD or in digital formats.
LEVEL	A synonym for volume. Audio editors will talk about the 'level' of a piece of audio, rather than how loud or quiet it is. The levels from different outputs (microphones, recordings, etc.) are controlled and combined by a MIXING DESK.
MEDIUM WAVE	Mono radio transmission which may suffer from the intrusion of other stations, especially at night.

MIXING

Combining sounds (usually voice, effects, music). Originally via the use of the DRAMATIC CONTROL PANEL, which used a series of knobs for different sources. This progressed to a MIXING DESK with a series of faders, and in the twenty-first century mixing is also carried out through digital editing; see MULTI-TRACK.

MULTI-TRACK

Digital editing software enabling an audio editor to mix multiple audio feeds by displaying them as separate tracks and adjusting their levels as required.

MUSIC LINK

A short burst of music between scenes to signify the end of one and the start of another. Often used to signal a shift in mood, location or time.

NOISY

Used to refer to old recordings where there is extraneous sound due to the recording method (e.g. tape hiss or crackles on a worn disc).

OFF MIC

Speaking outside a microphone's most sensitive area of pick-up, but still audible. Often used to suggest distance or, by moving from off-mic to on-mic, to suggest movement towards the listener.

OVERMODU-
LATION/
OVERMODDED

Where the sound source is louder than that with which the recording device can cope, leading to a distinctive form of distortion.

PLAYOUT

The action of playing audio (via a control desk or other system) to a transmitter.

PRODUCER/
DIRECTOR

Usually one and the same person in radio, the terms are often interchangeable. Generally 'producer' is the preferred term. In the case of Shakespeare's plays, the producer/director is also frequently the textual editor. Occasionally, especially in more recent productions, there will be a separate director and producer, but this is rare.

QUAD-
RAPHONY/
QUAD

Forerunner of surround sound, a method of audio recording and reproduction using four channels (four speakers receiving different sounds) covering front and rear, left and right, creating the effect of three-dimensional sound for the listener.

RADIOPHONIC SOUNDS	Sound effects and music created by the BBC Radiophonic Workshop (1958–98) using pioneering methods including manipulating tape and using test oscillators. Most famously used to create the original theme tune to *Doctor Who* (1963–), the Workshop was also responsible for effects for *The Goon Show* (1951–60) and *The Hitchhiker's Guide to the Galaxy* (1978–80).
RAJAR	Radio Joint Audience Research, the official body in charge of measuring radio audiences in the UK.
RECEIVED PRO-NUNCIATION/ RP	A form of English speech without regional variation, generally linked to public school education.
REVERB	Abbreviation for reverberation, the continuation of a sound after its source has stopped. An ACOUSTIC that most listeners would think of as echo. Used to help signify space: no REVERB would suggest an outside location; a lot might suggest a cave. Also used in a similar way to DISTORT.
SPOT EFFECTS	Sound effects generated live by a studio manager. Typical examples include doors opening/shutting, footsteps, water splashing, as well as less obvious sounds such as dried peas tipped from side to side in a box to mimic sea breaking on shingle and scrunching cellophane to sound like a blazing fire.
STUDIO/ CUBICLE	A studio is a space for performance; a cubicle is the room (usually adjoining and connected by a glass window) where the technical team is based during recording or live broadcast. The term STUDIO can also be shorthand for a studio day, the time spent recording.
STUDIO CUE-LIGHT	Also called a LIGHT CUE or a FLICK. A light switched on briefly by the producer or studio manager that indicates that the microphone is live and the actor should begin speaking.
STUDIO MANAGER/SM	A job title covering a number of technical roles, such as overseeing the recording of a production, controlling the microphones, playing in sound effects or music, or generating spot effects. Studio managers also play out the finished recordings on

the day of broadcast. Described by Elwyn Evans as 'the invaluable human bridges between the artistic and the engineering sides of radio'.

SURROUND SOUND
Used to describe sound reproduction that attempts to create a sense of the listener being surrounded by sound, putting them at the centre of the action. Often uses more than two speakers. Sometimes now referred to as spatial audio, 3D or immersive reproduction.

TALKBACK
A microphone in the technical CUBICLE connected to a speaker in the studio, enabling the producer to communicate with the cast.

VHF
Very High Frequency. Widely used in radio, VHF waves are not impaired by random electromagnetic noise ('static') and can be used by transmitters several hundred miles apart without interfering with one another.

WILD TRACK
Audio recorded without any speech. Often used in location recording, it means an editor has a background track of atmosphere (e.g. birdsong, wind, other natural noise) that can be used to patch together any inconsistencies in the edits.

Introduction: What Is Radio Shakespeare and How Does It Work?

I'm sitting in Christchurch Park in my home town of Ipswich, trying to get to grips with Shakespeare for an exam. I've got the text of *Richard II* in front of me, and in my ears, Samuel West and Damian Lewis. As I listen, something magical is happening. This 400-year-old language is lifting off the page. The words are making sense. I already enjoyed watching Shakespeare on the stage – but here was a new way to enjoy my favourite playwright that didn't require expensive theatre tickets and probably a long journey to Stratford-upon-Avon or London.

When I first started studying Shakespeare at undergraduate level, I turned to BBC audio recordings of the plays to help me understand Shakespeare's language. As a distance-learning student, reading them on my own sometimes left me feeling they were impenetrable. Audio helped unlock these texts for me – and I hope it will for others in the future.

That experience led to the development of this book. A passion for audio Shakespeare grew into a full-blown investigation into how it can be – and is – presented on radio. I'm not going to claim every production is a gem – who could claim that every stage production they've seen was perfect? But I will say that there are hugely enjoyable productions, ones that can tell us a lot about their source text, and those that speak to the era in which they were broadcast. Some do all these things at the same time.

Shakespeare is inextricably linked to the birth of broadcasting in the UK. The first time his words were spoken on air pre-dates the BBC. The actor Robert Atkins gave a 'dramatic recital' of act one, scene three of *The Merchant of Venice* on an experimental London station on 2 September 1922.[1] The BBC came into existence ten weeks later on 14 November and on 16 February 1923 scenes from *Julius Caesar* and *Othello* were performed.[2] The first broadcast of a full-length play, *Twelfth Night*, followed on 28 May.[3]

Since that date, the BBC has broadcast more than 400 full radio productions of Shakespeare's plays and continues to produce new ones. Around 150 recordings are held in its archive. Existing scholarship is limited and looks predominantly at what was broadcast, not how it sounded, taking a historical overview of Shakespeare on radio internationally. This book is different. It examines radio plays as 'texts' in their own right in a similar way to research into film and television productions. It looks specifically at the BBC's archive – the largest in the world and the most accessible. As well as exploring the script changes made for the medium, it also pays close attention to the sound of these productions, from voice, music and sound effects to the mixing and manipulation of those sounds, as well as the effect this has on the texts. And it sets these productions in their historical and critical context.

In this book you will notice the term 'production' is used to describe the BBC's radio versions of Shakespeare's plays, rather than 'adaptation'. This acknowledges the plays' origins in stage performance and is the industry standard term, but the choice here also reflects the lack of stability in what 'adaptation' means. There is far from an academic consensus over the word, or which of the myriad other terms might be more applicable: Ruby Cohn cites seventeen different words used to describe the 'rewriting of Shakespeare', and others have come up with many more.[4] Daniel Fischlin and Mark Fortier suggest that a production in any medium, including the theatre, might be an adaptation, while Margaret Jane Kidnie disputes this, stating that a play is a 'dynamic *process* that evolves over time in response to the needs and sensibilities of its users'.[5]

---

[1] 'To-night's Radio', *Daily News*, 2 September 1922, p. 5; 'Concert transmission to Enfield War Memorial Hospital', in *BBC Programme Index*, <https://genome.ch.bbc.co.uk/c62f62fbfb42040665ff9dc1b9b7da92> [accessed 14 August 2023].

[2] '369 Metres', *Pall Mall Gazette*, 16 February 1923, p. 8.

[3] 'Broadcasting – Performance of "Twelfth Night"', *The Times*, 28 May 1923, p. 10. See also Chapter 1.

[4] Ruby Cohn, *Modern Shakespeare Offshoots* (Princeton: Princeton University Press, 1976), p. 3.

[5] Daniel Fischlin and Mark Fortier, 'General Introduction', in *Adaptations of Shakespeare*, ed. by Fischlin and Fortier (Abingdon: Routledge, 2000), pp. 1–22 (p. 17); Margaret Jane Kidnie, *Shakespeare and the Problem of Adaptation* (Abingdon: Routledge, 2009), p. 2.

Novels presented as radio plays are readily recognised as adaptations: extensive editing and usually the invention of dialogue clearly shows they have been 'adapted'. For stage plays, the changes to the text are often minimal, making it harder to define. Within radio drama itself, the expression 'arranged for broadcasting' was used for many years, while contemporary radio producers tend to prefer 'dramatised', but this is usually in the context of novels and, as plays are already 'drama', it is not terribly helpful here.[6] Perhaps the most appropriate term for the production of Shakespeare's plays on BBC radio is 'transmedialization', described by Jan Baetens and Domingo Sánchez-Mesa Martínez as 'the mechanism or process that adapts a work that exists in a given medium to another medium'.[7] This makes clear that there is a change of medium, but that the play as an entity remains largely the same, in a similar way to taking a play text and putting it on a stage. However, it is not widely used and is liable to be confused with the more popular term 'transmedia storytelling', where a 'story unfolds across multiple media platforms'.[8] Returning to Fischlin and Fortier, we are left with the question of whether a 'production' is necessarily an 'adaptation' or not. As stage plays broadcast on radio are so rarely discussed by academics working in the field of adaptation, perhaps this book will help advance that debate.

In many ways, presenting Shakespeare on radio is much closer to the theatre than other media such as film and television. While producers may make additions and cuts to the text, as well as occasionally imposing a particular setting on it, radio productions usually retain more of Shakespeare's words than film and are unable to substitute pictures for text. Kenneth Graham and Alysia Kolentsis point out that on stage there is not 'some universal idea of *Hamlet* that we are witnessing, but a particular *production* of the play' (added emphasis).[9] The same could be said for radio, as John Drakakis notes: 'Nominally a radio adaptation may be regarded as the *production* of a particular text – an embodiment of an essence that is not

---

[6] Claire Grove and Stephen Wyatt, *So You Want to Write Radio Drama?* (London: Nick Hern Books, 2013), p. 213.

[7] Jan Baetens and Domingo Sánchez-Mesa Martínez, 'Literature in the Expanded Field: Intermediality at the Crossroads of Literary Theory and Comparative Literature', *Interfaces*, 36 (2015), 289–304 (292).

[8] Henry Jenkins, *Convergence Culture* (New York: New York University Press, 2006), p. 97.

[9] Kenneth Graham and Alysia Kolentsis, 'Introduction', in *Shakespeare On Stage and Off*, ed. by Graham and Kolentsis (Montreal: McGill-Queen's University Press, 2019), pp. 3–12 (pp. 4–5).

seen – although historically each text is itself the locus of divergent cultural forces' (added emphasis).[10] This last point is particularly noticeable in some of the later productions in this book, which move Shakespeare's texts to new locations and/or time periods and sometimes add new dialogue to reflect their new settings.

Radio productions have three virtues over other performances of Shakespeare. Firstly, the large number that are available to listen to, dating back many decades. Some are available for free through BBC Sounds and more than a hundred are accessible through Learning on Screen's Box of Broadcasts website.[11] The BBC's Shakespeare Sessions website also has a number which can be permanently downloaded to keep for free, while audiobook subscription service Audible holds many BBC productions, as well as some created by other production companies.[12] Secondly, unlike recordings of stage productions which cannot capture the same experience as being in a theatre, we are able to listen to these plays in the same medium as their original audience: sound. And thirdly, these productions provide an opportunity to understand not just how radio has presented Shakespeare but how Shakespeare was performed and received over the last century in the wider context. Many stage performances have been captured by radio and many Shakespearean actors better known for film or stage have taken roles in radio productions. In some cases, these recordings are the only examples of their work that have been preserved.

Radio has often been considered peculiarly appropriate for Shakespeare. The BBC's first director-general, John Reith, wrote in 1924: 'The plays of Shakespeare fulfil to a great extent the requirements of wireless, for he had little in the way of setting and scenery, and relied chiefly on the vigour of his plot and the conviction of the speakers to convey his ideas.'[13] One of the BBC's first producers, Cecil Lewis, wrote in the same year that 'no better plays for broadcasting could have been written'.[14] And radio playwright L. du

---

[10] John Drakakis, 'The Essence That's Not Seen: Radio Adaptations of Stage Plays', in *Radio Drama*, ed. by Peter Lewis (London and New York: Longman, 1981), pp. 111–33 (p. 131).

[11] 'BBC Sounds', BBC, n.d., <https://www.bbc.co.uk/sounds> [accessed 9 July 2024]; 'BBC Radio Shakespeare Curated Playlist', Box of Broadcasts [institutional login required], n.d., <https://learningonscreen.ac.uk/bob-curated-playlists/bbc-radio-shakespeare/> [accessed 9 July 2024].

[12] 'BBC Shakespeare Sessions', BBC, n.d., <https://www.bbc.co.uk/programmes/p06 55br3/episodes/player> [accessed 9 July 2024]; Audible, n.d., <https://www.audible.co.uk/> [accessed 9 July 2024].

[13] J. C. W. Reith, *Broadcast over Britain* (London: Hodder & Stoughton, 1924), p. 168.

[14] C. A. Lewis, *Broadcasting from Within* (London: George Newnes, 1924), pp. 61–2.

Garde Peach believed firmly that 'Shakespeare wrote the best broadcast plays' as 'Shakespeare is his own scenic artist, because the things the characters say and their reactions to the environment in which Shakespeare's fancy has placed them, *suggest* the scene to you in a way which makes painted canvas an offence'.[15] Radio therefore offers another advantage over visual media: listeners are not distracted by a director's *mise-en-scène*. As producer Felix Felton wrote: 'we want to take the listener, not to the "Garrick", the "Lyric" or the "New", but to fair Verona, [or] the shores of Illyria.'[16] These opinions continue to be held to this day. Current producer Emma Harding states that radio can be 'valuable and revealing': 'When you've only got the text to listen to, your mind is doing all this visual work. [. . .] I think we also respond to spoken language in a very different way from reading it on a page.'[17] As such, radio productions of these plays can offer fresh ways of engaging with the words of these texts, making a virtue out of the lack of visuals.

Radio is primarily an entertainment medium and broadcast plays are mainly created for that purpose but, like any performance of Shakespeare, they can provide both an insight into the text and a reflection of their moment of production. The fact that these performances have so far been left unexamined means that there is a large gap in the history of Shakespearean performance in the UK. Without examining a medium that has, at times, had millions of listeners, and continues to be enjoyed by hundreds of thousands, work in this area is skewed towards theatre, and to some extent film. This book corrects this imbalance, showing that BBC radio productions of Shakespeare's plays are not second-class adaptations in a 'blind' medium, but productions as clear and individual as those presented on film and in the theatre (and sometimes as flawed as productions in those other media can be too).

While this book endeavours to cover the entire history of the first hundred years of these productions, the BBC's audio archive is incomplete. The biggest gap is from the earliest period, where plays were not routinely recorded (indeed it was not possible to record

---

[15] L. du Garde Peach, 'Shakespeare Wrote the Best Broadcast Plays', *Radio Times*, 24 June 1927, p. 549.

[16] Felix Felton, *The Radio-Play: Its Technique and Possibilities* (London: Sylvan Press, 1949), p. 14.

[17] Emma Harding in Ronan Hatfull, 'Adapting *The Merchant of Venice* for Radio: An Interview with Emma Harding, Adapter and Director for BBC Radio Drama', *Shakespeare*, 17.4 (2021), 1–15, <https://doi.org/10.1080/17450918.2021.1960416> [accessed 6 October 2021], p. 4.

them for some time). Even when recording was possible, this did not necessarily mean they were kept for posterity. As one BBC executive described it, the archive is 'the stuff that the BBC forgot to throw away'.[18] In the immediate post-war period there is also a lack of variety in what was kept (e.g. three versions each of *King Lear* and *Antony and Cleopatra* but none of *A Midsummer Night's Dream* or *The Tempest* – all plays performed multiple times). The most recent missing production from the BBC archive is the 1970 *All's Well That Ends Well*.

Although all the extant productions have been listened to for this book, the sheer number involved means that it has only been possible to select a few to examine in detail as case studies. Some have been chosen on the basis of the attention they received either at the time of their broadcast or subsequently, such as John Gielgud's *Hamlet* (1948) which has received more critical attention than any other. Radio frequently appears to act completely independently of film and theatre, but on a few occasions there have been radio productions that coincide with those elsewhere. For example, that same production of *Hamlet* was broadcast shortly after the release of Laurence Olivier's Academy Award-winning film. And a radio production of *A Midsummer Night's Dream* (1970) was aired a few months before Peter Brook's famous 'white box', Stratford-upon-Avon staging. These productions have been included as case studies not for direct comparison between radio and film/theatre, but to reflect their respective moments of cultural context.

Most of the productions examined are 'full-length'. This does not necessarily mean full text, but plays that present the majority of Shakespeare's words, plot and characters (although, as in other media, some may be conflated). In 1949 Felton wrote that for a recent series of Shakespeare's plays 'it was decided to keep each play within the limit of the "two-hours' traffic"'.[19] This was deemed a 'listenable length'.[20] And most producers, before and since, have regarded a duration of around two hours to be appropriate, although there are shorter and longer productions here as well.

Finally, the choice of plays has attempted to reflect Shakespeare's full canon, ranging from examples of the most famous texts to those least commonly performed. Each chapter also features a production

[18] CHASE DTP, *Bill Thompson – BBC Archives, Head of Partnership Development – Plenary address*, online video recording, YouTube, 9 September 2015, <https://www.youtube.com/watch?v=wBx75Z_ID8g> [accessed 8 July 2024].
[19] Felton, p. 26.
[20] Felton, p. 26.

of *Macbeth* in order to offer direct comparison throughout. *Macbeth* was chosen not only because it is one of the most performed plays, but also because it has been given a number of different treatments over the century, often typifying the style of production at the time of broadcast. However, the repetition of other texts has been kept to a minimum, and I only return to a play if a new production is significant in some way.

In order to analyse these productions, a technique of 'close listening' has been devised, based on the elements of radio drama identified by Elke Huwiler: 'music, noises and voices and also technical features like electro-acoustical manipulation or mixing'.[21] Unlike other works on radio Shakespeare, this moves beyond a simple comparison of Shakespeare's texts and radio scripts and examines the productions as a whole. As well as identifying the elements that make up the overall sound of the play, I also assess the impact or effect of these choices. Throughout this book you will find timecodes given so you can listen to the same extracts if you wish. Details of the source of the archive audio are given in a footnote.

For the early case studies, where recording was not possible or not carried out, it may not be possible to completely recreate what they sounded like, but it is possible to establish many of the elements described above through written sources. Many scripts still exist: the BBC's Written Archives Centre and the Library of Birmingham's Shakespeare Collection hold between them copies of the majority of scripts for productions aired between 1929 and 1993. These not only identify cuts and changes to the text, but frequently include information about music, sound effects and even how the director would like the actor to play the part. Newspapers and magazines are a very useful resource for previews, reviews and letters from listeners, frequently discussing the acting and sound of productions. Other written sources include the *BBC Handbooks* and *Year Books* and memoirs and instruction books written by BBC staff, some dating back as far as 1924. In the first two decades of the BBC, radio was a new and exciting medium, unrivalled yet by television. As such, a great deal of written material exists about broadcasts and broadcasting at this time.

* * *

---

[21] Elke Huwiler, 'Storytelling by Sound: A Theoretical Frame for Radio Drama Analysis', *Radio Journal: International Studies in Broadcast & Audio Media*, 3.1 (2005), 45–59 (45).

The next section will help you understand how radio drama works, particularly in relation to Shakespeare. It looks at both the technical adaptation of stage plays to the medium and the technology that supports their broadcast. Many of the technical words and terms used here will appear throughout the book and can also be found in the glossary for easy reference. These are indicated in SMALL CAPS.

Adapting Shakespeare for Radio

Firstly, in the world of radio drama, the PRODUCER is often not just the person in overall charge of the production but also the director and sometimes the script editor/arranger too. Therefore, the actions of a producer will often include jobs that in other media would be carried out by other people. For the most part the term 'producer' is the term you will see used to refer to the person responsible for all these roles, and sometimes several others.

Like the majority of Shakespeare performances, cuts are made to the text. While a few BBC radio productions claim to be full text, such as the 1972 *Othello* with Paul Scofield or Kenneth Branagh's *Hamlet* (1992), it is rare to find a production completely unedited.[22] However, the amount of cutting can vary hugely. John Gielgud's 1948 *Hamlet*, which has a running time of three hours and twenty minutes, plus two intervals, still had around forty lines removed. However, the 1968 *Comedy of Errors* lasted for just eighty minutes, with scores of lines edited out. Across the last century, textual cuts have been controversial. In the *Radio Times* in 1935, under the headline 'Must Shakespeare be butchered by the BBC?', the critic and playwright Herbert Farjeon bemoaned what he saw as unjustifiable editing of texts, in particular a version of *Henry V* that he claimed was only seventy-five minutes long: 'the BBC calmly announced it as *Henry V*. *Henry the Two-Fifths* would have been more accurate.'[23] Producer Howard Rose later told the *Radio Times* 'the actual transmission time was an hour and fifty-five minutes'.[24] BBC Drama Director Val Gielgud also told the magazine:

[22] Robert Ottaway, '"I Have Undertaken Othello Now Because I Feel I Am Ready to Do It Justice"', *Radio Times*, 9 November 1972, p. 3; 'Radio 3 Celebrates with New *Hamlet* Production', *The Stage*, 23 April 1992, p. 17.

[23] Herbert Farjeon, 'Must Shakespeare Be Butchered by the BBC? An Attack by Herbert Farjeon', *Radio Times*, 30 August 1935, p. 13.

[24] Howard Rose in Val Gielgud, 'What the Other Listener Thinks – "Must Shakespeare Be Butchered . . .?" Val Gielgud Replies', *Radio Times*, 6 September 1935, p. 9.

[If] Mr Farjeon listens to broadcasts of Shakespeare in the uninspiring company of a pencil and a text, counting words feverishly in order to be able to tell me just how many have been excised in the interests of practical entertainment value, I should be more than glad to know how any individual listening in such conditions expects to get anything from a broadcast play except a feeling of acute exasperation, probably coupled quite literally with a pain in the neck![25]

Gielgud added that he believed the average listener was 'not prepared to listen for hours at a time to Shakespeare [. . .] because any listening to the spoken word is a business demanding acute attention and concentration'.[26] However, Farjeon was not alone in voicing dissatisfaction with the cutting of Shakespeare's texts and this remains a contentious issue in the twenty-first century, with critics still expressing a desire for longer productions and producers believing that most people would prefer a shorter play.

Textual edits are not just made to condense Shakespeare's works, although this is often a major reason for them. Producers also remove elements because they deem lines to be archaic and therefore not understandable, or because they allude to something highly visual that cannot easily be replicated on radio. Perhaps the most obvious instance of a visual element not translating well to audio is the dumb show in *Hamlet*. Most producers choose to ignore it and simply present the play-within-the-play, as John Tydeman does in his 1971 production.[27] Many other examples of all three forms of cutting will be found in the case studies in the following chapters. However, in the main, the textual cuts made are not dissimilar to those in the theatre. Textual additions, though, are frequently specific to radio.

Cecil Lewis stated in 1924 that 'having selected the play, the next question is to arrange it'.[28] In the case of radio, 'arrangement' often means having to take into account the visual aspects of the text such as action or location. For many decades this was achieved largely through narration, although this was unpopular. Edward Sackville-West wrote that it 'always makes for a drop in temperature of the programme',[29] while Elkan and Dorotheen Allan suggested 'the narrator of radio-drama is an intruder [. . .] preventing the listener

---

[25] Gielgud, *Radio Times*, 6 September 1935.

[26] Gielgud, *Radio Times*, 6 September 1935.

[27] Kenneth Branagh's 1992 production keeps the dumb show, but it is very difficult to comprehend.

[28] Lewis, *Broadcasting from Within*, p. 62.

[29] Edward Sackville-West, *The Rescue* (London: Martin Secker & Warburg, 1945), p. 9.

from thoroughly immersing himself'.[30] In 1950 producer Frank Hauser wrote that 'there is precious little good in critics wailing against the use of the narrator in principle, unless they *can* suggest an alternative'.[31] Unlike the adaptation of other plays or novels, there seems to have been particular pressure on producers to find a 'Shakespearean' way of creating narration. Hauser justified his use of it by stating that the text was 'taken from North's Plutarch, which is where Shakespeare got his material from in the first place'.[32] Other producers would do little more than have a narrator read aloud the stage directions, such as the combined productions of the three parts of *Henry VI* in 1971.[33] More unusually, Sue Wilson framed her production of *The Comedy of Errors* (1999) with the narration of the supposed BBC travel reporter Gervaise Ffoulkes who found himself 'caught up in some strange local customs'.[34] But in the main, the more recent the production, the less likely it is that it will use narration.

However, that does create a challenge for the producer as to how to convert something visual into something aural. In the case of location, this can often be done with music and sound effects. Purely visual scenes are trickier, though, without an 'intruder' explaining what is happening. A key example is the sword fight at the end of *Hamlet*. Hamlet and Laertes swap swords, but the characters' lines do not directly indicate this. In 1948 this was resolved with narration. Alongside the clashing of foils, the sounds of exertion and the murmuring of the court, producer John Richmond inserts the following:

> NARRATOR   Laertes takes Hamlet off his guard. He disarms and wounds him.
>
> *FX – brief clash of foils*

---

[30] Elkan and Dorotheen Allan, *Good Listening: A Survey of Broadcasting* (London: Hutchinson, 1951), p. 100.

[31] Frank Hauser, 'Can Shakespeare Be Broadcast?', *Radio Times*, 29 September 1950, p. 6.

[32] Hauser, *Radio Times*, 29 September 1950.

[33] *Henry VI – Part 1*, BBC Radio 3, 7 March 1971, <https://learningonscreen.ac.uk/ondemand/index.php/prog/RT39A2AC?bcast=119118228> and <https://learningonscreen.ac.uk/ondemand/index.php/prog/buf671d37?bcast=131985129> [in two parts, accessed 29 December 2020]; *Henry VI – Part 2*, BBC Radio 3, 14 March 1971, <https://learningonscreen.ac.uk/ondemand/index.php/prog/buf671d38?bcast=131985130> and <https://learningonscreen.ac.uk/ondemand/index.php/prog/buf4f51b8?bcast=119118895> [in two parts, accessed 29 December 2020].

[34] 'Comedy of Errors', *Radio Times*, 18 February 1999, p. 104.

Hamlet leaps in and wrests Laertes' sword from his hand and Laertes picks up Hamlet's. They've exchanged swords.

3:11:58[35]

But in Tydeman's 1971 version of the play, just five words of dialogue are added to explain the same situation:

FX – clatter of foils on the floor

LAERTES   My sword!
HAMLET   *My* sword now!

2:57:04[36]

Textual additions are also used to help convey who is present and who is being addressed. Examples include the addition of characters' names or relationships, or servants announcing their appearance or departure. *Antony and Cleopatra* (1942) has many examples of this. There is no recording but the script shows frequent insertions of this nature, such as names at the ends of lines (additions in italics):

CAESAR   Welcome to Rome, *Mark Antony.*
ANTONY   Thank you, *Octavius Caesar.*[37]

In a similar way, actors often make non-verbal sounds such as murmurs of agreement, groans of displeasure or even whimpers of pain to indicate their presence in a scene if they do not have any lines or have not spoken for some time.

Conveying the visual in sound does not necessarily require additional words, though. Sound effects have been deployed extensively. These can take several forms: live SPOT EFFECTS, created by a STUDIO MANAGER; recorded effects, played in on record, CD or now from a digital database; and RADIOPHONIC SOUNDS, non-realistic effects created by sound engineers. Producer Martin Jenkins was a pioneer of using spot effects to graphically capture the sound of murder and mutilation. For the sound of decapitations he used 'a cabbage, a knife and a cup of water, for the spurting blood'.[38] Techniques like

---

[35] *Hamlet*, BBC Third Programme, 26 December 1948 (unpublished, BBC Sound Archive).
[36] *Hamlet*, BBC Radio 3, 31 October 1971 (unpublished, BBC Sound Archive).
[37] William Shakespeare, *Antony and Cleopatra*, in The *Norton Shakespeare*, 3rd edn, ed. by Stephen Greenblatt and others (London: W. W. Norton, 2016), 2.2.30–1. All subsequent references to Shakespeare's plays will be given within the text and refer to this edition of the Complete Works unless otherwise stated.
[38] 'Vivat Rex', *Radio 4 and 4 Extra Blog*, <https://www.bbc.co.uk/blogs/radio4/2012/04/radio_4extra_vivat_rex.html> [accessed 3 January 2021].

this help clarify situations where the text only suggests what is happening and is not explicit. In *Titus Andronicus*, when Aaron cuts off Titus's hand, Titus merely says: 'Lend me thy hand and I will give thee mine' (3.1.186).[39] However, in Jenkins's 1973 production there is no doubt what has happened, as there is the sound of chopping, 'bones' crunching and liquid running (1:16:24). Moments which are not clear from the text alone, once supported with sound effects, require no further words to explain the action.

Recorded effects are usually used as background, rather than detail. Writing about radio drama in general, John Drakakis comments: 'A crude example might be the sound of the ubiquitous BBC seagull, first introduced in the early days of radio and used conventionally to suggest a particular location and atmosphere.'[40] In Shakespeare's plays, a more common sound is that of crows, particularly in productions of *Macbeth*, effectively doing the same job as the seagull but creating a more sinister environment.[41] In plays featuring battle scenes, appropriate recorded sounds are also frequently used, although, as in the 2020 *Henry IV, Part 1*, these are often augmented with shouts and sounds of exertion from the cast (1:43:50).[42]

While spot and recorded effects are usually attempting to replicate real sounds, Elwyn Evans points out that 'not all effects are meant to be realistic'.[43] This is particularly the case with radiophonic effects. Louis Niebur suggests that 'beginning in the early 1950s, radio audiences began to tire of the relentless barrage of "realistic" sound effects in radio drama'.[44] In 1958, the BBC Radiophonic Workshop was founded. It is probably best known now for creating the original theme tune to the television programme *Doctor Who* (1963–). However, it also provided an antidote to traditional radio sound effects, with 'menacing and other-worldly' sounds

---

[39] *Titus Andronicus*, BBC Radio 3, 28 October 1973, <https://learningonscreen.ac.uk/ondemand/index.php/prog/RT3ACE12?bcast=119250895> [accessed 13 September 2021].

[40] John Drakakis, 'Introduction', in *British Radio Drama*, ed. by Drakakis (Cambridge: Cambridge University Press, 1981), pp. 1–36 (p. 30).

[41] The sound of crows has been added to productions ranging from *Henry V* (1976) to *Cymbeline* (2006) and can be found in every audio production of *Macbeth* covered as a case study in this book.

[42] *Henry IV, Part 1*, BBC Radio 3, 26 April 2020, <https://learningonscreen.ac.uk/ondemand/index.php/prog/15E8E24C?bcast=131789644> [accessed 13 September 2021].

[43] Elwyn Evans, *Radio: A Guide to Broadcasting Techniques* (London: Barrie & Jenkins, 1977), p. 131.

[44] Louis Niebur, *Special Sound* (New York: Oxford University Press, 2010), p. 14.

considered 'particularly useful for the heightening of tension'.[45] The Workshop created its sounds and music by 'manipulating tape and test oscillators', as well as using 'found sounds, synthesisers and eventually samplers'.[46] Unusual noises such as these are put to good use in *Hamlet* (1971) during the 'closet scene' (act three, scene four) when Hamlet can see the ghost of his father but Gertrude cannot. The ghost's appearance is signalled by radiophonic effects (1:48:55) and they are used throughout the scene to indicate the ghost's presence, as well as heightening Ronald Pickup's performance as the prince.

Like effects, music is used to create and maintain atmosphere in radio Shakespeare productions. Val Gielgud states that 'music can intensify the dramatic atmosphere of a scene—it can even conjure up the physical picture of that scene—as nothing else can'.[47] However, the style of music varies greatly, from the melodic, pseudo-Elizabethan to more abstract, modernist pieces. Much of what has been used in the production of Shakespeare's plays has been specially written. The importance of choosing and using this correctly is brought home by Felton, who writes that 'in an ideal world every radio-producer would be a trained musician'.[48] Evans would probably have applauded the sentiment, complaining that 'early producers plastered music all over their plays'.[49] He particularly bemoans the use of the MUSIC LINK, something popular in early productions and used as 'inter-scene punctuation'.[50] In a medium without the facility to fade to black or bring down a curtain, music has often been used to create an equivalent end to a scene although, as Evans indicates, not always successfully. The 1964 *Troilus and Cressida* particularly relies on this device, sometimes even within scenes. Act one, scene one not only begins with a music link, to separate it from the prologue (0:02:55), but also has links before and after Troilus's soliloquy (1.1.85–99; 0:06:40, 0:07:42).[51] Similarly Kenneth Branagh relies heavily on music links to separate the scenes in his three 1990s

---

[45] 'BBC Radiophonic Workshop founded', *History of the BBC*, <https://www.bbc.com/historyofthebbc/anniversaries/april/bbc-radiophonic-workshop> [accessed 13 September 2021]; Evans, p. 131.

[46] 'BBC Radiophonic Workshop founded', *History of the BBC*.

[47] Val Gielgud, *Radio Theatre: Plays Specifically Written for Broadcasting* (London: Macdonald, 1946), pp. xiii–xiv.

[48] Felton, p. 127.

[49] Evans, p. 150.

[50] Evans, p. 149.

[51] *Troilus and Cressida*, BBC Third Programme, 25 September 1964 (unpublished, BBC Sound Archive).

productions: *Hamlet* (1992), *Romeo and Juliet* (1993) and *King Lear* (1994).[52]

Vocal performance is another key technique in transferring Shakespeare's plays to radio. This was recognised from the very earliest days. Lewis writes: 'It does not follow that a well-known actor on the stage will be successful on the microphone. Extreme sensitivity of vocal colour is essential.'[53] He adds that 'a certain mellowness of speech' can be an asset but 'an acutely unpleasant voice may be the making of some thankless or humorous part where the voice is not used to give pleasure, but to provoke or amuse'.[54] More recently, Alan Beck comments that 'the microphone has a magnifying effect [. . .] You often need to underplay and be more subtle, and you rarely use the projection needed for stage.'[55] Radio producer Donald McWhinnie observes that 'the producer must not only find the right interpreter for each part, he must have an ear to the final orchestration of the cast as a whole. Since there are no costumes, each actor must be readily identifiable by voice alone.'[56] Sometimes this basic fact eludes producers. When Tydeman chose Paul Scofield and Nicol Williamson for his production of *Othello* (1972), he was delighted with his 'magnificent cast'.[57] But once the two actors were in a room together, Tydeman realised he had a problem: 'When we had the read-through, I thought "Oh, god". They sounded very alike. Same timbre.'[58] The solution for Tydeman was to ask Scofield to adjust his vocal tone as Othello, with the actor adopting the audio equivalent of blacking-up, thankfully a practice that has long since ceased.[59] However, this demonstrates the importance of the art of voice casting on radio.

Shakespeare's plays also have a distinctive requirement in vocal performance that is rare in other radio drama: cross-gender disguise. While on stage costume can indicate that a female character has taken on the appearance of a boy, on radio this has to be conveyed in

[52] *Hamlet*, BBC Radio 3, 26 April 1992, <https://learningonscreen.ac.uk/ondemand/index.php/prog/RT437D24?bcast=120071753> [accessed 24 September 2021]; *Romeo and Juliet*, BBC Radio 3, 25 April 1993, <https://learningonscreen.ac.uk/ondemand/index.php/prog/RT44104D?bcast=120118097> [accessed 18 March 2021]; *King Lear*, BBC Radio 3, 10 April 1994, <https://learningonscreen.ac.uk/ondemand/index.php/prog/RT44A592?bcast=120168103> [accessed 24 September 2021].
[53] Lewis, *Broadcasting from Within*, p. 62.
[54] Lewis, *Broadcasting from Within*, p. 62.
[55] Alan Beck, *Radio Acting* (London: A & C Black, 1997), p. 64.
[56] Donald McWhinnie, *The Art of Radio* (London: Faber, 1959), p. 126.
[57] John Tydeman, private phone conversation, 18 February 2020.
[58] Tydeman, private phone conversation, 18 February 2020.
[59] *Othello*, BBC Radio 3, 12 November 1972, <https://learningonscreen.ac.uk/ondemand/index.php/prog/RT3A618D?bcast=119210276> [accessed 23 July 2021].

other ways, such as voice. To indicate Rosalind's transformation into Ganymede in *As You Like It*, both Sarah Badel and Imogen Stubbs in the 1978 and 1997 productions respectively shift their voices into a deeper register, making it easier for the audience to understand that the character they are playing is pretending to be male.[60] The use of children is also rare in radio Shakespeare productions before the twenty-first century. Usually child characters, such as Arthur in *King John* (1967) and the Page in *Henry IV, Part 2* (1995), are played by women, reversing the Elizabethan and Jacobean tradition which saw women played by boys.[61]

While radio actors generally work around a single microphone, it does not mean their performances are static. McWhinnie explains that the producer 'will map out in his mind how to dispose his actors in relation to the microphone, remembering that variation and ingenuity in their placing will convey, unconsciously, the impression of depth and dimension'.[62] This is particularly important with stereo and SURROUND SOUND productions. Alison Hindell, who started producing for the BBC in the late 1980s, explains how her predecessors dealt with this (pictured overleaf):

> In the 70s, when they were first introducing stereo, they had very complicated grid patterns marked on the floor of the studio like a chess board, and then producers would very laboriously block the play so that somebody would move from D4 to E3 in order to say this line that much closer or further away or in a particular space in the producer's head.[63]

The proximity of the actor to the microphone is a particularly useful tool for soliloquies and asides, with CLOSE MIC performance creating a more intimate sound. Additionally producers can add effects to an actor's voice, such as DISTORT, which is commonly used to simulate phone calls, intercoms and news broadcasts.

While this is not an exhaustive list of techniques, it summarises many of the ways producers have adapted Shakespeare for radio over the decades and sets the scene for the productions examined in the following chapters. Alongside these techniques there have

---

[60] *As You Like It*, BBC Radio 3, 1 January 1978, <https://learningonscreen.ac.uk/onde mand/index.php/prog/RT3C9A0E?bcast=119429460> [accessed 10 March 2020]; *As You Like It*, BBC Radio 4, 1 September 1997, <https://learningonscreen.ac.uk/onde mand/index.php/prog/RT46B966?bcast=120340622> [accessed 10 March 2020].

[61] For more on women playing boys, see Chapter 3.

[62] McWhinnie, p. 127.

[63] Alison Hindell, private Zoom conversation, 17 June 2021.

Figure 1 Actors in Broadcasting House working on a stereo grid.
© BBC Archive

been significant changes in the technical methods of production and broadcasting which have also contributed greatly to the creation and reception of Shakespeare's plays on radio.

Broadcasting Shakespeare on Radio

The BBC's first Shakespeare scenes in February 1923 were broadcast from Marconi House in the Strand in a 'small room' that 'was originally a cinematograph theatre'.[64] Three months later when the first full play, *Twelfth Night*, was broadcast, the organisation had moved to larger premises at Savoy Hill which served them for nearly a decade. Asa Briggs states that the new studio was '38 feet by 18 feet, and it was very heavily draped [. . .] to damp reverberation. For the same reason there was a thick, heavy carpet on the floor.'[65] However, while this may have helped the acoustics, 'perfect reproduction' was not possible.[66] Peter Eckersley, the BBC's first chief engineer, wrote

---

[64] Lewis, *Broadcasting from Within*, p. 29.
[65] Asa Briggs, *The History of Broadcasting in the United Kingdom: Volume I – The Birth of Broadcasting* (Oxford: Oxford University Press, 1995), p. 193.
[66] Lewis, *Broadcasting from Within*, p. 47.

that 'nearly all the crude microphones and loudspeakers of the early days responded to middle and cut off bass and top [low and high sounds]'.[67] In addition, most people listened at home on headphones that would 'respond to certain frequencies more than to others'.[68] As such, the 'niceties of the voice' were 'practically all lost'.[69] Therefore, no matter what techniques actors and producers employed, listeners to early broadcasts could not get the full effect of the performance.

The use of sound effects and music was also limited. The BBC's Director of Programmes, Arthur Burrows, described the difficulties of providing such additions without a dedicated effects studio or even microphone: 'The variation in intensity of accompanying sounds is obtained by opening and shutting the doors between the studio and the property-room.'[70] A similar procedure was adopted for 'some of the instrumental music in Shakespeare's plays' which was 'performed in a room outside with the door open two or three inches only'.[71]

Initially, broadcasts were made at relatively low power, meaning that listeners could only tune in within a limited distance from a transmitter, unless they had a particularly sensitive receiver. The BBC therefore established a series of separate stations in major cities across the country, each creating its own output and broadcasting from studios similar to Savoy Hill. More than fifty Shakespeare plays were produced by these regional stations, with Cardiff the most prolific, airing more than twenty. However, it was not long before fully UK-wide broadcasting was launched. From 1930, productions were broadcast on the National Programme and from this point on, while regional stations did still occasionally do their own Shakespeare plays, the majority were broadcast from London.[72]

The next big change came in 1932 with the opening of the purpose-built Broadcasting House in Portland Place, London – still the BBC's main home today. The new studios allowed for much grander productions and enabled producers to control the LEVEL and MIX of various sounds from different studios. Actors would mainly perform in the largest studio, 6A, described as occupying the height

[67] P. P. Eckersley, *The Power Behind the Microphone* (London: Jonathan Cape, 1941), p. 107.

[68] A. C. Shaw, 'The "Real Thing" v. Broadcast. The Art of Reproduction', *Popular Wireless Weekly*, 18 October 1924, pp. 363–4 (p. 364).

[69] Shaw, *Popular Wireless Weekly*, 18 October 1924.

[70] A. R. Burrows, *The Story of Broadcasting* (London: Cassell, 1924), p. 100.

[71] Burrows, p. 100.

[72] Asa Briggs, *The History of Broadcasting in the United Kingdom: Volume II – The Golden Age of Wireless* (Oxford: Oxford University Press, 1995), p. 28.

of two floors.[73] There were also four smaller studios: '6B and 7B were the "live" studios. 6C and 7C were the "dead" studios.'[74] Gielgud explains that the 'live' studios had a normal ACOUSTIC while the 'dead' had specially treated walls 'giving the impression of a confined space', such as a prison cell or for 'aural "close-ups"'.[75] In addition, there were four effects studios. Studio 6D was described as being 'as exciting as a magician's cave', offering a wide variety of equipment to generate spot effects.[76] Adjoining it was 6E, the 'Gramophone Studio' with six turntables for MIXING a variety of sounds.[77] There were also 'Secondary Effects and Gramophone Studios, 7D and 7E' and two 'Echo rooms', where 'artificial echo' could be added to the output of any studio.[78] Music came from the Military Band studio on the eighth floor.

This set-up may seem complicated, but it enabled a producer to fully control the sounds they wanted to hear. To do this, they used a DRAMATIC CONTROL PANEL which had 'rows of vulcanite knobs controlling the strength of individual studio output' so that a producer could mix the sounds, as well as STUDIO CUE-LIGHTS telling an actor when they should speak.[79] Gielgud explains that a producer 'listened to the output from his studios through a loudspeaker facing him, and communicated with his actors through a microphone at his elbow [. . .] The advantages were obvious. Performances could, indeed, were compelled to be, judged entirely aurally.'[80]

Staff began moving to the new premises in the spring, with the first official programme broadcast from 'BH' on 15 May 1932.[81] The first Shakespeare play was three weeks later: *Hamlet*, starring John Gielgud and directed by his brother, Val.[82] As there are no Shakespeare recordings from Savoy Hill or the early days of Broadcasting House, it is difficult to tell how much difference the new studios made to the production. However, *The Stage* reported that it was 'a superb achievement' and 'a great advance' on the previous play, *Othello*, although there is no indication whether this

[73] 'The Studios', in *BBC Year-Book 1932* (London: BBC, 1931), pp. 69–76 (p. 74).
[74] Val Gielgud, *British Radio Drama 1922–1956* (London: George G. Harrap, 1957), p. 55.
[75] Gielgud, *British Radio Drama*, p. 55.
[76] Mark Hines, *The Story of Broadcasting House: Home of the BBC* (London: Merrell, 2008), p. 64.
[77] *BBC Year-Book 1932*, p. 74.
[78] *BBC Year-Book 1932*, p. 74; Gielgud, *British Radio Drama*, p. 55.
[79] Gielgud, *British Radio Drama*, p. 57.
[80] Gielgud, *British Radio Drama*, p. 56.
[81] Hines, p. 20.
[82] 'Hamlet', *Radio Times*, 3 June 1932, p. 604.

Figure 2 Production team working at a dramatic control panel in Broadcasting House. Val Gielgud in foreground. © BBC Archive

was due to the more sophisticated facilities.[83] In fact, although much more complex productions were now possible, it seems that it may have taken a while for producers to take full advantage of them. The *BBC Year-Book 1933* commented that the 'potentialities' of the new studios 'are not likely to be fully explored for some time to come'.[84] However, within two years producers were making the most of the new studios.

Scripts from this period list detailed sound effects and music cues. In the case of the 1935 *Macbeth*, producer Peter Creswell even noted exactly where each performer and sound would be coming from:

ANNOUNCEMENT IN 6C

ANNOUNCER   A shortened version for Broadcasting of Shakespeare's Tragedy 'MACBETH' with Victor Hely-Hutchinson's music, conducted by .... etc., etc.

[83] 'Cues and Comments', *The Stage*, 9 June 1932, p. 11.
[84] 'Development in Drama', in *BBC Year-Book 1933* (London: BBC, 1932), pp. 171–6 (p. 173).

(Overture from 8A)
(Fade into storm 6D and 6E)
(6D and 6E down to background.
FLICK 6A for Macbeth)

MACBETH   (distant) So foul and fair a day I have not seen.
(on flick in 6A)
BANQUO   How far is't call'd to Forres?[85]

'Flick' here is to indicate the use of the studio cue-light. The script goes on to show that scene two came from studio 6B and scene three, in which Lady Macbeth reads the letter from her husband, from 6C: the 'dead' studio, used for intimate scenes. This level of script detail is unusual compared to Creswell's contemporaries, but it gives an idea of the complex choreography required to make the best use of the new studios. As Eric Maschwitz, head of the BBC's Variety Department, later put it: 'Radio Drama, hitherto earthbound, was finding wings; like the cinema before it, it was on its way to escaping from the limitations of the theatre.'[86]

No audio exists of Creswell's *Macbeth* and routine recording of dramatic productions was not yet taking place. The BBC did have the facility to record audio at this time via Blattnerphones, an early form of tape recorder.[87] However, they were 'used exclusively for "bottling" examples of significant broadcast material'.[88] It would be some years before plays were regularly recorded for broadcast, and many more before they were systematically archived.

The next major change to BBC radio Shakespeare production was forced upon it by the Second World War. Radio Drama was moved out of London, briefly setting up in Evesham, before moving again to Manchester.[89] Gielgud states that the 'technique of production was compelled to be radically simplified'.[90] Plays were produced in single studios, 'working under conditions only to be comprehensively categorised as "lash-up"'.[91] However, not everyone thought the change in production methods was a bad thing. H. Bishop from the Institution of Electrical Engineers believed that there had

[85] William Shakespeare, *Macbeth*, ed. by Peter Creswell (unpublished, Library of Birmingham S334.1935Q), p. 1.
[86] Eric Maschwitz, *No Chip on my Shoulder* (London: Herbert Jenkins, 1957), p. 54.
[87] Hines, p. 64.
[88] Paddy Scannell and David Cardiff, *A Social History of British Broadcasting: Volume One, 1922–1939 – Serving the Nation* (Oxford: Basil Blackwell, 1991), p. 146.
[89] Gielgud, *British Radio Drama*, p. 95, p. 99.
[90] Gielgud, *Radio Theatre*, p. viii.
[91] Gielgud, *Radio Theatre*, p. viii.

previously been a tendency for 'broadcasts to become technically over-elaborate', although his dislike of these productions seems to have been rooted in the engineering headaches they caused for his members.[92]

This new, simpler style of production became the norm and after the bombing of Broadcasting House there was no way back. It was hit a number of times, but the worst was on 15 October 1940. A bomb hit the building, killing seven people and causing damage 'from the third to the eighth floors', completely destroying the drama suite.[93] This meant that even when it was deemed safe for the department to return to London, they were without their usual facilities. However, rather than being rebuilt exactly as before, the new studios had a simplified layout. There was still a small 'dead' studio, but the four small studios on the sixth floor were combined, 'capable of subdivision to taste by means of curtains and special screening and different types of flooring and wall-treatment'.[94] The producer's control-room now had a glass window so that they could have visual contact with their actors, although there was also a blind that could be pulled down if the producer wanted 'visual isolation'.[95] The new studio space was much more flexible and also had 'a number of permanent "spot" Effects—a staircase, doors with bolts and locks, a small water-tank, a gravel surface, and so on' built in.[96] There was also a new mixing unit which 'linked to a number of microphone-points instead of a number of studios'.[97] This revised studio set-up is largely the way studio-based radio drama is still recorded in the twenty-first century, with the exception of the period during the Covid-19 pandemic.

In early 2020, entertainment production across the world shut down. In the case of radio, it was quickly determined that some sort of home recording could be done instead. Some plays, including John Webster's *Duchess of Malfi* (2021), were created using a combination of Zoom for visual contact and software specially created by BBC engineers to record the sound. However, no Shakespeare plays were recorded this way. By the time that Gaynor Macfarlane came to produce *The Tempest* (2021), it was still unsafe for everyone to

---

[92] H. Bishop quoted in F. C. Brooker, *Engineering Division Training Manual* (London: BBC, 1942), pp. 217–18.

[93] Asa Briggs, *The History of Broadcasting in the United Kingdom: Volume III – The War of Words* (Oxford: Oxford University Press, 1995), p. 268; Hines, p. 103.

[94] Gielgud, *British Radio Drama*, p. 119.

[95] Gielgud, *British Radio Drama*, p. 119.

[96] Gielgud, *British Radio Drama*, p. 119.

[97] Gielgud, *British Radio Drama*, p. 119.

be in one room, but people could leave their homes. She hired an independent voice-over studio and each actor had their own booth, linked to each other via video camera and a screen.[98] This enabled a high-quality sound recording to be made, and some limited, 'live' interaction between actors, but also restricted the number of people in a scene. This was the first major change to studio technique in at least seventy years and a one-off. Since that production, techniques have reverted to pre-pandemic recording.

Although by the end of the war the BBC could, and sometimes did, record productions for broadcast, many plays continued to be performed live. And as recorded productions could not be edited, they also sounded live, including the occasional fluffed line or rustle of paper. If plays were recorded, it was mainly for the purpose of repeating productions, rather than archiving. For example, the 1962 *Love's Labour's Lost* was aired six times but no longer exists in the archives, presumably because nobody thought they would want to broadcast it again. Several other productions suffered the same fate.[99]

Briggs states that 'in 1960 about half the sound programmes broadcast for the British audience were broadcast live [. . .] By the mid-1970s there were very few programmes that were not recorded.'[100] With advances in recording technology, 'mixing now became far easier', and since EDITING had become possible, it had developed into 'an art'.[101] As recording on ¼-INCH TAPE became standard, producers were able to make a 'quick slice with a razor blade' to remove errors and join various takes together.[102] After editing, music or effects could also be added to the audio by playing the recording back through a mixing desk and DUBBING it on to a fresh tape, while playing in the additional sounds simultaneously. David Wade notes that it gave 'the director a far greater measure of control over the performance he eventually obtains: provided time allows, sequences can be done and done again, mistakes eliminated, balance perfected'.[103] However, tape was bulky; a standard

---

[98] Gaynor Macfarlane, private Zoom conversation, 3 February 2022.

[99] The 1947 productions of both parts of *Henry IV* were broadcast four times each, as was the 1953 *As You Like It*, the 1957 *Cymbeline* and the 1959 *Tempest*, but none of them have been kept.

[100] Asa Briggs, *The History of Broadcasting in the United Kingdom: Volume V – Competition* (Oxford: Oxford University Press, 1995), p. 833.

[101] Briggs, *Volume V*, p. 834.

[102] John Tydeman, 'The Producer and Radio Drama: A Personal View', in *Radio Drama*, ed. by Peter Lewis (London and New York: Longman, 1981), pp. 12–27 (p. 26).

[103] David Wade, 'British Radio Drama since 1960', in *British Radio Drama*, ed. by Drakakis, pp. 218–44 (p. 241).

10½-inch reel would only hold half an hour of audio, so most plays required at least four reels. Playing them out on air also required skill from the studio manager to ensure there was no gap or overlap between one tape ending and the next starting.

Alongside steadily improving recording and editing techniques, broadcasting technology also developed. MEDIUM WAVE broadcasting suffered 'serious [atmospheric] interference after dark', although Briggs states that there was 'no public demand for VHF' initially.[104] However, attitudes changed and the BBC opened its first VHF station in May 1955.[105] The *BBC Handbook 1956* told readers the new service would enable them 'to enjoy the heightened pleasure of hearing the programmes as they really should be heard'.[106] The *Handbook* quoted an unnamed radio critic as saying: 'The difference (listening on VHF) was like looking at an object through spectacles before and after they had been polished.'[107] This may be why those within the BBC appreciated it. Wade comments: 'A play received on VHF can then be heard as its performers and director intended – every nuance of speech, every sound effect, even uneasy silences.'[108]

In addition to radio reception improving, there was also a slow move towards stereo broadcasting. As early as 1924 it was being contemplated.[109] But it was another forty years before BBC radio drama began to embrace the technique, thanks to the work of 'pioneering' producer Raymond Raikes.[110] However, not everyone approved. McWhinnie complains that 'one of the disadvantages of stereophony, to my mind, is that it brings the precise sense of left and right to the radio illusion; in other words, places us in front of an invisible stage'.[111] This was precisely what Raikes liked, making use of it specifically in his 1968 production of *The Comedy of Errors* by using sound effects to create a virtual stage with the port of Ephesus on one side and the abbey on the other, as well as using left and right to distinguish between the two pairs of twins.[112]

---

[104] Briggs, *Volume V*, p. 840.
[105] Briggs, *Volume V*, p. 841.
[106] *BBC Handbook 1956* (London: BBC, 1956), p. 115.
[107] *BBC Handbook 1956*, p. 115.
[108] Wade, 'British Radio Drama since 1960', p. 241.
[109] Lewis, *Broadcasting from Within*, pp. 137–9.
[110] Margaret Horsfield, 'Shakespeare on Radio' (unpublished masters dissertation, Shakespeare Institute (University of Birmingham), 1978), p. 32.
[111] McWhinnie, p. 127.
[112] For more on Raikes's use of stereo in *The Comedy of Errors*, see Chapter 3.

Following the introduction of stereo, there have been a number of attempts to take the idea of space and sound even further. Six years after Raikes's *Comedy of Errors*, the first QUAD Shakespeare play was broadcast: *The Tempest* (1974), produced by Ian Cotterell.[113] David Hendy explains that QUADRAPHONY 'doubled the number of speakers to four. The aesthetic appeal of this lay in being able to place listeners in the centre of a 360-degree performing area: they would be sitting, quite literally, in the thick of the action.'[114] In 1977 the BBC was broadcasting 'about one "quad" programme a week' but 'without a system of encoders and decoders [. . .] there was no such thing as a domestic radio set able to receive four bands of information simultaneously' and 'the technology foundered'.[115] However, while surround sound was abandoned in the short term, the idea of creating an immersive experience did not disappear altogether, although it was several decades before a producer would look at using it again for Shakespeare.

Almost simultaneously with the interest in quad, the BBC was experimenting with BINAURAL sound. Binaural recording uses a pair of microphones fixed into a life-sized model of a head at the location of the ears, in an attempt to mimic the way we hear sound. When using headphones, a listener to binaural audio gets a sense of being in the middle of the action in a similar way to quad but, because it only requires two channels, it can be broadcast on conventional stereo systems. Agnieszka Roginska and Paul Geluso describe binaural as '"you are there", first-person perspective, in contrast to the loudspeaker "they are here"'.[116] The first plays to use binaural were broadcast in the 1970s, but it was not until the twenty-first century that it was used for Shakespeare. Hindell's 2017 *Richard II* is the only production to date to use the technology and she says her studio manager felt that 'it's technically very complicated for not necessarily a big reward or a big difference'.[117] As stereo editing and mixing has become more sophisticated in the digital age, it is now possible to create something akin to surround sound without complicated transmitting and receiving equipment or specialist microphones.

---

[113] For more on Cotterell's use of quad in *The Tempest*, see Chapter 3.
[114] David Hendy, *Life on Air: A History of Radio Four* (Oxford: Oxford University Press, 2007), p. 197.
[115] Hendy, *Life on Air*, p. 197.
[116] Agnieszka Roginska and Paul Geluso, eds, *Immersive Sound: The Art and Science of Binaural and Multi-Channel Audio* (Abingdon: Routledge, 2018), p. 3.
[117] Hindell, private Zoom conversation, 17 June 2021.

Digital technology has transformed the recording and editing of audio. Producer Clive Brill was one of the first to embrace it with his 1991 production of *A Midsummer Night's Dream*.[118] Brill recalls using a twenty-four-track system, allowing him to mix many different audio sources at one time; far more than would be practical to do through a conventional mixing desk. In the twenty-first century, producers and their studio managers can have an almost inexhaustible number of tracks. ProTools, the industry standard editing software, offers more than 2,000, although producers would be unlikely to use even as many as 100.[119] Digital technology has also made it easier to edit out unwanted sounds. Sound designer David Thomas says the software Izotope RX is 'basically like Photoshop for sound', enabling him to perfect background sound in the edit.[120]

Digital technology has also made location recording much easier. As recording equipment has got progressively smaller and digital storage (such as hard drives and SD cards) has increased in capacity and decreased in price, taking actors out of the studio has become much more practical. No longer is a BBC outside broadcast van needed: portable equipment can be taken to almost any location.[121] However, just because a production is recorded outside the studio, it does not necessarily mean that it is complete in itself. Often it benefits from additional sound treatment or effects in the edit. Thomas says: 'If you're in a castle, you might have a [REVERB] but not quite the right reverb so you might have to fiddle that a bit.'[122] And in real life, other sounds may not live up to expectations either: 'You end up layering. For *A Midsummer Night's Dream* [2011] you do want to colour it slightly and put in a few more birdies. You take the listener with you on a journey rather than it being a pure record of the recording.'[123] Location recording for Shakespeare's plays has happened occasionally in the twenty-first century, but the majority of producers still choose to record in a studio.

Broadcasting continues to be available in analogue form on FM and, until recently, on Long and Medium Wave on Radio 4. However, listeners can also now choose to listen on DAB. This does not

---

[118] For more on Clive Brill's editing of *A Midsummer Night's Dream* (1991), see Chapter 4.

[119] Dave Tyler, 'Exploring increased voices, tracks, and I/O in Pro Tools 2021.6', *Avid*, <https://www.avid.com/resource-center/exploring-increased-voices-tracks-and-io-in-pro-tools-2021-6> [accessed 16 September 2024].

[120] David Thomas, private Zoom conversation, 22 April 2021.

[121] For more on location recording, see Chapter 5.

[122] Thomas, private Zoom conversation, 22 April 2021.

[123] Thomas, private Zoom conversation, 22 April 2021.

suffer from interference like its predecessors and offers 'CD-quality sound'.[124] It has now overtaken AM and FM transmission in terms of listeners, but other forms of device are also rising in popularity.[125] Angeliki Gazi, Guy Starkey and Stanislaw Jedrzejewski note that 'Radio "receivers" are no longer only dedicated hi-fi tuners or portable radios with whip aerials in the traditional sense, but they are now also assuming the shape of various multimedia-enabled computer devices'.[126] During the twenty-first century, BBC radio Shakespeare productions became available to listen to online, but are also now downloadable via the BBC Sounds app.[127]

* * *

Shakespeare's plays have been produced on radio in many anglophone countries, including the USA, Canada, Australia and Ireland. But none have created anything like as many productions as the BBC in the UK, nor do they have comparable archives. That is not to say they are not worthy of further research – far from it. But they are not the subject of this book. Neither are the BBC's World Service productions. There is more than enough material to explore from its domestic broadcasts.

While the production of Shakespeare's plays on radio has never been fully investigated, there have been a few academics who have championed this medium and paved the way for this book. Douglas Lanier and Michael P. Jensen have both written about American broadcasts. Eve-Marie Oesterlen has summarised the BBC's domestic broadcasts, while Susanne Greenhalgh has written a number of articles and book chapters about them. But, as Lanier states, 'the importance of radio to the history of Shakespeare and mass media has long been underestimated'.[128] Greenhalgh comments that research has so far been 'infrequent and remains under-developed'

---

[124] 'BBC national digital radio coverage improves in five areas', *BBC Media Centre*, <https://www.bbc.co.uk/mediacentre/latestnews/2014/bbc-dab> [accessed 22 September 2021]; Stephen Lax, 'Different Standards: Engineers' Expectations and Listener Adoption of Digital and FM Radio Broadcasting', *Journal of Radio & Audio Media*, 24.1 (2017), 28–44 (31).

[125] 'RAJAR Data Release, Quarter 1, 2023', *RAJAR*, <https://www.rajar.co.uk/docs/news/RAJAR_DataRelease_InfographicQ12023.pdf> [accessed 17 August 2023].

[126] Angeliki Gazi, Guy Starkey and Stanislaw Jedrzejewski, 'Introduction', in *Radio Content in the Digital Age*, ed. by Gazi, Starkey and Jedrzejewski (Bristol: Intellect Books, 2011), pp. 9–21 (p. 10).

[127] For more on this, see Chapter 5.

[128] Douglas Lanier and Michael P. Jensen, 'Radio', in *Shakespeares after Shakespeare*, ed. by Richard Burt (Westport: Greenwood Press, 2007), pp. 506–84 (p. 506).

and that it offers 'that rare phenomenon in Shakespeare studies, a history still in the process of being outlined and documented'.[129] This book finally documents a history that is long overdue for recognition.

The following five chapters move chronologically through the history of the BBC's Shakespeare plays on radio from the very first production through to the third decade of the twenty-first century. They look at the common themes of each era and the issues that appear to have been driving the sort of productions made, as well as how they might reflect the critical thinking of their era. They are also situated within contemporary performance. As well as an overview of the era there are five case studies for each period, examining productions in detail and exploring in depth how producers have presented Shakespeare for their audiences.

Chapter 1 looks at the BBC's earliest radio Shakespeare productions, from its inception through to the end of the Second World War in 1945. Because there is only a limited amount of audio available from productions broadcast during this era, the earliest case studies use documentary evidence to build up a concept of what they sounded like. The chapter then moves on to those for which extracts of audio exist, finishing with the first play for which a full recording is available, *As You Like It* (1944). It also looks at how these productions engage with some of the approaches taken to the plays by literary critics of the day. This chapter argues that, despite the comments of some modern scholars, radio productions of Shakespeare were always presented as radio drama, however primitive at the outset. From the very first production, producers and actors aimed to present full audio plays, not simple poetry readings. These early pioneers might not always have been successful in presenting Shakespeare this way, but the evidence suggests this was always their aim.

Chapter 2 concentrates on the post-war period from 1946 to 1966. All the case studies featured are those for which the full audio exists – around a fifth of those broadcast. This chapter shows that the now well-established BBC was showing confidence in its production of Shakespeare, especially with the introduction of a new station, the Third Programme, which broadcast many of these plays.

---

[129] Susanne Greenhalgh, 'Listening to Shakespeare', in *Shakespeare on Film, Television and Radio: The Researcher's Guide*, ed. by Olwen Terris, Eve-Marie Oesterlen and Luke McKernan (London: British Universities Film & Video Council, 2009), pp. 74–93 (p. 74); Greenhalgh, 'Shakespeare and Radio', in *The Edinburgh Companion to Shakespeare and the Arts*, ed. by Mark Thornton Burnett and Adrian Streete (Edinburgh: Edinburgh University Press, 2011), pp. 541–57 (p. 544).

Producers also appear to have been trying to fulfil a prediction by Reith that radio would popularise Shakespeare. More productions on more networks, essentially available for free, increased access to the plays in a way never seen before.

The start of the period covered by Chapter 3, 1967–87, was one of change in the BBC. Radio was reorganised, with the addition of a new channel, Radio 1, and the renaming of the existing three. As part of this process, Shakespeare's plays could no longer be found across all networks, and while the new Radio 4 still broadcast some, Radio 3 became their real home. This may have fostered an age notable for the rise of the radio Shakespeare 'auteur': producers who imprinted their own personal style on their work. From 1971 onwards, the BBC holds a complete archive of its radio Shakespeare plays, providing a wide selection to choose from as well as the opportunity to listen to a variety of plays by each producer, enabling the identification of their own, unique take on them, much as one would expect from a leading theatre or film director.

Chapter 4 begins as the twentieth century draws to a close and examines the years 1988–2001. During this period, the BBC, like other arts organisations, seemed keen to take advantage of the cultural capital offered by Shakespeare, firstly by releasing cassettes of their archive plays, then by commissioning productions starring perhaps the leading Shakespearean actor of his generation, Kenneth Branagh, and finally by the creation of the 'Shakespeare for the Millennium' series on Radio 3. Coincidentally (or not), Shakespeare was voted 'Personality of the Millennium' by listeners to the BBC's flagship news programme, *Today*, on Radio 4.

The final chapter concentrates on the most recent productions, looking at the way Shakespeare has been presented on BBC radio during the twenty-first century. Covering the years 2002–23, it coincides with the rise in availability of digital radio, the first productions available on demand, and the creation of BBC Sounds, enabling listeners to download the plays and listen to them anytime, anywhere. This has been a period of new creativity among radio producers, who have also been able to take advantage of the possibilities offered by digital recording and editing. It has seen a greater diversity of casting than ever before, and producers presenting Shakespeare's plays in a wider variety of styles, including contemporary and futuristic settings. This reframing of Shakespeare on BBC radio perhaps also indicates the direction in which productions will head in its second century.

The conclusion of this book is really the start of what I hope will be an ongoing conversation about this academically under-represented aspect of dramatic performance in the history of Shakespeare's plays. The wealth of material uncovered by this research shows that there is plenty of scope for further investigation. And the production of Shakespeare's plays on BBC radio is an ever-evolving practice, influenced not only by technology but also by audience and critical reaction, and the thinking of those involved in bringing these works to the airwaves. Radio has a unique connection to its audience: far from being a 'blind' medium as people have often labelled it, it can produce visually engaging productions – albeit with the pictures entirely generated in the listeners' imaginations. And it puts emphasis on Shakespeare's words – both their sound and their meaning – in a way no other medium does. Radio Shakespeare is a specific genre within radio drama, as well as a form of Shakespearean production in its own right. Now that it has been 'outlined and documented', as Greenhalgh puts it, the work of putting these performances into the canon alongside their stage, film and television counterparts really begins.

First Steps and Early Success: 1923–45

The first six months of the BBC were a frenzy of innovation. Every new type of programme had to be developed almost entirely from scratch. While there had been limited broadcasting prior to the organisation's creation, nothing had been attempted on this scale. Wireless had been something for hobbyists; now it quickly became a new form of entertainment. In the opening weeks listeners were introduced to children's programmes, concert music from small ensembles crammed into the BBC's first London studio, and even an opera relayed from Covent Garden. Programming quickly became more sophisticated, with the small team continually experimenting with new ideas, pushing the limits of what was possible within the medium. It was not long before they turned their attention to drama.

Even before the launch of the BBC, those involved in the very earliest British broadcasts understood that to be successful, radio drama required more than just a group of actors reading aloud. By the time the BBC attempted its first full radio play, it was clear this would involve a specially adapted script, music and sound effects. This chapter shows that from their inception, performances of Shakespeare's plays on BBC radio were always conceived as full productions in audio. While there were undoubted difficulties in translating works intended for the stage to the airwaves, and some techniques were more effective than others, no producer ever viewed it as just people standing around a microphone. They might not always have been successful in presenting Shakespeare as a radio play (as opposed to a simple 'reading') but the evidence suggests this was always their aim. Later generations would develop these principles as technology improved, leading to increasingly sophisticated productions over the century.

A month before the BBC officially launched, staff at an experimental wireless station in Writtle near Chelmsford decided to present their listeners with 'the balcony scene from Cyrano de Bergerac'.[1] Their studio was no more than a hut in a field and this scene was deemed the most suitable thing to broadcast as it 'is played on stage in semi darkness with virtually stationary players'.[2] Tim Wander explains the actors' scripts were 'complete with instructions in brackets imploring the speaker to read with "voice raised", "voice discrete" [*sic*] or "voice passionate"'.[3] In addition, 'a young actress, Miss Agnes "Uggy" Travers and her brother came to help the engineers with their lines'.[4] This first attempt at drama may have involved amateur players, but there was already an understanding that the subject matter needed to work for the medium and that the players needed to do more than simply read aloud; they needed to act with their voice. These principles would be developed the following year at the new BBC.

Prior to the first full production, the BBC broadcast a number of short scenes from Shakespeare's plays. In February 1923, listeners heard professional actors Shayle Gardner and Hubert Carter in 'The Quarrel Scene' and 'Mark Antony's Oration' from *Julius Caesar*, as well as 'Othello's Defence'.[5] And on Shakespeare's birthday in April, there was a special night of extracts presented by the British Empire Shakespeare Society, including excerpts from *The Merchant of Venice*, *The Merry Wives of Windsor*, *Henry VIII*, *Much Ado About Nothing* and *As You Like It*.[6] The actors had already presented the scenes earlier in the day on the stage of the Haymarket Theatre.

At the time of this broadcast, the BBC's London operation was still based at Marconi House in the Strand, where 'working conditions and competition for studio time must have made experiments with studio productions of plays practically impossible'.[7] However, within days, the BBC received an incentive to try. The West End theatres had been allowing excerpts of their plays to be presented on

---

[1] Tim Wander, *2MT Writtle – The Birth of British Broadcasting* (Stowmarket: Capella Publications, 1988), p. 75.
[2] Wander, p. 75.
[3] Wander, p. 75.
[4] Wander, p. 75.
[5] '369 Metres', *Pall Mall Gazette*, 16 February 1923, p. 8.
[6] 'Broadcasting – A Shakespeare Night', *The Times*, 23 April 1923, p. 10.
[7] Christina S. L. Pepler, 'Discovering the Art of Wireless: A Critical History of Radio Drama at the BBC, 1922–1928' (unpublished doctoral thesis, University of Bristol, 1988), p. 28.

air but 'changed their attitude to broadcasting'.[8] The Entertainments Industry Joint Broadcasting Committee had agreed a resolution: 'That the broadcasting of plays, music, songs, or other entertainments is prejudicial to the interests of all connected with places of public entertainment, and that such steps shall be taken as might be necessary to protect such interests.'[9] If the BBC wanted to continue to offer drama it would have to find a new source of plays and a new location to present them.

The latter was already in the pipeline. On 1 May 1923, the BBC began broadcasting from new studios in Savoy Hill, much better suited to drama, with more space and better acoustics. And while the theatres may have been opposed to allowing excerpts of their own productions on the radio, actors did not seem to be so unwilling to perform. Among those who had taken part in the British Empire Shakespeare Society broadcast in April were Cathleen Nesbitt, Nigel Playfair, Gerald Lawrence and Henry Caine. These four would go on to be members of the cast of the first full-length play, adapted by Nesbitt. By presenting its own productions, the BBC also opened up the opportunity to broadcast plays specifically tailored to the medium: no longer were they restricted by what the theatres were offering and willing to share.

When Nesbitt started work on preparing *Twelfth Night* for broadcast in 1923, she had no model to follow. However, it seems that right from that first broadcast, she and her colleagues realised two things. Firstly, that to present a play on the radio, the cast had to do more than merely read the script out loud. They needed to perform it, using their voices to convey anything from simple emotion to lively movement. Secondly, that radio required different skills to the theatre. It was not just that the listeners could not see the actors, but that the whole medium interacted differently with its audience. In addition, one other element is clear: these plays were always intended as entertainment.

Comments from both listeners and producers highlight this fact. Less than six months after *Twelfth Night*, a reader of the *Radio Times* wrote to congratulate the BBC on the 'excellent performance' of *The Merchant of Venice*, adding: 'I would like to make a plea for more Shakespeare plays to be broadcast [. . .] I have never

[8] Briggs, *Volume I*, p. 256.
[9] 'Broadcasting and the Theatres – Entertainment Industry's Opposition', *The Times*, 28 April 1923, p. 8.

enjoyed listening so much.'[10] The magazine's editor responded that 'many letters of congratulation have been received on our various Shakespeare Recitals'.[11] And in 1924, the *Western Mail* received at least twenty letters about the broadcasting of a series of Shakespeare plays on the BBC's Cardiff station. The correspondence began with a letter from someone calling himself 'Paterfamilias', who wrote: 'We are not interested in wandering through "thirty-seven Shakespearean plays in strict chronological order".'[12] This was followed the next day by a letter from 'Six Sufferers' saying 'we do not want Shakespeare at all'.[13] But others were in favour of the broadcasts. 'Indignant' wrote: 'I am exceedingly interested in the Shakespearean plays which we have been privileged to listen to.'[14] J. Dugenot added: 'Might I be allowed to express my thanks to the Cardiff Station Repertory Company for the excellent performance of "The Merry Wives of Windsor".'[15] Others 'have marvelled, and still marvel, at the wonderful talent', or wrote that Shakespeare plays 'interest me much more than continual music'.[16]

Some of the responses started to get quite personal. 'Indignant' wrote again, saying that 'Six Sufferers' were making themselves look ridiculous and 'libelling their respective mental capacities'.[17] 'Paterfamilias' re-entered the fray, saying: 'I am *not* against the broadcasting of Shakespeare [. . .] but I am indignant at the way it is being done,' although he does not specify what was wrong.[18] The row went on for several weeks, culminating in the station director, Major Arthur Corbett-Smith, giving an address to Cardiff Rotarians, saying: 'We have tried to share beautiful music and poetry with you, not as Welshmen or as Englishmen, but as members of one human family.'[19] He added: 'I don't think we are "highbrows." [. . .] You must not think because we give you symphonies and Shakespeare's

---

[10] G. M. Pope, 'A Plea for Shakespeare', *Radio Times*, 9 November 1923, p. 238.

[11] Pope, *Radio Times*, 9 November 1923.

[12] 'Cardiff Broadcasting Programme', *Western Mail*, 14 February 1924, p. 10. There is no record of this plan, although the station did begin by performing some of the earlier plays and did not broadcast the late plays.

[13] 'Cardiff Broadcasting Programme', *Western Mail*, 15 February 1924, p. 9.

[14] 'Programmes Approved and Appreciated', *Western Mail*, 16 February 1924, p. 5.

[15] 'Broadcasting – Worship, Handel and Opera', *Western Mail*, 22 February 1924, p. 5.

[16] Admirer, 'Programmes Approved and Appreciated', *Western Mail*, 16 February 1924, p. 5; G. H. W., 'Cardiff Broadcasting', *Western Mail*, 18 February 1924, p. 9.

[17] 'Cardiff Broadcasting Programmes', *Western Mail*, 19 February 1924, p. 7.

[18] 'Cardiff Broadcasting', *Western Mail*, 27 February 1924, p. 9.

[19] 'Wireless Programmes Critics – Cardiff Director Speaks to Rotarians', *Western Mail*, 11 March 1924, p. 7.

plays it is because we are "highbrows."'[20] Corbett-Smith's declaration was echoed just over a decade later by producer Peter Creswell, when a similar row erupted in the *Radio Times*. He told readers about a letter he had received signed from 'An Unemployed Miner in the Rhondda Valley'.[21] In it, the man wrote: 'I had no idea before that Shakespeare was so exciting.'[22] Creswell adds: 'One need not labour the point, but I had rather have had that letter than volumes of praise from all the professing "Shakespeare lovers" in this world.'[23] For producers such as Corbett-Smith and Creswell, the aim was clearly to entertain.

Producers employed a number of techniques to try to make their productions entertaining. From the outset, music and sound effects were part of their toolkit. Playfair appeared in two of the BBC's first Shakespeare plays and went on to produce radio drama. Within months of *Twelfth Night* (1923) he recognised that a 'new craft will be developed, and new methods evolved' to transfer plays from stage to the airwaves.[24] By the 1930s, and particularly after the move to Broadcasting House with its much-improved facilities, producers became increasingly adept at doing this. A reviewer in the *Yorkshire Evening Post* of the 1933 production of *Julius Caesar* praised the portrayal of the murder and crowd scenes, adding that 'he must have been a most unimaginative listener whose mind did not conjure up a vivid picture of the scene as the conspirators gathered around Caesar'.[25] The reviewer added that 'a word of thanks should be said for the music—just enough and of the right quality'.[26] This was aided by the new band studio in Broadcasting House, which allowed not only for more musicians, but also for greater control over the mixing of music with speech and effects. Robert Chignell, who composed music for *Julius Caesar* (1931) and *Coriolanus* (1933), was acutely aware that his music could 'take the place of the eyes of the listener in order that he may unconsciously imagine (it can only be that) through his mind's eye what a character or a scene or object might,

[20] 'Wireless Programmes Critics', *Western Mail*, 11 March 1924.
[21] Peter Creswell, 'What the Other Listener Thinks – "Must Shakespeare Be Butchered?"', *Radio Times*, 27 September 1935, p. 9.
[22] Creswell, *Radio Times*, 27 September 1935.
[23] Creswell, *Radio Times*, 27 September 1935.
[24] Nigel Playfair, 'How Plays Will Be Broadcast', *Radio Times*, 14 December 1923, p. 429.
[25] G. C. H., 'Commentary on Broadcasting', *Yorkshire Evening Post*, 11 December 1933, p. 4.
[26] G. C. H., *Yorkshire Evening Post*, 11 December 1933.

perhaps, look like'.[27] Visualising character could also be aided through voice, although this was a more contentious issue.

In the 1930s, Shakespeare's plays were regularly broadcast on Sundays, reportedly so that 'fine casts can be engaged'.[28] This generally meant using actors from the London stage. It undoubtedly secured coverage for the radio productions in newspapers and magazines, and would have attracted listeners, but not everyone felt this was the right course of action. Farjeon wrote: 'it seems to me a bull-headed mistake to recruit speakers so heavily from the stage, where so much depends on physical appearance.'[29] However, there was a bigger problem. Many actors from the stage were unable to understand the different technique required for radio. Barbara Couper, who performed in nine Shakespeare plays for the BBC from the 1920s to the 1940s, was well aware of this: 'You cannot bluff the microphone as you might an audience—the former is the more subtle of the two.'[30] She was also frustrated by the idea that 'there are some who think anyone can act for the microphone—"My dear, they just stand and read!"'.[31] This was echoed by her husband, BBC Shakespeare actor and producer Howard Rose: 'The broadcasting of radio plays by no means consists of merely reading them. They have to be given with all the completeness and finish of a theatre play so far as the speaking, and, indeed, the acting is concerned.'[32] Newcastle producer Gordon Lea agreed, stating that 'voice is the all-important factor' and needs to be 'flexible enough to interpret any shade of emotion'.[33] It also needed to be distinctive, something producers recognised as important, but sometimes struggled to achieve.

In the case of the 1934 production of *A Midsummer Night's Dream*, producer Val Gielgud undertook what was probably the BBC's first piece of cross-gender casting. Margaret Rawlings was chosen to play Oberon, with pre-publicity suggesting she had 'the sort of deep, strong contralto voice that will contrast admirably' with the young male characters and that of Titania, played by Fay

---

[27] Robert Chignell, 'Music for Radio Plays', in 'Sidelights on Radio Drama', *Radio Times*, 30 August 1935, pp. 6–9 (p. 7).

[28] Collie Knox, 'Listen to the Jaltarang – and Other Things in India's Broadcast', *Daily Mail*, 5 December 1933, p. 20. See also 'Shakespeare on the Wireless: Mr Godfrey Tearle as Macbeth', *The Times*, 20 September 1935, p. 10.

[29] Farjeon, *Radio Times*, 30 August 1935.

[30] Barbara Couper, 'The Radio Actor's Job', *Radio Times*, 30 August 1935, pp. 8–9.

[31] Couper, *Radio Times*, 30 August 1935.

[32] Howard Rose, 'Producing a Radio Play', *Radio Times*, 30 August 1935, p. 8.

[33] Gordon Lea, *Radio Drama and How to Write It* (London: George Allen & Unwin, 1926), p. 38.

Compton.[34] The *Radio Times* explained that the choice of casting by Gielgud was due to 'consideration for the exigencies of voice-differentiation over the microphone'.[35] Unfortunately Rawlings did not play the role on the day. Instead, a last-minute change meant Compton played the part, with one critic commenting that 'it might have been better in this case to have had it played by a man, for Miss Compton's voice was entirely feminine, and in the scenes with Titania there was by no means sufficient differentiation of voices'.[36] The production was also notable for having a cast where women outnumbered men by three to two: no other Shakespeare production to date has had a cast with more women than men. The dominance of male voices in productions of this era was commented upon by Joyce Grenfell in her review of *Antony and Cleopatra* (1942): 'Because of the necessary overweight of men's voices it would have made a change to have used a woman for the concise introductory remarks between scenes.'[37] However, her comment went unheeded and when narrators were used they were always male.

One way of differentiating between voices is to use accents. However, the RP (Received Pronunciation) voice was very much the sound of both theatre and radio in the first half of the twentieth century. Occasionally an all-purpose yokel or cockney accent could be heard, but they were not always consistently used. In *As You Like It* (1944), Phebe the shepherdess speaks in RP, but the shepherd Silvius uses an inconsistent, generic yokel voice. Audrey, the country wench, and Corin the old shepherd both adopt undefined rural accents. But Adam the servant is RP. Accent here seems to be at the discretion of the individual actor. It also makes Orlando's line to Rosalind 'Your accent is something finer than you could purchase in so removed a dwelling' (3.2.314–15; 1:12:44) seem a nonsense, as so many of the voices are as fine as hers. This may, at least partly, be due to attitudes towards accent in the acting profession at the time. T. H. Pear stated in 1956 that 'in twenty-five years of radio and many more of theatre-plays, speech prototypes and stereotypes have been built up'.[38] He argued that 'a generation has grown up which not only accepts but copies prototypes and stereotypes suggested by the BBC and the colleges of dramatic art'.[39] It may have been the

[34] 'Both Sides of the Microphone – Female Oberon', *Radio Times*, 8 June 1934, p. 741.
[35] 'Both Sides of the Microphone', *Radio Times*, 8 June 1934.
[36] 'Wireless Notes', *Manchester Guardian*, 18 June 1934, p. 10.
[37] Joyce Grenfell, 'Radio', *The Observer*, 8 March 1942, p. 7.
[38] T. H. Pear, *English Social Differences* (London: George Allen & Unwin, 1955), p. 97.
[39] Pear, p. 88.

case that, at a time when listeners were used to hearing certain social groups represented by certain accents, and when many 'real' accents were rarely reflected on radio, the non-specific, rural voices here would not have seemed out of place.

Listeners would have heard at least some genuine regional accents in Shakespeare productions during the BBC's first decade when they were being produced by stations outside London. There were even Welsh-language versions of *A Midsummer Night's Dream* (1938), *Macbeth* (1938) and *The Merchant of Venice* (1939), with two more productions in the 1940s and 1950s. The Cardiff station was undoubtedly the most prolific in those early years, but the other regional stations also aired their own Shakespeare plays. Glasgow and Manchester both broadcast *A Midsummer Night's Dream* using scripts prepared by Nesbitt.[40] Birmingham marked Shakespeare's birthday with *Othello* in two parts, lasting more than two and a half hours.[41] And Sheffield broadcast a three-hour production of *A Midsummer Night's Dream* from the city's Hippodrome.[42] However, once Val Gielgud became head of drama, the broadcasting of Shakespeare's plays was centralised in London. Briggs states that Gielgud 'had feared that Regional drama would not reach "a high standard"' and Gielgud himself wrote that 'occasionally Regional Drama fell short by allowing reach to exceed grasp'.[43] He was no more complimentary about the BBC's national stations, stating that drama in Scotland, Wales and Northern Ireland was 'limited both in quality and importance' when compared to 'metropolitan standards'.[44] Those standards included producing plenty of Shakespeare: Gielgud wrote that when he took over the drama department he was given a directive 'that at least eight of Shakespeare's plays should appear in our programmes each year'.[45] Although there were sometimes only between four and six such plays annually, the department did hit its target more than once in the 1930s, and in 1934 outdid itself with a total of ten.

Gielgud said that he and his producers found out which plays worked best as audio by 'trial and error', discovering that 'in

---

[40] 'A Midsummer Night's Dream', *Radio Times*, 9 November 1923, p. 233; 'A Midsummer Night's Dream', *Radio Times*, 23 November 1923, p. 301.
[41] 'Shakespeare Birthday Performance of "Othello," the Moor of Venice', *Radio Times*, 18 April 1924, p. 140.
[42] 'A Midsummer Night's Dream', *Radio Times*, 14 November 1924, p. 371.
[43] Briggs, *Volume I*, p. 151; Gielgud, *British Radio Drama*, p. 131.
[44] Gielgud, *British Radio Drama*, p. 128.
[45] Val Gielgud, *Years in a Mirror* (London: Bodley Head, 1965), p. 180.

general terms the plays of fantasy and imagination—in particular *A Midsummer Night's Dream* and *The Tempest*—might almost have been written for the "insubstantial pageant" of "thin air"'.[46] This was supported by listeners, including the *Yorkshire Evening Post* reviewer who commented on *The Tempest*'s suitability for radio 'by virtue of its fancifulness, and its play with airy sounds, of the stuff that good broadcasts are made on'.[47] Producers also recognised that radio had a different relationship with its audience than that of the stage. Lea, writing in 1926, suggests that radio offers 'a means of truer interpretation, a medium of finer artistry and a clearer path to truth'.[48] He goes on to point out that while 'hundreds of thousands of people' were listening, they were 'not gathered together in one place, but individualized in their own homes'.[49] This may be why Shakespeare's plays have increasingly been presented in intimate settings, as domestic dramas or focusing on the inner turmoil within the minds of the characters.[50] In 1942, Barbara Burnham's editing of *Antony and Cleopatra* does this by focusing the story on the lead characters, cutting several scenes involving soldiers or battle, including the drinking scene on Pompey's galley, as well as those featuring Antony with Octavia.[51] The cuts also remove some of the passages highlighted by contemporary literary critic Caroline Spurgeon as important. She states: 'The group of images in *Antony and Cleopatra* which, on analysis, immediately attracts attention as peculiar to this play, consists of images of the world, the firmament, the ocean and vastness generally.'[52] She goes on to add that 'this vastness of scale is kept constantly before us by the use of the word "world", which occurs forty-two times, nearly double, or more than double, as often as in most other plays'.[53] Burnham cuts more than a quarter of these references. Consciously or not, this choice brings the play more in line with others, perhaps helping the audience to concentrate on the intimate tragedy of the protagonists, rather than the international impact of the couple's relationship.

---

[46] Gielgud, *Years in a Mirror*, p. 180.
[47] G. C. H., *Yorkshire Evening Post*, 11 December 1933.
[48] Lea, p. 38.
[49] Lea, p. 38.
[50] For examples, see *King Lear* (1974) in Chapter 3 and *Macbeth* (2015) in Chapter 5.
[51] The following scenes are cut entirely: 2.4, 2.7, 3.1, 3.3, 3.4, 3.5, 3.9, 4.7, 4.11. There are also other, shorter cuts.
[52] Caroline F. E. Spurgeon, *Shakespeare's Imagery and What It Tells Us* (Cambridge: Cambridge University Press, 1935), p. 350.
[53] Spurgeon, p. 352.

This chapter charts the 'long chain of development' of radio Shakespeare during the first two decades of the BBC.[54] It establishes that from the very first play, producers used a combination of music, effects and acting technique to engage listeners with the drama. This later became controversial, with many critics feeling that the BBC's productions prioritised this and failed to 'concentrate on the fine speaking of his poetry': an issue that continues to be debated by critics to this day.[55] While the ways early producers conveyed Shakespeare's plays may have been primitive at times, there was a clear emphasis on radio drama as a new genre and the following case studies demonstrate how successive producers attempted to achieve this.

The opening example is the first ever Shakespeare play on the BBC, *Twelfth Night* (1923). Although this was broadcast long before recording was taking place, journalists were invited to watch it go out and detailed written accounts indicate how it sounded and was received. This is followed by *Macbeth* (1935) and while, again, there is no audio, documents describing Creswell's meticulous preparation as well as contemporary and subsequent comments from critics and listeners provide a clear sense of how the production sounded. Leslie Howard's performance as Hamlet in 1938 follows: the first production for which audio is known to exist. Howard had much stage experience in the role, as well as having appeared in an American radio Shakespeare play the previous year, and brings both these skills to his performance. The following year, after the outbreak of war, radio drama was truncated, but Shakespeare's plays continued to be broadcast, albeit in a very much shortened form, as illustrated by *Othello* (1939), of which most of the audio is still held by the BBC. The final case study is *As You Like It* (1944), the first complete recording in the archives and an illustration of the tensions at play within radio Shakespeare, in terms of both script and performance.

It is not clear who first came up with the idea of doing a full-length play, or when, although Briggs states that Cecil Lewis, deputy director of programmes at the time, was extremely interested in drama and 'obtained the services of Miss Cathleen Nesbitt' to adapt and produce several of Shakespeare's plays for radio.[56] She was to be responsible for the first five plays broadcast from London and as such can be seen as the originator of radio drama in the UK.

---

[54] *BBC Year-Book 1930* (London: BBC, 1930), p. 164.
[55] Grace Wyndham Goldie, 'Profit and Loss on the Air', *The Listener*, 16 October 1935, p. 658.
[56] Briggs, *Volume I*, p. 256.

Twelfth Night (1923)

The BBC was only six months old when *Twelfth Night* was broadcast and its small staff 'were mostly executants as well as administrators'.[57] Therefore, 'plays were handled for the most part by outside producers'.[58] In this case, Nesbitt. While *Twelfth Night* was not full text, it did last two hours, so her first job would have been to prepare a suitable script for the broadcast. This does not survive, but it appears to have been a combination of cutting the text and adding narration. According to the actors' trade paper, *The Stage*: 'The play has been specifically arranged in order to adapt it to the medium. The matter that links up the scenes has been either specially written for this purpose or adapted from Lamb [*Tales from Shakespeare*].'[59] And after the broadcast a reporter from the *Daily Telegraph*, who was at Savoy Hill for the performance, wrote: 'It was not deemed advisable to present the piece in its entirety, but merely in a series of scenes, the necessary links for the full understanding of the story being provided by an interlocutor.'[60] Meanwhile, a correspondent for the *Belfast Telegraph* reported that the 'only loss was the duel scene'.[61] It seems that Nesbitt may have intended making further changes, but was deterred from doing so by George Bernard Shaw. Lewis had contacted the great writer, asking him to introduce the production. Shaw not only declined but criticised the script for a 'prologue' that was 'beyond human patience', as well as Nesbitt's plan to swap around the opening two scenes.[62] Shaw told them to 'read the play straight through just as Shakespear [*sic*] (who really knew better than you) wrote it'.[63] Perhaps Nesbitt took this on board, as none of the reviews of the production mention the switch, suggesting she may have returned to the play's usual opening with lovesick Orsino, despite the fact that Viola's shipwreck would have made a potentially much more arresting start on radio.

Before the broadcast, the doom-mongers were predicting the play to be a failure. The prospect of changes to Shakespeare's text

[57] *BBC Year-Book 1930*, p. 155.
[58] *BBC Year-Book 1930*, p. 164.
[59] 'Broadcasting', *The Stage*, 24 May 1923, p. 8.
[60] 'Broadcasting Shakespeare – "Twelfth Night" by Wireless', *Daily Telegraph*, 29 May 1923, p. 12.
[61] 'Shakespeare by Wireless', *Belfast Telegraph*, 29 May 1923, p. 5.
[62] C. A. Lewis, 'G. B. S. Lectures the B.B.C.', *Radio Times*, 14 November 1924, p. 357.
[63] Lewis, *Radio Times*, 14 November 1924.

filled Farjeon with dread, and he gloomily told readers of the *Sunday Pictorial*: 'The play is to be cut, and the scenes are to be linked together by non-Shakespearean explanations, which sounds ominous.'[64] Farjeon was later to become one of the BBC's fiercest critics when it came to radio Shakespeare, and it seems that even before the first broadcast he had reservations. He was not alone in his concerns. The *Sheffield Daily Telegraph* warned: 'Shakespeare by wireless must be a poor substitute for the play on the stage. And poor substitutes are not popular with the public and never will be.'[65]

The actors were professionals, with the exception of the BBC's own Arthur Burrows, who took the role of the Sea Captain, and possibly Mabel Tait, who played Maria. She does not seem to have had any theatrical credits before this performance, but she had won a British Empire Shakespeare Society elocution competition the year before and later went on to appear in a number of other plays for the BBC.[66] Accounts suggest the cast adapted to radio acting remarkably well, especially Playfair, who took the role of Andrew Aguecheek. 'R. C. W.' from the *Daily Herald*, who was also present on the night, described the end of act one, scene three, where Sir Toby urges Sir Andrew to caper 'higher' (1.3.126), stating that 'they rose to the occasion nobly. [. . .] So well did they play this, that if my eyes had been shut, I should have sworn that Sir Andrew was not standing motionless, as he really was, but capering to the ceiling.'[67] The writer does not explain how Playfair did this, although comments from the distinguished actress Dame May Whitty, who was listening at home, suggest voice was probably a factor: 'One visualised the foolish, timorous knight though one could not see him, and that was because the speaker used the upward inflection almost continually.'[68] She also had praise for many of the rest of the cast, particularly commending Herbert Waring as Malvolio: 'One realised the pomposity and fatuousness of the character, and one saw that painful smile and the yellow stockings cross gartered.'[69] She also found Enid Rose, playing Olivia, 'satisfying', adding that 'one felt the melancholy, the

---

[64] Herbert Farjeon, 'In the Limelight – Broadcasting Shakespeare', *Sunday Pictorial*, 20 May 1923, p. 18.

[65] 'The Wireless War', *Sheffield Daily Telegraph*, 22 May 1923, p. 6.

[66] 'Speaking Shakespeare – Mr Ainley's Awards for Elocution', *The Times*, 29 July 1922, p. 12.

[67] R. C. W., 'Shakespeare in Modern Dress – How "Twelfth Night" Was Played for Wireless', *Daily Herald*, 29 May 1923, p. 7.

[68] Dame May Whitty, 'The BBC Plays', *Popular Wireless*, 23 June 1923, p. 688.

[69] Whitty, *Popular Wireless*, 23 June 1923.

feeling of weariness and distaste, the gradual quickening of interest in the saucy boy who comes as Orsino's messenger, and the graciousness and simple dignity of the great lady'.[70] Nesbitt, who played both Viola and Sebastian, was praised by R. C. W., who admired her 'velvety tones' as well as the 'resonant voice of Orsino (Gerald Lawrence), and the capable singing of Norman Notley'.[71] After the broadcast, a reporter from the paper spoke to Lawrence about the experience: 'There is a sort of fascination in playing before an invisible audience. One feels that at the back of it (the big receiver) there are thousands of people listening. [. . .] But of course you miss your audience.'[72] For the first performance of its kind, the cast seems to have not only coped well with the new medium but also impressed at least some of the critics.

Despite the move to the new studio, technology remained very basic. The production did include music by Henry Purcell performed on a harpsichord.[73] But it is unclear what, if any, sound effects were used, with a retrospective article on the BBC's history suggesting that 'sound effects in this first year of broadcasting were still in a rudimentary stage'.[74] The actors also had to be thoughtfully positioned, as *Popular Wireless* magazine noted that 'the artistes must have been placed very carefully in the studio so that no drowning effects were caused by a strong voice being placed nearer to the microphone than one not so powerful'.[75] The reception for those listening over the airwaves appears to have been patchy. St. John Ervine, another of the journalists invited to watch the performance, noted that when he was in the room with the actors, Nesbitt's voice was 'beautiful', but when he was given a chance to listen over the wireless, he heard 'tinny and sometimes unintelligible noises' from the speaker and Nesbitt sounded 'at one moment [to have] a pebble in her mouth, and, at another moment, that she had unaccountably contracted a lisp'.[76] Whitty was also aware that not everyone heard the same performance: 'I gather that there is enormous variety in the instruments used; that while one person using a head telephone gets the voice

[70] Whitty, *Popular Wireless*, 23 June 1923.
[71] R. C. W., *Daily Herald*, 29 May 1923.
[72] 'What It Feels Like – Actor's Impression of Play to Invisible Audience', *Daily Herald*, 29 May 1923, p. 7.
[73] 'Broadcasting', *The Times*, 28 May 1923, p. 10; R. C. W., *Daily Herald*, 29 May 1923.
[74] *BBC Year-Book 1930*, p. 164.
[75] 'Topical Notes and News – Voices Well-balanced', *Popular Wireless*, 9 June 1923, p. 609.
[76] St. John Ervine, 'At the Play – Listening-in to Shakespeare', *The Observer*, 3 June 1923, p. 11.

very clearly, [for] others listening to a horn [. . .] the sound is metallic and like a bad gramophone record.'[77] Reception quality would
be an issue for many years to come, although on the whole this does
not seem to have deterred listeners; perhaps the novelty of the new
medium overrode its drawbacks.

This first production certainly appears to have been a success with
its audience. The *Belfast Telegraph* reported:

> At the Broadcasting station Shakespeare was applauded by telegram
> for the first time. The first messenger arriving at the end of Act 2
> announced from King's Lynn that the performance was an 'enthral-
> ling, wonderful, triumphant success.' Actors and actresses read the
> applause while they said their lines.[78]

Wireless Weekly told readers that the play 'has been received with a
perfect chorus of praise from the Press and from listeners-in. About
five hundred letters were received by the BBC couched in the most
laudatory vein, all asking for more.'[79] The correspondent acknowledged that 'about five communications' were negative but added that
'five hundred for and five against is a pretty decisive indication of
popular favour'.[80]

Without a full script or any audio it is difficult to know how the
production might have reflected critical thought about the play at
the time. George Brandes's comment that '*Twelfth Night* is perhaps
the most graceful and harmonious comedy Shakespeare ever wrote'
might indicate why it was chosen.[81] The reviews and comments on
the broadcast certainly suggest that it was entertaining. However, as
its adaptor was a theatre actress, rather than an academic, it seems
likely that Nesbitt drew inspiration from the stage and not contemporary critical thinking. When the BBC started recruiting university-
educated producers a short while later, the influence of Shakespeare
academics became more evident.

Twelfth Night may have taken advantage of the better facilities
available at Savoy Hill compared to Marconi House, but it was still
far from ideal for performing Shakespeare. However, within a few
years plans were being drawn up for a new, purpose-built home for
the BBC in London: Broadcasting House. And by the time Creswell

---

[77] Whitty, *Popular Wireless*, 23 June 1923.
[78] 'Shakespeare by Wireless', *Belfast Telegraph*, 29 May 1923.
[79] 'Broadcasting News', *Wireless Weekly*, 13 June 1923, p. 114.
[80] 'Broadcasting News', *Wireless Weekly*, 13 June 1923.
[81] George Brandes, *William Shakespeare: A Critical Study* (London: William Heinemann, 1905), p. 233.

came to present his production of *Macbeth* in 1935, he and his colleagues were using this new studio complex to its full extent.

Macbeth (1935)

Macbeth was Creswell's twelfth Shakespeare production for the BBC and he put much preparation into his work. The script has the most detailed annotation of any during this period and includes a seventeen-page essay to the cast.[82] Although no audio exists, these documents, along with reviews and letters of the time, indicate how this production sounded. The *Manchester Guardian* told readers that Creswell would 'attempt to convey over the microphone the manner in which Shakespeare's first producers created the characters, and to accomplish this he has made considerable research'.[83] In his guidance to the cast, Creswell states:

> These notes are actually the result of very intensive study, first of the actual 1623 Folio (the only authoritative version from which all others have been drawn), of a number of modern editions including the Arden and the Furness Variorum and a legion of commentators from Doctor Johnson to [A. C.] Bradley, [R. H.] Case, and [Harley] Granville Barker.[84]

Granville-Barker's 'Preface to *Macbeth*' in *The Players' Shakespeare* seems to have been particularly influential, with Creswell frequently paraphrasing the critical essay, including the descriptions of both Macbeths.[85] He also echoes Granville-Barker's dislike of the 'tradition' of playing the Porter as 'a candidate for an inebriates' home' and the fact that 'Shakespeare never once calls them [the weird sisters] witches'.[86]

---

[82] Peter Creswell, 'From the Producer to the Members of the Cast. A Few Preliminary Notes and Suggestions about *Macbeth*', in Shakespeare, *Macbeth*, ed. by Creswell (unpublished, Library of Birmingham S334.1935Q).

[83] 'Wireless Notes – Godfrey Tearle as Macbeth', *Manchester Guardian*, 12 October 1935, p. 14.

[84] Creswell, 'A Few Preliminary Notes', pp. 1–2.

[85] For Macbeth, see Creswell, 'A Few Preliminary Notes', p. 3, p. 9, and Harley Granville-Barker, *More Prefaces to Shakespeare* (Princeton: Princeton University Press, 1974), p. 60, p. 73. For Lady Macbeth, see Creswell, 'A Few Preliminary Notes', p. 8, and Granville-Barker, p. 73.

[86] See Creswell, 'A Few Preliminary Notes', p. 13, p. 16, and Granville-Barker, p. 84, p. 61n.

Creswell used his academic research not only to determine how he wanted the characters to be played, but also to help him decide on how to cut the play for broadcast. In an article in the *Radio Times* he comments on the 'passages that most commentators suspect as being interpolations by Middleton or Rowley or Wilkins or all three', adding: 'I have cut only such passages as I myself, in the light of this evidence, have come to regard as doubtfully Shakespearean.'[87] This might suggest Creswell viewed his script preparation as an academic exercise, but there may have been another reason for his decisions. Radio critics, in particular Farjeon, had taken exception to the fact the BBC was editing Shakespeare's plays for broadcast, with running times rarely more than two hours. Creswell's assertion that what he was presenting was the 'real' Shakespeare might have been intended to justify his cuts and fend off potential criticism.

Creswell's edits include removing the first two scenes of the play, opening with Macbeth's first line (1.3.36). This may again be inspired by Granville-Barker, who suggested it would make 'an interesting and very possible, and indeed a most dramatic, beginning'.[88] However, Creswell cuts about thirty lines from the Porter's scene, text that both Bradley and Granville-Barker believed was written by Shakespeare.[89] Creswell's notes offer no explanation, but it seems likely it may have been for reasons of taste and decency, rather than textual validity, as they include the reference to the 'farmer who hanged himself' (2.3.4), and the Porter's observations on the things drink provokes – including a desire for sex and the inability to perform (2.3.21–34).

Creswell's apparent reliance on academic writing does not mean that he was not also thinking in terms of the needs of radio. In the *Radio Times* article he gives a highly visual description of the play he is presenting: 'through this ensanguined mist, lit by the glare of their cauldron fire or fitfully illuminated in storm and tempest, are dimly seen those shapes of horror, the Weird Sisters.'[90] To convey this, Creswell uses music, sound effects and different acoustics to create a sophisticated mix, with the script detailing how each of these elements should be combined. The murder of Banquo in act three, scene three is an example of this. The scene opens with: 'Music in 8A. Sinister motif. Fade up night effects in 6D and 6E. Fade to

[87] Peter Creswell, 'Shakespeare's Stark Tragedy', *Radio Times*, 4 October 1935, p. 6.
[88] Granville-Barker, p. 61.
[89] A. C. Bradley, *Shakespearean Tragedy* (London: Macmillan & Co., 1952), p. 397; Granville-Barker, p. 63.
[90] Creswell, *Radio Times*, 4 October 1935.

background.'[91] Creswell sets up the atmosphere with both music
and a mix of recorded and live effects, before fading them down to
enable his audience to hear the speeches clearly. Just before the Third
Murderer's line 'Hark, I hear horses' (3.3.8), there is the instruction to 'Fade in walking horses', a recorded effect.[92] This is faded
down as the First Murderer says 'His horses go about' (3.3.11). At
the Second Murderer's cry of 'A light, a light!' (3.3.15), Creswell
instructs 'Pause – hold "night" effects'.[93] Finally, after the First
Murderer's line 'Let it come down!' (3.3.18), there are more spot
effects.[94] Although the details of these are not specified, it seems
safe to assume they would have simulated the attack on Banquo.
Creswell uses what amounts to an effects 'score', just as a composer
would score a piece of music, to support and enhance the dialogue
and create a vivid picture in the listener's imagination.

This seems to have had mixed success. The reviewer in *The Times*
felt Creswell overused effects and music, stating that the production was 'a virile, if somewhat rather too noisy, affair'.[95] Critic Basil
Maine accused Creswell of being 'preoccupied' with effects and
'irrelevant fanfares'.[96] However, the review in the *Daily Telegraph*
was headlined 'Impressive Broadcast of Macbeth' and praised the
'imaginative background' supplied to each scene in the form of
'incidental music and appropriate noises', particularly in the 'second
scene with the witches [which] was full of atmosphere'.[97] The writer
was less impressed with Godfrey Tearle as Macbeth, though, finding
themselves 'hampered occasionally by the very thing that was the
production's greatest beauty—the range of Godfrey Tearle's magnificent voice'.[98] In particular it was 'sometimes not immediately certain,
when he was using his upper register, that he was still speaking'.[99]
This may have been due to the limits of either the broadcasting
equipment or the reviewer's wireless set, or both. However, this was
not the only criticism of Tearle. *The Times* had reservations: 'In the
early scenes, his Macbeth is too much inclined to declaim, and it is

[91] Shakespeare, *Macbeth*, ed. by Creswell, p. 24.
[92] Shakespeare, *Macbeth*, ed. by Creswell, p. 24.
[93] Shakespeare, *Macbeth*, ed. by Creswell, pp. 24–5.
[94] Shakespeare, *Macbeth*, ed. by Creswell, p. 25.
[95] 'Broadcast Drama: Macbeth', *The Times*, 14 October 1935, p. 21.
[96] Basil Maine, *The BBC and its Audience* (London: Thomas Nelson & Sons, 1939),
    p. 103.
[97] W. A. D., 'Godfrey Tearle and Flora Robson: Impressive Broadcast of Macbeth', *Daily
    Telegraph*, 14 October 1935, p. 10.
[98] W. A. D., *Daily Telegraph*, 14 October 1935.
[99] W. A. D., *Daily Telegraph*, 14 October 1935.

not until Duncan has been killed that a portrait of the man begins to emerge.'[100] And Maine also had harsh words for Tearle, saying he 'could not believe in his Macbeth for a single moment'.[101] He added: 'His every pause was a weighty footnote. His intonation of "Not yet" in answer to "Is the king stirring?" and "Is't far you ride?" carried the unmistakable undertone of a villainous "Ha! Ha!"'[102] Tearle was a well-known stage actor and reviews of his theatrical performances echo this description of his playing style, something particularly unsuited to radio, where more intimate acting is usually most effective. However, this was not his first Shakespeare play for the BBC, having previously played three leading roles for Creswell. And comments made by Tearle the year before *Macbeth* suggest the pair had a good working relationship: 'Both he and I felt that we were there to interpret Shakespeare and to find a producer who wants to be an interpreter of Shakespeare, rather than an adaptor of Shakespeare to his own extravagant ideas, is a relief in these days.'[103] Despite Creswell's radio-specific use of sound, he seems to have been less aware that the performance of his actors also needed to be suited to the medium.

There were also a number of general comments from reviewers about the cast's delivery of the text. Maine felt that the production 'failed because neither word-sense nor word-music was glorified, but impoverished rather'.[104] And Grace Wyndham Goldie commented that the production did not fulfil the need for 'fine speaking', complaining that '[n]obody seemed to be bothering very much about the verse'.[105] She continued: 'In the minor parts there were all kinds of accents which varied from the best Oxford to something perilously near Cockney: the only unity seemed to be in a failure to reveal the rhythms of the lines that were being spoken.'[106] However, her criticism seems to be as much about class as the ability of the actors, with some voices deemed unacceptable for the job.

Creswell's *Macbeth* made the most of the current technology, combining sound effects and music in an attempt to create a production that would entertain his audience and be faithful to what

---

[100] 'Broadcast Drama: Macbeth', *The Times*, 14 October 1935.

[101] Maine, p. 103.

[102] Maine, p. 103.

[103] Edith Evans and Godfrey Tearle, 'They Will Play the Two Leading Parts', *Radio Times*, 9 February 1934, p. 371.

[104] Maine, p. 103.

[105] Wyndham Goldie, *The Listener*, 16 October 1935.

[106] Wyndham Goldie, *The Listener*, 16 October 1935.

he believed was the genuine text of Shakespeare's play. However, this was no pompous, academic production. Creswell's intentions are perhaps best summed up in a letter he wrote to the *Radio Times* the month before this production, as part of the ongoing argument about the cutting of Shakespeare's plays. Creswell told readers that he 'strongly suspect[ed]' that, like him, Shakespeare's '"intention" was no more than to entertain his public'.[107] And it seems he was not alone in wanting to entertain on the radio. Leslie Howard had already had experience of the American way of doing Shakespeare on air when he came to the BBC and brought with him a less reverential attitude to the text.

Hamlet (1938)[108]

Howard was an established film star when he made his only appearance on the BBC in a Shakespeare play. He was also very familiar with the text of *Hamlet*, having played the part on Broadway and toured the production around the USA.[109] While in America he had also appeared in a radio production of *Much Ado About Nothing* for CBS.[110] This was part of a series of Shakespeare plays, all just an hour long, featuring 'a galaxy of stars' from Hollywood.[111] These productions were firmly populist, with introductions proclaiming that they would be bringing 'the great dramatist's work to a larger audience than we have ever reached before'.[112] It seems likely his experiences in America had an impact on his attitude to performing the play in England.

Howard gave an interview to the *Radio Times* in which he described Hamlet as 'a normal man, intelligent, subtle, but certainly not neurotic'.[113] He saw the character as a man of action, with hesitation a sign of reasonable caution, rather than cowardice, citing the play-within-a-play as critical: 'From this point the gloves are off, and

---

[107] Creswell, *Radio Times*, 27 September 1935.
[108] *Hamlet* (extract – act 3, scene 1), 2 January 1938 (unpublished, BBC Sound Archive, 0F025573).
[109] 'Both Sides of the Microphone – Hamlet and Cantor', *Radio Times*, 31 December 1937, p. 4; 'Leslie Howard in "Hamlet"', *Radio Times*, 31 December 1937, p. 7.
[110] *Much Ado About Nothing*, Columbia [CBS], 19 July 1937, <https://www.youtube.com/watch?v=yBxg8pBPlrs> [accessed 17 January 2021].
[111] Michael P. Jensen, *The Battle of the Bard: Shakespeare on U.S. Radio in 1937* (Leeds: Arc Humanities Press, 2018), p. 43.
[112] *Much Ado About Nothing*, Columbia, 19 July 1937.
[113] 'Leslie Howard in "Hamlet"', *Radio Times*, 31 December 1937.

he has to meet violence with violence.'[114] A review of the production in *The Times* describes Howard's Hamlet as 'an exciting character to listen to, with a crisis always upon him, and urgent in all his business' with 'the drama within Hamlet's mind [. . .] of rather less importance than usual' and the play 'active, bustling, an affair of moves and countermoves'.[115] The reviewer concluded: 'This may well be better, for the purpose of a broadcast performance, than too subtle an inspection of motives or too individual a solution of the play's psychological mysteries.'[116] Rejecting the character's psychological aspects in favour of a more active protagonist was not without critical support. Bradley suggests: 'This melancholy is something very different from insanity, in anything like the usual meaning of that word. [. . .] It's a totally different thing from the madness which he feigns.'[117] It is also possible that psychoanalysis played a part in the development of Howard's version of the character. The summary of Hamlet in Sigmund Freud's *The Interpretation of Dreams* bears some similarities with Howard's, stating that 'Hamlet is far from being represented as a person incapable of taking any action'.[118]

Howard is not credited as adaptor; that was producer Barbara Burnham.[119] But it seems likely that after Howard's extensive experience with the play he would have influenced the editing of the text. Some of the cuts are common to many productions of *Hamlet*, such as the scene between Polonius and his spy Reynaldo. However, other edits are more surprising. Hamlet's advice to the players (3.2.1–44) and Polonius's 'pastoral-comical, historical-pastoral' speech (2.2.324–8), two of the better-known sections of the text, are removed. The loss of this last speech prompted a listener to write to the *Radio Times*, accusing Burnham of 'faulty cutting', to which she replied: 'Too much of Polonius (when you don't see him) makes him tedious, and that is why we preferred to cut the tragical-historical speech.'[120] But she admitted that was not the only reason she cut the text: 'I should have liked two and a half hours, with two *proper*

---

[114] 'Leslie Howard in "Hamlet"', *Radio Times*, 31 December 1937.

[115] 'Broadcast Drama – "Hamlet" by William Shakespeare', *The Times*, 3 January 1938, p. 10.

[116] 'Broadcast Drama', *The Times*, 3 January 1938.

[117] Bradley, *Shakespearean Tragedy*, p. 121.

[118] Sigmund Freud, *The Interpretation of Dreams*, ed. and trans. by James Strachey (New York: Basic Books, 2010), p. 282.

[119] William Shakespeare, *Hamlet*, ed. by Barbara Burnham (unpublished, Library of Birmingham S317.1938Q).

[120] 'What the Other Listener Thinks – Faulty Cutting?', *Radio Times*, 21 January 1938, p. 9.

three- to five-minute intervals, but had to make the best of a bad job in the time allowed.'[121] Her cuts do help speed up the play, however, and create the sense of urgency commented on by *The Times*.

The BBC must have considered Howard's performance important as it is the first excerpt from a full play to exist in the archives. The extract begins at the start of act three and incorporates Hamlet's 'To be or not to be' soliloquy. Listening to it gives some indication of the way Howard presented Hamlet. Rather than being a contemplative reflection on his situation, Howard's delivery suggests a man preparing to take action. He leaves a slight pause after 'And by opposing' but then says 'end them' with force and speed (3.1.59). He runs 'Devoutly to be wish'd' straight on to 'To die' (3.1.63), putting emphasis on the idea that Hamlet would like to escape everything through death. He begins 'To sleep: perchance to dream' harshly and says 'ay, there's the rub' (3.1.64) with a tone of voice that suggests that he has no need to speculate on an afterlife; he knows it will be bad. When he says 'conscience does make cowards of us all' (3.1.82), his emphasis on 'conscience' suggests that what he actually means is fear of death. Throughout the soliloquy his delivery is firm and assured. He is a man talking himself into what he must do next, not a man dithering over his course of action.

The audio extract continues with his encounter with Ophelia. At her entrance, Howard whispers 'The fair Ophelia' (3.1.88). His voice is soft and loving but, when he addresses her, his tone becomes harsh, as if he is determined to make Ophelia fall out of love with him. Ophelia herself, played by Hermione Hannen, has a soft, light voice, although there is a slight edge when she says 'you know right well you did' about the gifts he gave her, and on 'Rich gifts wax poor when givers prove unkind' (3.1.96, 100). Howard pauses before he softly says 'I did love you once', again suggesting genuine love. He hesitates after 'believed me' and stutters over 'I loved you not', suggesting pent-up emotion and the reverse of what he says (3.1.115–17). He finishes the speech with what seems like a genuine warning about men, with the insertion of 'all' after 'We are arrant knaves' and continuing with 'believe none of us. Go thy ways to a nunnery' (3.1.126–7). There is then a long pause before he adds, angrily, 'Where's your father?' (3.1.127). Ophelia audibly winces, before attempting an offhand 'At home, my lord' (3.1.128). But her tone makes it clear she is lying, and the mood of the scene

[121] 'What the Other Listener Thinks', *Radio Times*, 21 January 1938. The play's duration was one hour and fifty-five minutes.

changes, with Hamlet now railing at her. After his exit, Hannen cries through Ophelia's monologue, again suggesting a love match between the pair.

Writing in 1930 about the latter part of the play, William Empson states: 'It is easy to forget Ophelia's situation, and feel that she was a sweet pathetic creature, and it was somehow natural that she should be crazy.'[122] This suggestion that Ophelia is *not* 'sweet pathetic' sits well with this production. Aside from the evidence from this short audio extract, the reviewer in *The Times* said: 'Miss Hannen's Ophelia was emotional but often impressive', while Grenfell wrote in *The Observer*: 'her madness was lightly suggested, a madness to wring the heart.'[123] This Ophelia may ultimately become a victim but has at least some agency and personality in the earlier parts of the play.

The audio extract also includes a little of Basil Radford's portrayal of King Claudius. In his film roles the actor has been described as 'amiable, avuncular' and as having 'perfected the slightly flummoxed, unfailingly courteous, public-school, civil-servant type'.[124] However, in *Hamlet* he is closer to Howard's description of Claudius as 'a strong man; clever, able, hard-headed'.[125] This is not unlike G. Wilson Knight's description of Claudius as having 'clear and exact thought and an efficient and confident control of affairs'.[126] The review in *The Times* said Radford's Claudius 'appears as a powerful and dominating figure, a Renaissance statesman'.[127] This is particularly clear in the audio extract. After he has eavesdropped on Hamlet and Ophelia, he is contemptuous of the idea that Hamlet is in love and sounds concerned but not afraid that his nephew poses 'some danger' (3.1.159–64).

Radio critics enjoyed the production but did raise issues that were already becoming regular concerns about the broadcasting of Shakespeare on radio, including the delivery of poetry and how to convey who was speaking and where the scene was set. *The Times* reviewer said that it was not 'possible to put the poetry first', adding:

[122] William Empson, *Seven Types of Ambiguity* (London: Chatto & Windus, 1949), p. 212.
[123] 'Broadcast Drama', *The Times*, 3 January 1938; Joyce Grenfell, 'Broadcasting – Leslie Howard as Hamlet', *The Observer*, 9 January 1938, p. 9.
[124] David Quinlan, *The Illustrated Directory of Film Stars* (London: B. T. Batsford Ltd, 1981), p. 389; Brian McFarlane, *The Encyclopedia of British Film* (London: Methuen, 2003), p. 544.
[125] 'Leslie Howard in "Hamlet"', *Radio Times*, 31 December 1937.
[126] G. Wilson Knight, *The Wheel of Fire* (London: Routledge, 2001), p. 36.
[127] 'Broadcast Drama', *The Times*, 3 January 1938.

'There was no violence done to it, but equally it never became the prime mover of the play.'[128] This, they felt, was a missed opportunity: 'it might be argued that this was to neglect the special contribution which broadcast drama might make to the appreciation of Shakespeare.'[129] And Grenfell, who advocated following the text while listening, stated that without doing so 'it must have been nimble work catching on to the characters. A brief announcement of the setting "A room of State" or "In Polonius' House" would have made things easier.'[130] However, *The Times* reviewer contradicted her, stating that 'it was remarkable how little in the way of auditory background, of scenery for the ear, was necessary to make it entirely comprehensible'.[131] This also indicates a limited use of sound effects.

Howard's interpretation may well have been influenced by his stage experience but, as he had previously acted on radio, his performance seems well suited to the medium, making use of the intimacy of the microphone. However, other actors were yet to grasp the difference between radio and the stage, notably Henry Ainley, who would take the leading role in *Othello* the following year.

Othello (1939)[132]

During the late 1930s, the BBC's productions of Shakespeare's plays on radio were generally around two hours long. But after the declaration of war in 1939, there was a significant change. The last pre-war play, *King Lear*, in May of that year ran to 125 minutes. The first play during the conflict, a combination of *1 Henry IV* and *2 Henry IV*, was just thirty. This was largely because the BBC deemed drama 'superfluous' at a time of national crisis and drama production was limited to 'not more than half an hour'.[133] In addition, the department was moved out of London, first to Evesham, then to Manchester. Val Gielgud recalls that 'by mid-October, however, things had begun to straighten themselves out [. . .] with the distinguished help of Henry Ainley and Leslie Banks [I was able] to put the

---

128 'Broadcast Drama', *The Times*, 3 January 1938.
129 'Broadcast Drama', *The Times*, 3 January 1938.
130 Grenfell, *The Observer*, 9 January 1938.
131 'Broadcast Drama', *The Times*, 3 January 1938.
132 *Othello* (extract – act 5, scene 2), a.k.a. 'Put Out The Light', 2 December 1939 (unpublished, BBC Sound Archive).
133 Gielgud, *British Radio Drama*, p. 97.

first wartime Shakespeare on the air'.[134] Despite the upheaval, the script of the thirty-minute *Othello* has survived, along with a twenty-four-minute chunk of audio from the production.[135]

Unlike previous scripts, there are no instructions for engineers or actors, such as sound effects, music or studio locations, while the stage directions have been left in. Although clearly act four, scene three and act five, scene two of *Othello*, the production was billed as 'Put Out The Light'. Gielgud may have thought it was topical, as it was broadcast three months after the start of the blackout, but it seems to have left reviewers puzzled, including Wyndham Goldie, who commented: 'heaven knows why [it was given], the belittling, revue-sketch title.'[136] The choice was appropriate, though, as the two scenes cover Desdemona's conversation with Emilia as she prepares for bed, including the Willow Song, and then Othello's murder of his wife – with the line 'Put out the light' (5.2.7). Choosing to perform just the end of the play not only made sense when presenting such a truncated production, but also meant that the audience would hear what some regarded as the highlights. Bradley wrote that the scene where 'Desdemona and Emilia converse, and the willow-song is sung', was 'where pathos [. . .] reaches its height'.[137] He also believed that the second half of the play 'is immeasurably more exciting than the first'.[138] In addition, it meant that the play focused on the relationship between Othello and Desdemona, concurring with Wilson Knight's view that '*Othello* is eminently a domestic tragedy'.[139]

Desdemona dominates the first half of this production until her death, and there is very little of Iago, just ten lines. However, the largest part is that of Othello, played by Ainley, who was a highly respected theatre actor. This might explain why the audio extract does not begin until the second scene, opening with Othello's line: 'It is the cause' (5.2.1). Ainley had played Othello on radio seven years earlier and had left an indelible impression on Gielgud: 'The importance of reasonable proximity to the microphone was so lost upon Henry Ainley that it was necessary to station a couple of Effects boys, one at each elbow, to lead him back into position whenever

[134] Gielgud, *British Radio Drama*, p. 98.
[135] William Shakespeare, *Othello*, ed. by anon. (unpublished, Library of Birmingham S341.1939Q).
[136] Grace Wyndham Goldie, 'Critic on the Hearth – Broadcast Drama: Here's Great Acting', *The Listener*, 7 December 1939, p. 1,141. See also Guy Fletcher, 'This Week's Radio Miscellany', *Radio Times*, 24 November 1939, p. 7.
[137] Bradley, *Shakespearean Tragedy*, p. 61.
[138] Bradley, *Shakespearean Tragedy*, p. 55.
[139] Wilson Knight, *The Wheel of Fire*, p. 123.

he moved to address an imaginary auditorium.'[140] Listening to his
performance in 1939, it is easy to picture this scene. His delivery is
melodramatic, with much vibrato in his voice, and it has the feel of a
stage performance. His delivery of 'Oh! Oh! Oh!' (5.2.193) is almost
like listening to someone sing a musical scale from high to low, three
times in a row.

The *Radio Times* wrote that attracting Ainley to the part was 'a
remarkable achievement for wartime broadcasting'.[141] And his status
is also reflected in the review of the play in the *Manchester Guardian*:
'Mr Ainley gives the feeling which is not the case with most actors
that it would be perfectly satisfactory to hear him alone simply reciting passages from the play.'[142] The reviewer added that his voice
had 'an extraordinary range of tone and is one of the most musical
they [the listeners] are ever likely to hear'.[143] Wyndham Goldie was
less sure, asking: 'was this Othello? Othello was a murderer. And
there is in Mr Ainley's splendid voice, even when it rages, a mellow
richness which speaks an inner satisfaction and which continually
denies the dark violence of Othello's impulse to destroy.'[144] She was
still very impressed, though, saying Ainley had 'magnificence'.[145]
Ainley's delivery was certainly very dramatic, if perhaps not very
believable, and his declamatory style may have pleased those who
had not always felt radio productions delivered Shakespeare's poetry
to full effect.

Wyndham Goldie was less convinced by those she referred to as
'secondary actors', such as Hermione Hannen as Desdemona, who
she described as going 'to her death-bed with the prattling gaiety
of a Mayfair miss undressing after a party'.[146] Unfortunately the
audio of the Willow Song scene does not survive, but in the extract
of Desdemona's murder, this does not seem to be a fair description of her performance. Hannen's Desdemona shares some traits
with her Ophelia the year before. Once again, she has a slight edge
to her voice at times. She is also forceful in her defence of her life.
Initially she sounds afraid when Othello says 'I would not kill thy
soul' and she responds, 'Talk you of killing?' (5.2.32–3). But when

[140] Gielgud, *British Radio Drama*, p. 123.
[141] 'Both Sides of the Microphone – Great Names', *Radio Times*, 17 November 1939,
    p. 5.
[142] 'Review of Broadcasting: Mr Henry Ainley as Othello—A Scrapbook Revival',
    Manchester Guardian, 6 December 1939, p. 8.
[143] 'Review of Broadcasting', *Manchester Guardian*, 6 December 1939.
[144] Wyndham Goldie, *The Listener*, 7 December 1939.
[145] Wyndham Goldie, *The Listener*, 7 December 1939.
[146] Wyndham Goldie, *The Listener*, 7 December 1939.

the handkerchief is mentioned she is firm in denying she gave it to Cassio, almost shouting the word 'no' (5.2.49). She remains strong when she says 'Ay, but not yet to die' (5.2.52), but as the scene progresses she sounds more frightened, desperately begging, 'Kill me tomorrow; let me live tonight' (5.2.80). Strangely, her murder is silent. Neither Ainley nor Hannen makes any noise, and there are no sound effects or music to give any indication that he has smothered her. It is an anti-climax in a scene that had been building between the two actors and must also have been confusing for any listener who did not know the play.

Wyndham Goldie had mixed views about Martita Hunt's performance as Emilia: 'though excellent in her outburst at the end was, at the beginning, merely Kensington to Desdemona's Mayfair'.[147] Hunt was an actor described as 'playing all kinds of commanding roles (if they weren't commanding when she got them, they certainly were when she'd done with them)'.[148] She gives the same impression in the audio extract. She virtually screams at Othello 'Thou dost belie her' (5.2.130) and spits out 'ignorant as *dirt*' (5.2.159). She shouts 'odious *damned* lie', and the repetition of 'lie' is particularly strong. However, Hunt's performance, possibly influenced by playing opposite Ainley, also veers towards the melodramatic. Her speech beginning 'Villainy! Villainy!' (5.2.185–8) borders on the hysterical. Unlike Desdemona, Emilia does make a noise when she is killed, a strange wail-cum-whimper-cum-scream.

Othello was the last half-hour production of the war. Less than a fortnight later *The Listener* reported that 'the state of affairs was only temporary'.[149] Briggs writes that the nation had been 'robbed of its theatre' due to the closure of the West End, and the expectation was that the BBC should be filling the gap.[150] The next play, *Macbeth* with Godfrey Tearle once again in the lead, was an hour long, and for the following two years or so, most productions hovered around that length or a bit longer. However, by 1944 productions were back up to two hours or more, including a virtually full-text production of *As You Like It*.

---

[147] Wyndham Goldie, *The Listener*, 7 December 1939.
[148] McFarlane, p. 327.
[149] 'Broadcast Drama in Wartime', *The Listener*, 14 December 1939, p. 1,162.
[150] Briggs, *Volume III*, p. 89.

As You Like It (1944)[151]

The year 1944 saw the release of Laurence Olivier's film of *Henry V*, later described by Daniel Rosenthal as 'Shakespeare as propaganda'.[152] However, the BBC had already presented its own propaganda versions of the play in 1942 and 1943, starring Olivier and Esmond Knight respectively. Both productions featured on the front cover of the *Radio Times* in the weeks they were broadcast. In the case of Olivier, the magazine declared: 'No better prelude to St George's Day this year could be found than the burning words of King Harry on the eve of Agincourt—"Be copy now to men of grosser blood, and teach them how to war."'[153] Knight's appearance was previewed with: 'In 1415 the men wore armour, and in 1943 the armour is borne by the vehicles, but the same spirit informs the steel.'[154] The *Radio Times* also highlighted the fact that Knight was 'playing his first big radio part since he lost his sight when serving on the *Prince of Wales* during the *Bismarck* action'.[155] However, the response from the radio audience 'showed that the majority wished to have their minds taken off the war when listening to a play on the wireless'.[156] Therefore instead of heroic battles, in 1944 the BBC went for entertainment, with productions of the great tragedies and comedies, including *As You Like It*, the earliest full-length Shakespeare play held in the BBC archives.

The production starred Edith Evans and Michael Redgrave, who had played Rosalind and Orlando on stage together at the Old Vic in London eight years earlier. However, the *Manchester Guardian* reviewer was unimpressed with their radio version, stating that 'Edith Evans, though a brilliant actress, has not the right voice for a broadcast of Rosalind'.[157] They added: 'Everything depends upon the voice, and her voice, for all its vitality, has marked mannerisms which stand out strongly in radio and are not the mannerisms which

---

[151] *As You Like It*, BBC Home Service, 8 September 1944 (unpublished, BBC Sound Archive).
[152] Daniel Rosenthal, *Shakespeare on Screen* (London: Hamlyn, 2000), p. 42.
[153] 'This Week – Laurence Olivier', *Radio Times*, 17 April 1942, p. 1.
[154] 'Special Programmes – Echo of Agincourt', *Radio Times*, 26 February 1943, p. 1.
[155] C. Gordon Glover, 'Introducing – At Agincourt', *Radio Times*, 26 February 1943, p. 5.
[156] *BBC Handbook 1941* (London: BBC, 1941), p. 22.
[157] 'Broadcasting Review', *Manchester Guardian*, 13 September 1944, p. 6.

would suggest the character of Rosalind.'[158] By contrast, Redgrave's performance seems perfectly suited to radio. Whenever he is 'on mic', regardless of whether he has any actual lines, he makes his presence felt, often through non-verbal noises. In the wrestling scene, Orlando and Charles do not speak during the bout but they are continually panting, grunting and slapping (0:16:20–40). Redgrave does something similar when Orlando and Adam are in the forest, grunting as if with the exertion of lifting Adam (0:45:51).

In addition to Redgrave's non-verbal noises, his line delivery is markedly different to that of Evans. The contrast is particularly striking when Rosalind, as Ganymede, and Orlando meet in the forest (3.2.274; 1:11:05). Redgrave gives a naturalistic performance, gently laughing at Rosalind's comments (e.g. 1:11:59, 1:12:20, 1:12:31) and speaking in a soft tone. His questions seem to have just come to him. Evans, on the other hand, declaims Rosalind's witticisms with relish. Although not writing about this specific production, Spurgeon describes the scene as 'a kind of "set piece" to amuse the audience', and this is how Evans treats it.[159] Unlike Redgrave, Evans also does nothing to help the audience understand the visual aspects of the play, such as the fact that in this scene Rosalind is disguised as a boy. Although Evans demonstrated a lower vocal tone when playing the Nurse in *Romeo and Juliet* earlier the same year, she uses a high, feminine register for both Rosalind and Ganymede.[160] The effect of the clash of styles between Evans and Redgrave may principally be down to their different approaches to radio acting, but it also implies there is something inherent in the text itself. J. B. Priestley suggests Rosalind exhibits 'playfulness, girlish high spirits', while Orlando is 'bewildered'.[161] While not written about this production, these are good descriptions of the performances here.

The play was produced by Mary Hope Allen. She had been part of the Research Section at the BBC, which had been 'experimenting with new ways of making radio features and drama'.[162] However, this production was anything but experimental, probably due to

---

[158] 'Broadcasting Review', *Manchester Guardian*, 13 September 1944.
[159] Spurgeon, p. 76.
[160] *Romeo and Juliet*, BBC Home Service, 30 June 1944 (unpublished, BBC Sound Archive – extract).
[161] J. B. Priestley, *The English Comic Characters* (London: Bodley Head, 1928), p. 30.
[162] Kate Murphy, *Behind the Wireless: A History of Early Women at the BBC* (London: Palgrave Macmillan, 2016), p. 133.

the fact that it had been 'arranged for broadcasting' by Farjeon.[163] Nine years earlier he wrote: 'isn't it a fact that the more you cut Shakespeare, the harder he becomes to follow.'[164] In this production Farjeon omits just seven lines from the whole text (1.2.43–9). He also does little in the way of 'arranging'. There is the insertion of the phrase 'reading of a paper' at the end of Corin's line 'Here comes my young Master Ganymede, my new mistress's brother' (3.2.75–6; 1:02:58). This makes clear Rosalind has found one of Orlando's poems. And in the final scene, Rosalind's lines to her father and Orlando are alternated, to make it clearer who she is addressing:

ROSALIND	To you I give myself, for I am yours.
DUKE SENIOR	If there be truth in sight, you are my daughter.
ROSALIND	To you I give myself, for I am yours.
ORLANDO	If there be truth in sight, you are my Rosalind.

5.4.107–10; 2:11:40

However, there appears to be no attempt to adapt the text for radio, other than the addition of narration, but this is essentially the stage directions at the start of each scene, for example:

NARRATOR	An orchard. Orlando and Adam. (1.1)
NARRATOR	The Forest of Arden. The banished Duke, Amiens and outlaws. (2.1)
NARRATOR	The Forest. Touchstone and Audrey. Jaques at a distance. (3.3)

Felton condemned this sort of intervention, writing that 'in adaptations of Shakespeare, phrases like "The Prince Speaks" produce an undesirable effect of duplication'.[165] Its use here is not only largely redundant, but also interrupts the flow of the play. It could have been replaced with imaginative use of sound, such as birdsong for the forest or an echoey acoustic for the palace, but effects throughout are limited. This includes entrances and exits, which are not marked with footsteps or door sounds, two standard methods by this period. This means it is not always clear who is present, such as when Rosalind and Celia plan to run away. As there is no indication that Duke Frederick has left after banishing Rosalind (1.3.85; 0:24:37), it appears they are discussing their plans in front of him. The only exception to audio entrance cues is Touchstone,

---

[163] Herbert Farjeon, 'As You Like It', *Radio Times*, 1 September 1944, p. 16.
[164] Farjeon, *Radio Times*, 30 August 1935.
[165] Felton, p. 88.

whose fool's bells are heard on his first entrance (1.2.38; 0:10:32) and again elsewhere, but infrequently and inconsistently (2:02:42, 2:07:16).

Songs are a key part of *As You Like It*, with Enid Welsford stating that 'music is only less important than pictorial effect'.[166] In radio versions of the play, where the pictorial effect has to be conjured by the listener's imagination, music is often prominent, such as the 2015 production which has specially composed folk music by Johnny Flynn. In 1944 all the songs are retained and set to traditional tunes, ranging from 'It was a lover and his lass', with music by Shakespeare's contemporary Thomas Morley, to 'Under the Greenwood Tree' and 'Blow, blow, thou winter wind', both set by eighteenth-century composer Thomas Arne, best known for 'Rule, Britannia!'. The music evokes a past age and a sense of patriotism, perhaps important at this point in the war. It also suggests a nod to populism, in keeping with the fact that radio drama had 'begun to challenge variety programmes, always excepting the inimitable "Itma" [*It's That Man Again* (1939–49)], for sheer quantitive popularity'.[167]

This production of *As You Like It* sits stylistically at a crossroads in radio Shakespeare. Although it had long been recognised that the medium required a different style of acting to the stage, throughout much of the BBC's first twenty years some actors continued to give performances better suited to a large auditorium, including the likes of Ainley, Tearle and, in this case, Evans. But this was changing, with post-war radio performances delivered much more intimately. Redgrave, who would go on to take leading roles in five more Shakespeare plays for BBC radio, is much closer to Felton's desire that actors should give 'honest and truly-felt' performances.[168] And it was not just actors who were beginning to embrace the possibilities of the medium. Although there is no suggestion of tension between Farjeon and Allen, and they did continue to work together, they also represented opposite ends of the spectrum in terms of radio drama production. Farjeon preferred to leave the text unaltered, while Allen's style 'was lyrical and avant-garde'.[169] It would be many decades before this latter term could be applied to the BBC's treatment of Shakespeare on radio, but the post-war era certainly saw

---

[166] Enid Welsford, *The Court Masque* (Cambridge: Cambridge University Press, 2015), p. 282.

[167] Val Gielgud, 'No Mood to Bother with the Radio Play?', in *BBC Year Book 1945* (London: BBC, 1945), pp. 53–5 (p. 55).

[168] Felton, p. 133.

[169] Murphy, p. 134.

greater use of music and sound effects, and a developing maturity as to how to present these plays in an engaging and understandable fashion.

* * *

The BBC's early output of Shakespearean drama was prolific, with more than 150 productions between the start of broadcasting and the end of the Second World War. During this time, producers, actors and technicians were learning how to translate Shakespeare into the new medium, as well as exploring the potential of radio more generally. Audiences were learning how to use their new equipment and were adjusting to a new way of consuming drama. However, while some of the BBC's early attempts at presenting these plays may have been primitive, it is evident that from *Twelfth Night* (1923) onwards, there was a clear aim to offer listeners a genuinely dramatic experience, rather than what one reviewer described as 'a Shakespeare reading on a luxurious scale'.[170] Many of the issues they encountered continued into the next period of BBC radio Shakespeare, a golden age for such plays, with another 120 productions broadcast across three networks in the space of twenty years, plus scores of repeats. The whole canon was produced, with the exception of *The Comedy of Errors*, which was long held to be impossible on radio and did not get its first airing until 1968. There were also several works of 'Shakespeare Apocrypha' and John Gielgud gave his final performance in the title role of *Hamlet*, possibly the most significant and influential production of a Shakespeare play ever recorded. The next chapter will look at this production, along with a number of others from the period, including one featuring a man Val Gielgud described as 'the finest actor in broadcasting with whom I have ever worked'.[171] And he was not describing his brother.

---

[170] W. A. D., *Daily Telegraph*, 14 October 1935.
[171] Gielgud, *Years in a Mirror*, p. 181.

Chapter 2

Post-War Boom: 1946–66

In 1924, Reith wrote that 'wireless will render a highly important service in popularising Shakespeare'.[1] The twenty-year period following the Second World War was when the BBC came closest to fulfilling his prediction. The large number and wide variety of productions during this period gave audiences the opportunity to hear plays that would rarely be performed in theatres, particularly outside London and Stratford-upon-Avon. Most of these productions were broadcast on the network perceived as the most highbrow, but it still meant that performances of Shakespeare's plays were freely accessible to the majority of the public. During this period producers also began to place more emphasis on performance and story, rather than poetry and textual fidelity. The case studies in this chapter demonstrate how productions changed, from full-text with narration and little use of sound effects and music, to those making greater use of music, effects and additional dialogue to translate the plays to audio. The impact of this was to create productions that were more likely to engage a wider range of listeners, through both their more imaginative use of the medium and their clarity of storytelling, ensuring listeners understood what was happening. This chapter also shows that the combination of the BBC's prolific, widely available output and its producers' work to create productions that were creatively engaging and comprehensible offered listeners greater accessibility to Shakespeare's plays in performance, having a democratising effect on his canon.

The year 1946 saw the launch of a new BBC radio station. The Third Programme, the predecessor to today's BBC Radio 3, was

---

[1] Reith, p. 168.

not intended as a network for the elite but was for 'intelligent, receptive people in all classes' and aimed to build on the 'growth of public interest in the arts in wartime [. . .] and the virtually insatiable demand for serious literature and drama'.[2] The BBC's director-general, Sir William Haley, said he hoped the audience would include 'persons who value artistic experience all the more because of the limited opportunities they have of enjoying it'.[3] The week it launched, he wrote in the *Radio Times* that the network 'will devote occasional series of evenings to some related masterpieces, a Shakespeare historical cycle, all the Beethoven quartets, or a series of Mozart operas'.[4] That history cycle, featuring both tetralogies, was broadcast the following year. The first Shakespeare play on the Third, *Romeo and Juliet* with Edith Evans as the Nurse, was actually a repeat of a wartime production broadcast on the Home Service (now BBC Radio 4). But three weeks after that, the first production made for the Third, *Troilus and Cressida*, was aired, immediately signalling that the network would not just be somewhere to find the most commonly performed Shakespeare plays, but also his lesser-known works. In an article to mark the Third's thirtieth anniversary, theatre critic Robert Cushman wrote that 'the Home might knock off an *Othello* or a *Romeo and Juliet*' but for 'the less familiar plays [. . .] you tuned into the Third'.[5]

Every play in the Shakespeare canon except *The Comedy of Errors* was broadcast at least once during the two decades examined in this chapter. This is with the proviso that a combined, two-and-a-half-hour production of all three *Henry VI* plays constitutes a production of *1 Henry VI*; the other two plays in the trilogy received additional productions. Several works of 'Shakespeare Apocrypha' were also produced, including two versions of *Sir Thomas More* and two of *Edward III*, plus *Arden of Faversham*, *A Yorkshire Tragedy* and *The Merry Devil of Edmonton*. Many of the canon received multiple productions, including seven different versions of *The Tempest*, and six of *Macbeth*. There were at least two new productions of Shakespeare every year. It was not unusual for there to be more than six, and in Queen Elizabeth II's coronation year, 1953, there were eleven. In addition, plays were frequently repeated and

[2] Briggs, *The History of Broadcasting in the United Kingdom: Volume IV – Sound and Vision* (Oxford: Oxford University Press, 1995), p. 63, p. 60.
[3] Briggs, *Volume IV*, pp. 63–4.
[4] Sir William Haley, 'The Third Programme – An Introduction by the Director-General of the BBC', *Radio Times*, 27 September 1946, p. 1.
[5] Robert Cushman, 'Dramatic Entrances', *Radio Times*, 30 September 1976, pp. 9–10.

Shakespeare appeared on all three of the BBC's networks, including the Light Programme, the forerunner of BBC Radio 2, which was much better known for comedy and popular music. Never had so many of Shakespeare's plays been available, effectively for free (aside from the licence fee), to people of all social classes across the whole of the United Kingdom.

Although radio was – and still is – free to air, for almost the first fifty years of the BBC, listeners were required to buy a radio licence. At the start of this period, 1946, the cost was one pound: the equivalent of about fifty pounds now.[6] In 1947 a 'record figure of 10,740,350' people held one.[7] By 1966, more than sixteen million licences were issued, either for radio only or combined with television.[8] To put this into context, five years later at the time of the 1971 census, there were 18.7 million households in the UK.[9] With around 90 per cent of the UK population having a licence (and probably a few listening without), radio was easily accessible. But democratising Shakespeare was not just about whether people could afford to listen. Just because something is available, it does not necessarily follow that people will access it. As such, emphasis was put on creating productions that were engaging and comprehensible. In the 1947 *BBC Year Book*, Haley wrote that 'the BBC's pioneer work in spreading a love of music and drama, as well as of literature and the arts, has always had as its base a belief that the only sound and enduring enjoyment must come through understanding'.[10] He went on to admit that there had been complaints that 'the BBC tends to be governessy' and that the corporation 'could, at times, be a little less openly didactic' but added that enabling people 'to understand and therefore to have a well-based appreciation' was a purpose 'the BBC has no intention of abandoning'.[11] Throughout this period there was a desire that the arts were available to all. The *BBC Handbook 1959* states that 'the Drama Department tries to bring listeners a representative repertory of the world's great theatrical classics [. . .] that all but the most affluent and metropolitan would otherwise

---

[6] Briggs, *Volume IV*, p. 45.

[7] *BBC Year Book 1947* (London: BBC, 1947), p. 7.

[8] *BBC Handbook 1967* (London: BBC, 1967), p. 196.

[9] 'Indicator 36', *National Archives*, <https://webarchive.nationalarchives.gov.uk/ukgwa/20090703181924/http:/www.defra.gov.uk/sustainable/government/progress/national/36.htm> [accessed 8 September 2023].

[10] Sir William Haley, 'The Next Five Years in Broadcasting', *BBC Year Book 1947* (London: BBC, 1947), pp. 7–11 (p. 11).

[11] Haley, 'The Next Five Years', p. 11.

have little chance of judging in performance'.[12] This was apparently successful, with Humphrey Carpenter, 'biographer' of the Third and Radio 3, writing that the station 'spectacularly' attracted an audience of 'the young and the not well educated [. . .] in the early years of the Third'.[13]

Producers, critics and academics, then and now, have had their own ideas about how to create enjoyable productions while retaining Shakespeare's texts. Wade was concerned about what he described as 'accessibility', stating: 'By this I mean a play that will not put up any very great barriers of language or production technique [. . .] Listeners will understand what is being said to them – in a quite literal sense – and will know where the action is taking place.'[14] Other writers have had ideas on how to do this. Tim Crook states that 'success is wholly dependent on the quality of casting, direction, performance and production values'.[15] And Huwiler points to the importance of 'non-verbal sign systems' in contributing 'in a unique way to the generation of narrative meaning'.[16] However, Robert McLeish warns that 'if the "signposts" are too few or of the wrong kind, the listener becomes disorientated and cannot follow what is happening. If there are too many, the result is likely to be obvious, "cheesy" and "corny".'[17] Producers of this period used all these methods, some with greater success than others, to try to make their plays accessible.

One of the most common choices in the early years of this period was to use narration. Though it could be controversial, there are many scenes that make no sense without some sort of interpolation.[18] However, narration did serve the purpose of helping to convey to an audience what was going on when the text was not explicit, and some listeners welcomed it. K. Simmons wrote to the *Radio Times* asking for more: 'I think it would only be necessary to preface each scene with a phrase such as "A room in Angelo's house" or "The prison," to localise the scene and make the action more readily

---

[12] 'Programmes – Policy and Practice: Drama – Sound Radio', *BBC Handbook 1959* (London: BBC, 1959), pp. 89–91 (p. 90).

[13] Humphrey Carpenter, *The Envy of the World* (London: Weidenfeld & Nicolson, 1996), p. xiii.

[14] David Wade, 'Popular Radio Drama', in *Radio Drama*, ed. by Peter Lewis (London and New York: Longman, 1981), pp. 91–110 (p. 92).

[15] Tim Crook, *Radio Drama: Theory and Practice* (London: Routledge, 1999), p. 75.

[16] Huwiler, 'Storytelling by Sound', p. 57.

[17] Robert McLeish, *Radio Production*, 5th edn (Oxford: Focal Press, 2005), p. 243.

[18] See 'Adapting Shakespeare for Radio' section in the Introduction.

understood.'[19] The disputed benefits of narration may explain the brief popularity of *Pericles*, which was produced three times between 1953 and 1965. As a play with the built-in narrator of Gower, it enabled producers to legitimise the practice through Shakespeare's own words. Narration was not phased out until producers found other ways to signal place, character and visual 'business'. The insertion of the odd word or name had already become regular practice to indicate the presence of characters who would otherwise be silent or not easily identifiable, although this was later derided by Cushman: 'I always expected to hear a Shakespearean tragic hero announce "O, what a rogue and peasant slave am I, Hamlet."'[20] However, the additions and changes became more sophisticated as the 1950s and 1960s progressed, with producers increasingly using dialogue and sound, instead of narration, to convey visual elements.

The use of sound effects and, to a certain extent, music was quite limited in the 1940s and 1950s, despite both having the power to be highly evocative and to assist with storytelling. Effects in particular seem to have been avoided. There is the occasional sound of a door or footsteps, and the clashing of swords when required, but little else. *Macbeth* (1949) uses the sound of crows before and after the murder of Banquo (act three, scene three: 1:02:00, 1:03:16) to suggest menace, an effect that had already become a convention in Shakespeare's plays, particularly *Macbeth*.[21] Despite its use here, some producers had recognised that this was not the best use of effects, with McWhinnie describing 'stock sounds' as 'stereotyped'.[22] There also seems to have been resistance from listeners. S. Towl wrote to the *Radio Times* complaining: 'I wish to state that broadcast plays, talks, etc. are spoilt for me, and my friends, by the introduction of hideous noises [. . .] supposedly regarded as effects.'[23] Felton wrote that 'the first rule in the use of sound effects is to use them with economy'.[24] He believed a 'fussy succession' of sounds would be 'an irritation to the listener', adding that 'the less they are used, the more effective they are'.[25] Felton was firmly against the sort of soundscaping that would shortly be adopted for radio Shakespeare, complaining that collecting 'different noises' and 'lumping them'

---

[19] 'Listeners Write to the Radio Times', *Radio Times*, 17 June 1951, p. 35.
[20] Cushman, *Radio Times*, 30 September 1976, p. 9.
[21] Drakakis, 'Introduction', p. 30.
[22] McWhinnie, p. 91.
[23] 'Listeners Write . . . – Unwanted Effects', *Radio Times*, 14 January 1955, p. 33.
[24] Felton, p. 42.
[25] Felton, p. 44.

together would result in 'confusion', adding that 'the ear, unlike the eye, cannot assimilate a complex combination of impressions'.[26] The sound of other productions in the archive from this period suggests his comments reflect a wider belief held among his fellow producers, although later generations would reject this premise, with twenty-first-century research showing that sound effects are 'effective in stimulating images and in enhancing listener attention'.[27] Wider use at this time might have accelerated the move away from narration and made the productions easier to understand.

Music was an even more controversial issue. Val Gielgud wrote that 'there is nothing that can aid radio drama quite so powerfully as music'.[28] However, Felton was less certain: 'The use of music is the element in radio-dramatic production most frequently criticised by listeners.'[29] He was also concerned about music being 'thickly scored', adding that 'a special sort of "underwriting" is required' to prevent it from distracting the listener.[30] Holding the music back in the mix (i.e. playing it quietly) was also something he believed was ineffective. It appears this technique was attempted in *Antony and Cleopatra* (1954), presumably because the music was transferred from the stage, rather than specifically scored for radio. The composer, Antony Hopkins, had experience of writing for radio and was aware that 'opinions vary' on 'whether it is a good thing or a bad to use incidental music in a radio play'.[31] Overall, though, he agreed with Gielgud that adding it can 'help to enhance the atmosphere and kindle the imagination'.[32] There was also academic support for the idea that music could provide a direct route to the listeners' emotions. Carroll C. Pratt wrote that music created 'mood and feeling, not external fact and logical discourse', adding that 'nothing can express the height and depth and extent of emotion with anything like the artlessness of music'.[33] This was something that producers did come to realise.

---

[26] Felton, p. 42.
[27] Emma Rodero, 'See It on a Radio Story: Sound Effects and Shots to Evoked Imagery and Attention on Audio Fiction', *Communication Research*, 39.4 (2012), 458–79 (472).
[28] Gielgud, *Radio Theatre*, p. xiii.
[29] Felton, p. 110.
[30] Felton, p. 123.
[31] Antony Hopkins, 'How I Write Music for Radio', *Radio Times*, 23 January 1948, p. 4.
[32] Hopkins, *Radio Times*, 23 January 1948.
[33] Carroll C. Pratt, 'The Design of Music', *The Journal of Aesthetics and Art Criticism*, 12.3 (1954), 289–300 (289, 299).

Music could also be used to create very different productions of the same play. At the start of November 1951, the Third broadcast *The Tempest*. Less than four months later, at the end of February 1952, the Home Service also aired a version of the play. The producer in both cases was Raikes, but he used a different cast and different composer for each. While the productions themselves do not survive, recordings of the music do. The Third Programme version, composed by Anthony Bernard, opens with dramatic, discordant music, perhaps not out of place in its own right on the network. The Home Service production, with music by John Hotchkis, begins in much jollier mood with a more pastoral, old-fashioned style. While it is impossible to judge how these two plays sounded by this alone, the contrasting styles of music would suggest different treatments of the play, with music perhaps playing a key part in this. While Raikes's contemporaries were generally cautious about using music and effects, he went on to develop his own distinctive style of production which endeavoured to create entertaining, populist plays.[34]

Cast sizes at this time were large. The listings for *Macbeth* (1949) and *Antony and Cleopatra* (1954) both name more than thirty actors. Across the two *Henry IV* plays (1964) there is a cast of thirty-nine. These large ensembles are often put to good use, with anything from murmuring to full-blooded shouting helping to convey the atmosphere of court, crowd or battle. This was noted by listener Stanley Blake Reece, who wrote to the *Radio Times* saying: 'The visual presentation of Shakespeare on the stage, screen or television can never be as impressive as the excellent radio presentations that you have offered us.'[35] In his introduction to the 1959 production of *Coriolanus*, Ivor Brown makes a similar point, telling listeners: 'The mob may, on the stage, seem only to be a group, but [on radio] with a varying volume of sound, we can imagine ourselves to be right in the hurly-burly.'[36] The immersive nature of radio is something later producers harnessed to a greater extent, especially as technology advanced in the twenty-first century.[37] The use of ensembles not only gave size and scale to productions, but their reactions, whether through non-verbal noises, exclamations or even silence, could 'paint

---

[34] Raikes's later work is discussed in Chapter 3.
[35] 'Listeners Write to the Radio Times – Radio Shakespeare', *Radio Times*, 12 January 1951, p. 13.
[36] Ivor Brown, 'Introduction' to *Coriolanus*, BBC Home Service, 27 April 1959 (unpublished, BBC Sound Archive).
[37] See Chapter 5.

a picture and work on the listener's mind'.[38] This was another way in which producers were going beyond just a reading of the text to create an audio world to engage their audience.

During this period there was a strong connection between stage and radio, with the cast lists of extant productions in particular dominated by some of the most famous actors of their generation, including Donald Wolfit, Ralph Richardson and Paul Scofield. In addition, the BBC transferred nine productions from the Shakespeare Memorial Theatre in Stratford-upon-Avon to radio between 1950 and 1958. Leading actors including John Gielgud, Peggy Ashcroft and Michael Redgrave all reprised their stage roles for the microphone. These famous names may have helped attract listeners to their broadcasts, which could be considered as aiding the democratisation of Shakespeare by making their performances available to audiences who would not have been able to travel to Stratford. However, their success on radio varied and was dependent on their ability to adjust their style, not only in tone but also in conveying what cannot be seen. As Felton explained: 'The stage-actor has always to use the technique of the megaphone; in radio he can use the technique of the microphone.'[39] Subtlety has always been more effective on radio.

Gielgud, Scofield, Ashcroft and Evans (who twice more played the Nurse in *Romeo and Juliet* in this period) had a vocal quality that critics appreciated, reflecting an unspecified notion of the 'poetic' often mentioned in theatrical and radio reviews. Judging by the critical reaction, and the fact their plays are the ones that have been archived, it might be assumed that these actors were considered to give the best performances. This generally meant putting greater emphasis on the beauty of the words than the action of the drama. The effect of this is to reduce the dramatic power of the text in favour of the 'bloom and the pungency' of Shakespeare's words.[40] This was an issue contemporary producers were aware of, with McWhinnie complaining of 'the misguided school of Shakespearian study' that perpetuated 'the myth that what is really important in Shakespeare is the poetry'.[41] During this period, producers began to recognise that putting performance and story first was key to producing good audio

[38] Lawrence Raw, quoted in Richard J. Hand and Mary Traynor, *The Radio Drama Handbook: Audio Drama in Context and Practice* (London: Continuum, 2011), p. 114.
[39] Felton, p. 12.
[40] Philip Hope-Wallace, 'Broadcast Drama – Thanks for the Mummery', *The Listener*, 21 September 1950, p. 395.
[41] McWhinnie, p. 46.

drama: plays that are more entertaining, engaging and accessible to a wide range of listeners.

The desire from critics that Shakespeare should be spoken in a particular way could explain why some voices were deemed unacceptable. Just as, a generation earlier, Wyndham Goldie had complained of hearing 'something perilously near Cockney', Sheila Grant was similarly criticised for her interpretation of Mistress Quickly in *1 Henry IV* (1964).[42] These preconceived ideas about the 'right' and 'wrong' voices for Shakespeare may have also been connected to prejudice about accents. In 1955, psychologist T. H. Pear commented on the problem of 'unconscious bias' against people with 'working-class' and 'many provincial accents'.[43] In addition, Felton stated that 'the concentrated focus of the microphone demands a high standard of accuracy in the matter of dialect'.[44] Both these factors may have contributed to a dislike of voices that were not RP. One effect of uniformity of accent is a flattening of the hierarchical structures in the plays, perhaps explaining why Mistress Quickly is played cockney, albeit unconvincingly, to make a distinction between her, the knight Falstaff and Prince Hal. The lack of accents also fails to reflect the wide range of voices across Britain, especially as regional radio productions of Shakespeare had largely ended by this period. However, there is nothing to suggest listeners were put off by the fact that many were unlikely to hear voices similar to their own on air, perhaps because RP voices were the norm across radio, theatre and television for much of this time.

Accent is also a way of distinguishing different characters on radio, something McWhinnie recognised as important, stating that 'the beautiful voice' is not the most suitable for radio; instead 'the best voice is the most idiosyncratic'.[45] While accent was not generally used to differentiate characters, producers do seem to have understood the importance of having a variety of voices. There were even two cases of women playing men's parts, with Betty Linton as 'Philomena' in *Pericles* (1958) (Philemon in the original text) and Dorothy Gordon as Ariel in *The Tempest* (1959), although it would be decades before gender-blind casting became a regular feature of radio Shakespeare. However, producers were beginning to grasp the fact that radio enabled a greater variety of actors to play

[42] Wyndham Goldie, *The Listener*, 16 October 1935.
[43] Pear, p. 113.
[44] Felton, p. 129.
[45] McWhinnie, p. 126.

Shakespeare's characters than might have been deemed acceptable on stage or in film at the time, and that a wider range of distinct voices helped the audience differentiate the characters and follow the story.

While no producer in the post-war period paraded their academic knowledge to the public as Creswell had done with *Macbeth* in 1935, there are often indications that they were influenced by literary criticism. Plays frequently seem to reflect some contemporary or broadly recent scholarship, although rarely conform entirely. Redgrave wrote that it was important for 'the actor or producer or both' to have 'at least some nodding acquaintance with present-day Shakespearean scholarship', adding that he himself always had 'the Furness Variorum edition of the play [. . .] by me during the preparation of a part and during rehearsals'.[46] However, he is also somewhat dismissive of academics, stating that 'very few scholars [. . .] can envisage their theories being put into practice', adding that he was selective in what to use and what to disregard.[47] Although he was writing about the stage, it seems quite plausible that radio producers felt the same way. In particular, the later productions show fewer signs of academic influence, suggesting an intention to prioritise engaging listeners over textual fidelity and the accommodation of literary theory.

Over these two decades, technology changed little. Plays were now regularly recorded, although audio editing was not possible initially, and the BBC drama studio was largely unaltered for many years after its post-war rebuild. Editing the texts, though, was another thing. Fidelity to Shakespeare's scripts began to be relaxed and while productions from the late 1940s and early 1950s were often lengthy, with little in the way of additions other than narration largely based on stage directions, by the late 1950s the idea of cutting, rewriting or adding to Shakespeare's texts became a more common practice. These later productions are more effective at fulfilling what McWhinnie believed was the best sort of radio, something that 'evokes rather than depicts'.[48] As such, these productions could be said to engage listeners on a more emotional level, perhaps also making the plays more appealing to their audience.

---

[46] Michael Redgrave, 'Shakespeare and the Actors', in *Talking of Shakespeare*, ed. by John Garrett (London: Hodder & Stoughton, 1954), pp. 127–48 (pp. 134–5).
[47] Redgrave, pp. 134–5.
[48] McWhinnie, p. 41.

The case studies in this chapter begin with John Gielgud's highly lauded third appearance in *Hamlet* (1948). This is followed by *Macbeth* (1949), starring Stephen Murray. Although little-remembered in the twenty-first century, other than by fans of the radio comedy series *The Navy Lark* (1959–77), Murray was described by Val Gielgud as 'the finest actor in broadcasting with whom I have ever worked'; he added that Murray frequently 'carried almost the whole weight of the play on his shoulders [. . .] with skill, subtlety, certainty, and insight'.[49] The third case study is one of the productions that transferred from Stratford, *Antony and Cleopatra* (1954), which demonstrates some of the pitfalls of moving a play from one medium to another if insufficient effort is made in the transition. Paul Scofield's performance as Pericles (1958) is then examined, in a production that uses music and effects, along with cutting, reordering and rewriting of the text, to fashion a play that is designed for radio. Finally, both parts of *Henry IV* (1964) are discussed, a pair of productions where the producer makes full use of the medium.

More than a hundred different productions were broadcast in this twenty-year period. Many were repeated, some on multiple occasions, but not all were kept. Only about a fifth survive, but those that do help demonstrate the shift in dramatic production over this period. The most celebrated, and one of the earliest, is *Hamlet* (1948). In contrast to Leslie Howard's 'active, bustling' performance in 1938, Gielgud places emphasis on the delivery of the verse as poetry.[50] This may be one of the reasons it remained popular with critics for decades after its first broadcast.

Hamlet (1948)[51]

Laurence Olivier and John Gielgud dominated Shakespeare performance in the mid-twentieth century, and both played Hamlet in 1948. There has been an extensive critical response to Olivier's film: José Ramón Díaz-Fernández cites around a hundred publications that discuss it.[52] Far less has been written about the contemporaneous radio production starring Gielgud. It is estimated that the film

[49] Gielgud, *Years in a Mirror*, p. 181.
[50] 'Broadcast Drama – "Hamlet"', *The Times*, 3 January 1938.
[51] *Hamlet*, BBC Third Programme, 26 December 1948 (unpublished, BBC Sound Archive).
[52] José Ramón Díaz-Fernández, 'Shakespeare on Screen: A Bibliography of Critical Studies', *Post Script – Essays in Film and the Humanities*, 17.1 (1997), 91–146.

reached an audience of 'millions'.[53] However, although no audience figures appear to have been recorded for the radio production, it is quite possible it was heard by a similar number of people, with popular plays reaching 'an average audience of over 12 million in 1948'.[54]

Greenhalgh states that the 1948 radio *Hamlet* could be 'viewed as a deliberate answer to the artistic and institutional "butchery"' represented by Olivier's film, which uses only about half the text.[55] The radio adaptation, produced by John Richmond, is virtually uncut and its first broadcast ran for four hours and twenty minutes, including two intervals. The play was split at the points suggested by Granville-Barker in his *Prefaces to Shakespeare*: the end of act one and the end of act four, scene one.[56] However, the intervals were something that radio critic Philip Hope-Wallace deemed unnecessary, saying that 'pace and continuity should be the trump cards of radio Shakespeare'.[57] Overall, though, he was delighted: 'What a relief, in the avuncular avalanche of BBC Christmas bonhomie [. . .] "Hamlet" was like hearing Bertrand Russell after a week of Christmas card mottoes.'[58] The *Manchester Guardian*'s reviewer added that it was 'a highly intelligent, moving, and on the whole impressive production'.[59] Both suggest an intellectual quality to the production which may, at least in part, be due to Gielgud's performance in the leading role.

When Gielgud came to play Hamlet in 1948, he was no stranger to the part on stage or radio. He had played it twice before for the BBC, first in 1932, and again in 1940, and his stage performances are well documented.[60] Hope-Wallace described Gielgud's delivery of the text as giving 'a superb understanding of what makes the sound of Shakespeare unmatchable'.[61] He added: 'This was, in a way, the epitome of his whole performance and of the way it has grown these years; here was "the thing in itself", the line, once quicksilver,

---

[53] 'Hamlet to the General', *Time Magazine*, 16 October 1950, p. 96.

[54] Briggs, *Volume IV*, p. 631.

[55] Susanne Greenhalgh, '"A Stage of the Mind": *Hamlet* on Post-War British Radio', *Shakespeare Survey*, 64 (2011), 133–44 (137); Rosenthal, p. 22.

[56] Harley Granville-Barker, *Prefaces to Shakespeare, Volume 1* (London: Batsford, 1961), p. 46.

[57] Philip Hope-Wallace, 'Critic on the Hearth – Broadcast Drama: Uncle, Uncle!', *The Listener*, 30 December 1948, p. 1,024.

[58] Hope-Wallace, *The Listener*, 30 December 1948.

[59] 'Broadcasting Review', *Manchester Guardian*, 29 December 1948, p. 3.

[60] Mary Zenet Maher, *Modern Hamlets and Soliloquies: An Expanded Edition* (Iowa City: University of Iowa Press, 1992), p. 3.

[61] Hope-Wallace, *The Listener*, 30 December 1948.

now chiselled silver, the emotion sans emotionalism, the heart's voice itself—classical.'[62] These comments were echoed in reviews of later repeats. Peter Forster wrote: 'Here *in excelsis* are all Sir John's supreme qualities—the pathos, the Terry voice, the poetry.'[63] And actor Paul Daneman described Gielgud as an actor whose 'phrasing is incomparable' with a 'wonderfully supple voice'.[64] These insistent references to the Gielgud voice demonstrate the strong sense, particularly at the start of this period, that the poetry of the text was more important than story or character. This is perhaps surprising when literary critics seemed less concerned with this: John Dover Wilson pointed out that 'Shakespeare wrote not for readers but for auditors, who would have no time to consider his linked metaphors too curiously', while Granville-Barker stated that 'with Shakespeare dramatic *writing* was for convenience of record merely; his verse was not only conceived as speech, it was to be so born and only so meant to exist'.[65] Both suggest lingering, poetic delivery would be unhelpful to an audience.

Alongside his praise for Gielgud, Hope-Wallace had a dig at the idea that Shakespeare should be for everyone, questioning whether the production was 'vulgar enough' to be 'comprehensible to the lowest listening intelligence'.[66] He went on to suggest that if radio drama producers assume their audience has 'complete unfamiliarity with text and even story' it is necessary 'to intervene' by rewriting 'the text as a cinema organist rewrites Mozart or a missionary rewrites the Psalms of David in "business" English', adding that 'to object to this process is said to be undemocratic!'.[67] Additions to the text were made in the form of narration, but Hope-Wallace did not feel it was comprehensive enough, questioning Richmond's decision not to use it when Hamlet chooses to sit with Ophelia ('here's mettle more attractive', 3.2.100) and when Claudius drops the poisoned pearl into Hamlet's goblet ('this pearl is thine', 5.2.258). The narration generally does little more than give the stage directions, although at times it does provide what John Drakakis describes as 'an almost photographic visualisation of the scene for the listener'.[68]

[62] Hope-Wallace, *The Listener*, 30 December 1948.
[63] Peter Forster, 'The Best Hamlet of our Time', *Radio Times*, 17 April 1959, p. 7.
[64] Paul Daneman, 'The Genius of Sir John', *Daily Telegraph*, 15 April 1989, p. 15.
[65] John Dover Wilson, 'Introduction', in William Shakespeare, *Hamlet* (Cambridge: Cambridge University Press, 1968), pp. vii–lxvii (p. xxxviii); Granville-Barker, *Prefaces to Shakespeare 1*, p. 178.
[66] Hope-Wallace, *The Listener*, 30 December 1948.
[67] Hope-Wallace, *The Listener*, 30 December 1948.
[68] Drakakis, 'The Essence That's Not Seen', p. 124.

In particular he suggests that an unusually lengthy passage of ninety words at the start of act one, scene two, describing the entry of Claudius and courtiers in some detail (0:10:31), may have been a direct reference to Olivier's film.[69] However, there is nothing in the narration that can be exactly matched to the film, and it differs in several ways, such as the narrator stating that Claudius enters, when in the film he is seated. This suggests a desire to draw a comparison or even link the film and radio productions, rather than an actual intertextual relationship between the two. When the play was repeated in 1975, the narration again came under the spotlight, this time because it had been edited out. Reviewer Chris Dunkley wrote: 'no doubt this restored some lost purity to the play. I think the removal was a mistake, nevertheless, tending to reduce the comprehending audience to dedicated initiates.'[70] Comments from both Dunkley and Hope-Wallace highlight a supposed tension between 'purity' and comprehension, and the fine line producers had to walk in balancing these competing requirements.

Gielgud's fellow actors in this production all have distinctive voices, making it easy to tell who is speaking. In particular, creativity is used in the casting of the Player King and Queen. The Queen is played by Denise Bryer, a frequent radio actor who specialised in playing boys.[71] Her casting in *Hamlet* uses her vocal skills to create the illusion of a boy playing the Player Queen (1:40:30 onwards). Combined with the use of Hugh Griffith as First Player, who accentuates the musicality of his natural Welsh accent, there is a heightened sense of theatricality during the 'Murder of Gonzago' scene, making it easy to separate the play-within-a-play from the main action. There is also a sense of fun at times. When Esmé Percy, playing Osric, ad-libs 'He's enchanting!' (3:04:58) 'off mic' as he leaves after 5.2.157, Gielgud can be heard stifling a laugh in response. Hope-Wallace praised the 'very fine cast' but again his comments returned to the delivery of the verse: 'The reading was conventional in a modern way; but to try anything else (*i.e.*, an Elizabethan viewpoint and so on) is probably unwise in a one-sense medium like radio.'[72] In some ways his comments lack consistency, as he seems to want and praise good verse-speaking, but also recognises the problems

[69] Drakakis, 'The Essence That's Not Seen', p. 124.
[70] Chris Dunkley, 'Review', *Radio Times*, 27 March 1975, p. 74.
[71] Mairé Jean Steadman, 'The Presentation of Shakespeare's Plays on BBC Radio' (unpublished doctoral thesis, Shakespeare Institute (University of Birmingham), 1997), p. 120.
[72] Hope-Wallace, *The Listener*, 30 December 1948.

faced by a radio producer endeavouring to successfully convey character and plot, particularly to those unfamiliar with the play.

Like Michael Redgrave in the 1944 *As You Like It*, the actors regularly make non-verbal noises, such as 'hmm' or gasps, which help give a sense of the characters engaging with each other, as well as the public nature of the court scenes. Together with sound effects, they also make Laertes's entrance after the death of his father sound particularly impressive. First there is a crowd shouting from a distance (2:24:35). This builds to louder shouting, followed by banging and finally wood splintering (2:25:16), and continues under the dialogue of the King, Queen and Messenger (4.2.95.1–110), who have to shout towards the end to make themselves heard. This demonstrates how skilled radio production can convey what is happening without the need for narration, creating a textually faithful scene while also making it fully comprehensible to those not familiar with the text.

This production has become one of the most enduring Shakespeare plays ever broadcast on radio, repeated at least eight times over a forty-year period. Greenhalgh states that 'all the Hamlet-related programmes on the Third in the next few years would in some sense be in dialogue with this "entirety" production'.[73] When it was repeated in both 1949 and 1951, other programming was built around it, and for the 1959 repeat Forster wrote an article for the *Radio Times* entitled 'The Best Hamlet of our Time', declaring it was a production 'many consider as near the definitive as we are likely ever to get'.[74] However, Hope-Wallace did have some reservations about Gielgud, stating that a 'radio Hamlet' should be different to one on stage, adding that 'a finer *radio* actor could still have suggested, at the moment of the first re-meeting with Horatio, that extraordinarily moving effect of the heart lifting which Mr Gielgud always achieves on the stage'.[75] A few months after *Hamlet*, an actor who *was* highly experienced in radio took the lead in another of Shakespeare's most famous plays.

---

[73] Greenhalgh, '"A Stage of the Mind"', p. 137.
[74] Forster, *Radio Times*, 17 April 1959.
[75] Hope-Wallace, *The Listener*, 30 December 1948.

Macbeth (1949)[76]

In 1949 Stephen Murray accomplished something no one else has done before or since: he played the same lead Shakespearean role on radio and television in different productions within a month. His radio performance was recorded before his television appearance in mid-February, but aired two weeks after.[77] Murray wrote an article for the *Radio Times* comparing both media, highlighting the 'lack of visual aids' in radio, in particular when Banquo's ghost appears, but also the freedom to move in and out of the microphone, allowing an actor to 'switch in a moment from a low mutter to a full-throated shout' – something impossible with television microphones at the time.[78] Murray's comments highlight radio's need to make the action in the text clear to listeners, but also the benefits of radio in terms of performance. Murray went on: 'Shakespeare's dialogue is anything but naturalistic: the task of making it appear natural and sincere [on television] is a formidable one and does not occur in a broadcast [radio] version, where the convention of heightened, poetic language is much more easily accepted.'[79] However, unlike actors such as Gielgud and Paul Scofield (see *Pericles* below), Murray does not deliver the text in a heightened, poetic way. The previous year, W. E. Williams wrote that Murray spoke Shakespeare better than any other male actor, adding that he had 'a voice of exceptional expressiveness and [. . .] understands that the voice is a more potent means of impersonation than wigs or costume or makeup'.[80] However, Hope-Wallace felt he was 'dull and limited' and preferred Murray's performance later in the production, when he 'was able to "get a curve" on the poetry'.[81] As was by now an ever-present theme, there was conflict about what made a 'good' radio performance.

Murray's Lady Macbeth was Flora Robson, playing the part for the third time on radio and as commanding as previous reviews of her would suggest. Their relationship in scenes five and seven of act one has overtones of the literary criticism still popular in this

[76] *Macbeth*, BBC Third Programme, 6 March 1949 (unpublished, BBC Sound Archive).
[77] 'Television – Talk of the Week', *Radio Times*, 18 February 1949, p. 24.
[78] Stephen Murray, 'Acting Macbeth – from Television to Radio', *Radio Times*, 4 March 1949, p. 7.
[79] Murray, *Radio Times*, 4 March 1949.
[80] W. E. Williams, 'The Six Best Broadcasters of 1947', in *BBC Year Book 1948* (London: BBC, 1948), p. 9.
[81] Philip Hope-Wallace, 'Critic on the Hearth – Broadcast Drama – Murder Most Decent', *The Listener*, 10 March 1949, p. 419.

period, such as Bradley's comment that Lady Macbeth 'exerts the ultimate deciding influence on the action' in the first half of the play and Granville-Barker's description of Macbeth as a 'hanger-back' while his wife is 'the speeder on'.[82] Murray's Macbeth is generally quiet and thoughtful, delivering both 'If it were done when 'tis done' (1.7.1–28; 0:24:35) and 'Is this a dagger which I see before me' (2.1.33–64; 0:31:28) as thoughts spoken aloud, virtually in a whisper, although by the end of the second soliloquy he has the conviction to kill Duncan, in line with Wilson Knight's suggestion that the character 'undertakes the murder, as a grim and hideous duty'.[83] Murray also uses his quiet, naturalistic style to build audience empathy. When he tells Seyton 'She should have died hereafter' (5.5.17; 1:55:56) his voice is not 'devoid of tone', as recent critical thought suggested.[84] Murray sounds sad and weary, and it is only after this that he finally raises his voice, almost screaming 'Liar and slave' (5.5.35; 1:57:06) at the messenger telling him that Birnam Wood 'began to move'. Murray's Macbeth is deeply human, motivated by a desire to please his wife, and when she is dead, he loses all will to fight. He is not inherently evil, as suggested by literary critics such as Caroline Spurgeon.[85] Murray's interpretation is rooted in creating a character audiences can relate to.

Murray's voice is RP, but the rest of the cast are more varied, avoiding the problem of identification for the listener. Leon Quartermaine, as Banquo, sounds considerably older, with an avuncular tone. Macduff, played by Deryck Guyler, is gruff and loud. Williams described him as 'magnificent and poignant'.[86] Anthony Jacobs as Malcolm has a light voice, almost effete. The Porter is played as an old drunk by Jack Shaw, a radio stalwart who went on to be a regular in early radio soap opera *Mrs Dale's Diary* (1948–69). Williams praised the 'well-chosen company' as being of 'all-round excellence', in particular '"Boy, Son to Macduff," who spoke up in the valiant accent of a real boy and not in the hermaphrodite squeak of a pantomime elf'.[87] On radio, children were usually played by adult women at this time, in the case of Macduff's son by Patricia Hayes. Some were more convincing than others, but Williams's

---

[82] Bradley, *Shakespearean Tragedy*, p. 366; Granville-Barker, *More Prefaces to Shakespeare*, p. 73.
[83] Wilson Knight, *The Wheel of Fire*, p. 175.
[84] Mark Van Doren, *Shakespeare* (New York: Henry Holt, 1939), p. 264.
[85] Spurgeon, p. 328.
[86] W. E. Williams, 'Shakespeare and Radio', *The Observer*, 13 March 1949, p. 2.
[87] Williams, *The Observer*, 13 March 1949.

observation shows the importance of an authentic-sounding voice in aiding, rather than disrupting, the storytelling. However, Hope-Wallace did not share Williams's view of the performances. As with his criticism of Murray, he regarded any attempt at naturalistic delivery as an affront to Shakespeare's poetry: 'the speakers, taking their time, chopped their lines up in a way which suggested shortness of wind.'[88] While producers and actors were attempting to present realistic characters for their audiences, influential critics like Hope-Wallace continued to complain this was in conflict with the text.

The only characters who do sound alike are the witches, but this may have been an artistic decision, as they are played in a much more heightened way than the rest of the cast. Williams describes them as 'articulate as well as gruesome'.[89] Unlike Creswell's 1935 version, the witches' scenes remain intact, with the exception of Hecate. The production opens with forty-five seconds of sound effects of wind and storm with clattering thunder before the witches speak. When they do, echo is used on their voices, which are exaggerated, almost pantomimic. Portraying the witches very differently from the other characters serves to highlight the supernatural nature of their scenes, compared to the more realistic setting of the rest of the play. Elsewhere, the use of sound effects is limited, apart from storm noises which are heard throughout to denote evil. The discussion between Macbeth and his wife immediately after Duncan's murder is punctuated with thunder (0:36:09, 0:37:40, 0:38:28), and after Macbeth says 'Wake Duncan with thy knocking! I would thou couldst!' (2.2.77) there is a final, violent thunderclap (0:39:11). This technique would later be criticised by McWhinnie as 'dismal' – but it is effective.[90] However, in the case of the murder of Lady Macduff and her son (act four, scene two), there are no external noises. Instead, the listener hears the disturbing sounds of a struggle and the screams of mother and son (1:29:13). This concurs with Granville-Barker's assertion that the moment is 'abhorrent' and 'should be done very deliberately'.[91] The scene is augmented by the use of Norman Demuth's music as it ends: at first ominous, then a pause, before more music, this time pastoral in tone but still with an air of foreboding. This is unlike any other sequence in the play, which otherwise uses music sparingly. Felton states that music can have

---

[88] Hope-Wallace, *The Listener*, 10 March 1949.
[89] Williams, *The Observer*, 13 March 1949.
[90] McWhinnie, p. 91.
[91] Granville-Barker, *More Prefaces to Shakespeare*, p. 84.

'an inseparable emotional charge which could be used, like stage lighting, to create the appropriate mood'.[92] Here it heightens the murders, enhancing the storytelling and helping to engage listeners in the plot and characters.

Narration by adaptor M. R. Ridley is used liberally throughout the play, almost fifty times in total. It first appears at the end of the opening scene with the witches. The 'low-pitched marginal voice' of Duncan Carse has the stereotypical tone of a BBC announcer of the period, a form of RP without emotional engagement.[93] His flat narration is in contrast to the mood that has been created, with Hope-Wallace feeling that 'the constant incursions of the narrator [were] necessarily many but somewhat deadening'.[94] Williams did not feel narration was required at all: 'Shakespeare wrote for a bare stage; and he therefore incorporated in the text every single clue his audience needed to possess.'[95] He also assumed that as the broadcast was on the 'sophisticated Third' the audience did not need them. Again, producers faced difficult choices between offering an audience who might not know a text enough information to follow it, and concerns about how doing that might intrude on the play.

However, producer Wilfrid Grantham does not always feel the need to add narration. Like Richmond with *Hamlet* (1948), he also makes use of his large cast. After Macduff discovers the murdered Duncan, there is an increasing noise of people and confusion (after 2.3.71; 0:43:15 onwards), as well as the constant sound of a bell. And throughout the banquet scene with Banquo's ghost (act three, scene four) people can be heard in the background, initially cheerful (1:03:42), but as Lennox says 'What is't that moves your highness' (3.4.49; 1:06:29), the room falls silent, helping to indicate Macbeth's reaction even before he speaks. In both cases this reduces the need for narration.

Although Stephen Murray had performed with the Old Vic, he was not predominantly a theatre actor and became a familiar voice on radio, performing in more than 300 plays over several decades, including another performance as Macbeth in 1960, Leontes in *The Winter's Tale* in 1951 and 1966, and as the title character in *Timon of Athens* (1961 and 1975).[96] However, despite the acceptance that actors needed to give a 'radio' rather than 'stage' performance in

[92] Felton, p. 112.
[93] Williams, *The Observer*, 13 March 1949.
[94] Hope-Wallace, *The Listener*, 10 March 1949.
[95] Williams, *The Observer*, 13 March 1949.
[96] 'Television', *Radio Times*, 18 February 1949; McFarlane, p. 471.

front of the microphone, producers continued to look to the theatre for leading men and women, particularly Stratford-upon-Avon.

Antony and Cleopatra (1954)[97]

Before it became the home of the Royal Shakespeare Company, the Shakespeare Memorial Theatre was already widely respected, described by Gordon Crosse as 'a centre of the first importance [. . .] for those who believe that Shakespeare is truly honoured by the intelligent production and capable acting of his plays'.[98] In 1954, the theatre's production of *Antony and Cleopatra* from the previous year was transferred to BBC radio. It starred Michael Redgrave and Peggy Ashcroft and may have been deemed suitable for broadcasting as it had a setting 'of the simplest'.[99] However, a simple stage setting is still very different to an audio-only medium, and the transition between theatre and radio did not make many allowances for that. By broadcasting a production that originated from one of the most prestigious theatres in the country, the BBC gave millions of people the opportunity to hear highly acclaimed performances that might otherwise have been unavailable to them due to their location or financial situation. However, without the necessary adjustments to make it comprehensible, many listeners are likely to have found this production beyond them.

Critics of the stage production stated that theatre director Glen Byam Shaw had 'dispens[ed] with gloss and glamour, allow[ing] his actors to concentrate on the poetry'.[100] This is echoed in the only review of the radio production, from J. C. Trewin in *The Listener*. His brief summary concluded: 'The verse shone across the wide crest of the ranged empire.'[101] Literary critics of the time believed the play's strength lay in its words, with Mark Van Doren stating 'it is perhaps the richest poetry Shakespeare wrote'.[102] As radio critics valued the speaking of such poetry above making the plays fit for

---

[97] *Antony and Cleopatra*, BBC Home Service, 26 April 1954 (unpublished, BBC Sound Archive).

[98] Gordon Crosse, *Shakespearean Playgoing 1890–1952* (London: Mowbray, 1953), p. 88.

[99] 'At Stratford-Upon-Avon "Antony and Cleopatra"', *The Stage*, 30 April 1953, p. 10.

[100] 'Cleopatra's Glory – Memorial Theatre Triumph Reconsidered', *The Stage*, 17 September 1953, p. 8.

[101] J. C. Trewin, 'Sound Broadcasting – Drama: Here, There, Everywhere', *The Listener*, 6 May 1954, pp. 797, 799 (p. 799).

[102] Van Doren, p. 273.

radio, it is perhaps unsurprising that this production was virtually transferred wholesale from stage to studio, 'without elaboration', as Trewin put it.[103]

The stage production had been 'overwhelmingly successful', not only playing in Stratford and London, but then touring to Holland, Belgium and France.[104] Ivor Brown describes it as having had an 'intense and passionate realism', and also states that the French in particular found the production 'so unacademic, so untraditional'.[105] However, on radio the passion is not apparent and the production seems highly traditional, populated as it is with RP voices and concentrating on poetic delivery of the verse. The term 'unacademic' could be applied to some aspects of the production, though, and in particular to Ashcroft's performance. Wilson Knight describes Cleopatra as 'by turns proud and humble, a raging tigress and a demure girl'.[106] However, Ashcroft never shows any vulnerability, always portraying the 'proud' and 'raging' side of the character. Speeches such as 'I dreamt there was an emperor Antony' (5.2.75–91; 2:02:38) are spoken in a commanding style and although there is vibrato in her voice, the precision of her speech and RP delivery does not convey emotional truthfulness. One reviewer of her stage performance wrote that 'one cannot pretend that Miss Ashcroft is ideally suited to the part of Cleopatra', suggesting this was because she was not 'a great tragic actress'.[107] This summary seems apt for her radio performance too. There is nothing about it that makes the character sympathetic or tragic.

Wilson Knight describes *Antony and Cleopatra* as 'a play of sexual love'.[108] But despite Brown's assertion about passion, there is no evidence of it in this production. In the same year as this broadcast, a lecture by Redgrave was published in which he comments on this aspect of the play. He complains that reviews for stage performances blame the actress playing Cleopatra 'for not being sufficiently amorous'.[109] He also claims that there is 'no scene of love-making' in the play because of the 'limitations of boy-actors' when it was originally written.[110] While not directly referencing either his stage

[103] Trewin, *The Listener*, 6 May 1954.
[104] Ivor Brown, *Shakespeare Memorial Theatre 1954–56* (London: Reinhardt, 1956), p. 2.
[105] Brown, *Shakespeare Memorial Theatre*, p. 2.
[106] G. Wilson Knight, *The Imperial Theme* (Abingdon: Routledge, 2002), p. 290.
[107] 'Cleopatra's Glory', *The Stage*, 17 September 1953.
[108] Wilson Knight, *The Imperial Theme*, p. 219.
[109] Redgrave, p. 138.
[110] Redgrave, p. 137.

or his radio performances, this suggests he felt the need to justify the playing of the couple's relationship. Antony's death also contradicts contemporary literary criticism. Dover Wilson wrote it should excite 'pity in the highest degree'.[111] However, on radio, listeners may not have even realised he has died. There is just a quiet, short sigh under Ashcroft's belligerent speech (4.15.64; 1:53:20). It is only when she says 'We'll bury him' (4.15.90) that it is clear he is dead. While Redgrave and Ashcroft's playing of these scenes may have worked on stage, the characters' emotions are not convincingly conveyed on radio and would have benefited from more subtle performance, particularly on the part of Ashcroft, as well as sound effects and music.

The production did use music which, like the cast, was transferred from the stage. However, on radio it has little impact, largely because it is played at low level and is often very brief. Wilson Knight states that music is 'an important element in the play' and, in particular, during the drunken scene on Pompey's galley (act two, scene seven).[112] But while this is broadly played in this production, with lots of raucous male laughter, the only music is the song identified in the text as being sung by 'Boy' (2.7.114–19), here sung by a group of men (0:51:12). While musically it has the sound of a tavern catch and is sung riotously with overmodulation on the initial 'come', there is no embellishment of the six-line text and the whole performance lasts less than twenty seconds. While having the potential to create atmosphere and draw the listener into the world of the play, it is so brief it barely has a chance to do so.

The changes to Shakespeare's text were made by Byam Shaw for the stage, rather than by radio producer Peter Watts. However, many of these are the same as the cuts in the 1942 radio production, which suggests that both radio and stage saw the play in broadly similar textual terms. One difference between the two media is apparent, though, in the actors' voices. On stage, costume and physical appearance can help distinguish who is who. But on radio it is essential that characters sound different to each other. This production suffers significantly from uniformity of voice, possibly due to the preferred RP delivery of Shakespeare at this time. As such, it is often difficult to be sure who is talking. Even Redgrave is, at times, difficult to distinguish from the rest of the cast. One concession to radio is the

[111] John Dover Wilson, 'Introduction', in William Shakespeare, *Antony and Cleopatra: The Cambridge Dover Wilson Shakespeare*, ed. by Dover Wilson (Cambridge: Cambridge University Press, 2009), pp. vii–xxxvi (p. xxv).

[112] Wilson Knight, *The Imperial Theme*, p. 221.

addition of a narrator. Basil Hoskins was billed in the *Radio Times* as 'Plutarch the historian' and his script was based on Sir Thomas North's translation of Plutarch's *Lives of the Noble Grecians and Romans*. Drakakis suggests the narration was added 'to smooth the rapid transitions from one location to another', adding that it had the effect of 'diluting the dramatic conflict'.[113] It seems that in almost every aspect of the production the transfer to radio had a negative impact on the play, perhaps because it was little more than a stage production aired on radio, rather than a true audio production.

Antony and Cleopatra was one of the most popular plays with radio producers during this period with five different versions between 1948 and 1965, despite one reviewer stating that 'it may not be Shakespeare's most radiogenic play'.[114] Frank Hauser, who produced the 1950 radio version, wrote an article in the *Radio Times* headlined 'Can Shakespeare Be Broadcast?', discussing the difficulties in putting Shakespeare in general, and *Antony and Cleopatra* specifically, on radio. He concluded: 'the great Elizabethan verse-dramas were written for one kind of delivery, and that delivery happens to be the least suitable to our broadcasting set-up.'[115] However, not everyone found verse a problem. In the case of *Pericles*, verse may have been an advantage in conveying the 'fantasy' nature of the play.[116]

Pericles (1958)[117]

Pericles is less well known than many of Shakespeare's plays and this fact may have been part of its appeal to producers of this period: reviewers tend to make fewer criticisms of textual cuts to works they are less familiar with. At a time when narration was starting to lose favour, *Pericles* also provided a legitimate chorus in Gower. In addition, the 'saga of ships and storms, with sea-changes and almost miraculous risings from watery graves' gave producers an opportunity to conjure up some 'magic' on the airwaves.[118] The 1958

---

[113] Drakakis, 'The Essence That's Not Seen', p. 121.

[114] Hope-Wallace, *The Listener*, 21 September 1950.

[115] Hauser, *Radio Times*, 29 September 1950.

[116] Ian Rodger, 'Drama – Farce and Fantasises', *The Listener*, 14 August 1958, pp. 248–9 (p. 249).

[117] *Pericles*, BBC Third Programme, 9 March 1958 (unpublished, BBC Sound Archive).

[118] Roy Walker, 'Drama – Up She Rises', *The Listener*, 20 March 1958, pp. 514–15 (p. 515); Rodger, *The Listener*, 14 August 1958.

production in particular uses sound to create an engaging, comprehensible version of the play.

Paul Scofield played the title role, having previously done so
twice on stage. Literary critics of the day suggested 'Pericles has no
very sharply defined character' and 'is a passive figure'.[119] Scofield's
performance could be said to concur with this. His delivery of
Shakespeare's verse, like that of Gielgud, focuses on the poetry
rather than being naturalistic or dynamic. Even at times of high
emotion, such as the reunion with Marina (act five, scene one), he
is nothing less than steady. Writing about this scene, Wilson Knight
suggests that 'Pericles, half-awake, stammeringly repeats her strange
phrases'.[120] However, Scofield does not stammer (5.1.88; 1:55:45).
He barely slows his speech. He seems much more intent on sticking
to the verse than attempting to convey emotion. While this might
seem a barrier to listener engagement, the production uses another
technique that until this point had largely been under-employed in
the translation of text to radio to help create an emotionally engaging play: music.

Earlier productions of Shakespeare's plays use very little music.
Pericles, in contrast, uses a lot. Composer and conductor Marcus
Dods had a background in film and theatre, and put those skills
to good use, evoking a wide range of locations in music.[121] John
Arthos states that *Pericles* 'explores a whole wonderful world,
Antioch, Tarsus, Pentapolis, Tyre, so many of the great cities of the
past'.[122] In his review of this production, Rodger acknowledged the
benefits of presenting the play on radio: 'When the ear is doing all
the imagining the stage improbabilities of this play [. . .] are swept
aside.'[123] To convey these different locations, around sixty music
cues are used, encompassing a wide range of styles. The play opens
with a drum roll, fanfare and dramatic music, before moving on to
something more Elizabethan in style. This might suggest a sixteenth-
century setting, but the music changes from location to location.
In the opening scene the listener hears something almost military
(0:02:34), then a romantic, orchestral piece for the entrance of

---

[119] J. C. Maxwell, 'Introduction', in *Pericles: The Cambridge Dover Wilson Shakespeare*,
ed. by John Dover Wilson (Cambridge: Cambridge University Press, 2009), pp. ix–xxix
(p. xxvi); G. Wilson Knight, *Crown of Life* (Abingdon: Routledge, 2002), p. 73.

[120] Wilson Knight, *Crown of Life*, p. 63.

[121] Bruce Eder, 'Marcus Dods', in *AllMusic*, <https://www.allmusic.com/artist/marcus-
dods-mn0001571065> [accessed 23 June 2020].

[122] John Arthos, 'Pericles, Prince of Tyre: A Study in the Dramatic Use of Romantic
Narrative', *Shakespeare Quarterly*, 4.3 (1953), 257–70 (258).

[123] Rodger, *The Listener*, 14 August 1958.

Antiochus's daughter (1.1.13; 0:03:41), and when the riddle is read, a single, pulsating and reverberating chord is used to create an other-worldly effect (1.1.65; 0:07:17). During the rest of the play the music ranges from the pseudo-Middle Eastern, using what sounds like a traditional flute and drum, for the Mytilene brothel (1:25:05), to a halliard shanty sung in unaccompanied two-part harmony, signal-ling that act five begins on a ship (1:50:30). Music therefore creates a direct connection to place without the need for a precise location, meaning listeners do not need prior knowledge of the text or the geography of the eastern Mediterranean.

Wilson Knight identifies two points in the play where music becomes 'an active force' and is 'explicitly mystical'.[124] In this pro-duction, these scenes also seem to be linked musically. In the reviv-ing of the 'dead' Thaisa (3.2.87–95), there is more than a minute of slow, melancholic, romantic strings (1:08:39): a long period without speech for radio drama. When Pericles later hears the 'music of the spheres' as he recovers (5.1.217; 2:03:43), lush strings reappear, and while the music is not identical to that which revives his wife, it is very similar, perhaps deliberately trying to evoke a connection before their reunion in the final scene. McWhinnie states that 'music is inevitably the most potent artistic adjunct to speech, emotionally at least, because of its own emotional power'.[125] This production takes full advantage of this, engaging the listener not just through words and acting, but also through music.

It might be thought helpful for a producer to have a ready-made narrator in the form of Gower. Arthos suggests his speeches lend a 'formal elegance' to the play.[126] Lockwood West's delivery, like most radio narrators at the time, is very much in this style. However, in Shakespeare's text, Gower's speeches are often long and accompanied by dumb shows, neither of which work well dramatically on radio. Adaptor and producer R. D. Smith not only removes the dumb shows but also substantially cuts Gower's lines and frequently rewrites them, compressing the script. In the chorus at the opening of act two, twelve lines (2.0.5–16) are reduced to the un-Shakespearean 'Prince Pericles at Tarsus stays / But letters come him to amaze' (0:27:38). And a more elaborate version of this prac-tice can be found in the chorus in act four, scene four, where more than twenty lines are cut, seven are substantially rewritten, and

---

[124] Wilson Knight, *Crown of Life*, p. 73.
[125] McWhinnie, p. 64.
[126] Arthos, p. 262.

eight, from Marina's epitaph, are taken from Gower and given to Pericles. This practice of reallocating lines happens throughout the play. Pericles should read Antiochus's riddle at the start of the play, but instead he says 'let me *hear* the riddle', and a female voice recites it (1.1.65–72; 0:07:23). And when he arrives at the jousting tournament, he is not announced by Thaisa: the lines are subtly altered and he announces himself. This is the most heavily edited of the plays discussed in this chapter. As well as reducing the length, the editing speeds up the pace by increasing the interaction between characters, making it more conversational. It also makes it more engaging as audio drama, as McWhinnie asserts: 'radio must of its nature use words in the most compressed, condensed way' in order to be most effective.[127]

Pericles presents a dilemma to the producer in terms of content: it is 'Shakespeare's most sexually explicit play'.[128] A generation before this broadcast, Creswell cut some of the bawdier lines from the Porter in *Macbeth*. However, the sexual content in *Pericles* is far stronger and is maintained in this production. The incestuous relationship between Antiochus and his daughter is made clear both through the text itself and through Scofield's delivery of it, with his emphasis on words like 'bad', 'foul' and 'incest' (1.1.125–30; 0:11:09 and 1.2.76; 0:17:28). The brothel scenes in Mytilene are also unambiguous. They were much commented on by contemporary literary critics, with J. C. Maxwell writing that 'the best parts of them are genuinely funny' and Wilson Knight recognising their 'harsh, yet often richly amusing, satire'.[129] This radio production attempts to bring out the humour but also signal the danger facing Marina. Patricia Hayes, as the Bawd, adopts an exaggerated cockney accent while Boult, played by Malcolm Hayes, whistles as he enters and chuckles his way through his lines. Even when he threatens to rape Marina, his tone is jovial: 'Faith, I must ravish her' (4.6.10; 1:40:50); 'I must have your maidenhead taken off' (4.6.116; 1:45:54); 'To take from you the jewel you hold so dear' (4.6.140; 1:47:10). However, Jill Raymond's reaction as Marina indicates the horror of the situation. Her initial kidnap is punctuated with desperate screaming (1:24:06) and once delivered to the brothel she adopts a defiant tone against those holding her, fierce and disgusted (4.2.70–1; 1:28:58

[127] McWhinnie, p. 56.

[128] Maurice Charney, 'The Saintly Marina in *Pericles*', in *Shakespeare's Style* (London: Fairleigh Dickinson University Press, 2014), pp. 145–7 (p. 145).

[129] Maxwell, p. xxix; Wilson Knight, *Crown of Life*, p. 61.

and 4.2.75; 1:29:17). In addition, several interjections are added to the text, enabling Marina to stand up for herself. Raymond's performance as Marina makes the sexual violence genuinely threatening. However, played against the comedy characters of Bawd and Boult it is incongruous. These scenes highlight the conflict, inherent in the text itself, between violence and humour. This production attempts to present both, with the effect that neither works well, possibly undermining to some extent the audience engagement achieved through music and textual editing.

This production seems to mark the start of a change in the presentation of Shakespeare on radio. Its extensive and effective use of music helps tell the story and Smith does not seem to have felt constrained by textual fidelity, editing and rewriting the script to remove long passages of text in favour of more dramatic interactions. Another pair of productions where the producer used more textual editing and additions than his predecessors were the *Henry IV* plays broadcast to mark Shakespeare's quatercentenary.

1 Henry IV and *2 Henry IV* (1964)[130]

The BBC celebrated the 400th anniversary of the birth of William Shakespeare with six productions of his plays on radio across the year: two on the Home Service and four on the Third Programme, including the two parts of *Henry IV*. The plays were a popular choice that year with both Peter Hall and Joan Littlewood staging versions, Hall with John Barton and Clifford Williams at Stratford-upon-Avon, Littlewood at the Edinburgh Festival. Their general popularity and 'festive' comic nature seem well suited to a celebratory year.[131] Radio producer Charles Lefeaux described them as having 'an epic quality' and presenting 'an astonishing picture of life'.[132] However, his productions play more to the comic nature of Falstaff and his friends, perhaps making them more listener-friendly.

The two parts of *Henry IV* were broadcast on consecutive Friday nights in February. The idea that the plays were two halves of the

---

[130] *The History of Henry the Fourth, Part One*, BBC Third Programme, 7 February 1964 (unpublished, BBC Sound Archive); *The History of Henry the Fourth, Part Two*, BBC Third Programme, 14 February 1964 (unpublished, BBC Sound Archive).

[131] C. L. Barber, *Shakespeare's Festive Comedy* (Princeton: Princeton University Press, 1972), p. 4.

[132] Charles Lefeaux, 'Henry IV', *Radio Times*, 30 January 1964, p. 44.

same story was common in critical thinking.[133] Lefeaux wrote two articles for the *Radio Times* suggesting he also saw them as effectively one play, with the theme of the 'education of Hal'.[134] This loosely concurs with Harold C. Goddard, who states that 'Falstaff had been both Henry's tempter and his tutor', but is in conflict with S. C. Sen Gupta, whose book *Shakespeare's Historical Plays* came out the same year.[135] He states that the 'theme is not so much the education of Henry V [...] as the Fortunes of Falstaff'.[136] Falstaff in this production was Joss Ackland, aged thirty-five at the time. However, as it was radio, his age was immaterial, as his voice suited the part well. Ackland believably sounds considerably older, full of sack and rotund, although he was relatively slim. Goddard feared a stage Falstaff would be 'physically repulsive' due to his 'sheer material bulk'.[137] This might seem difficult to convey in sound, but P. N. Furbank stated that Ackland 'hit off the combination of physical grossness and intellectual nimbleness'.[138] However, he felt Ackland 'missed some richness' in Falstaff, adding that he 'has a perfect natural "fat" laugh, but he was never a very dominating figure; he was never an extravagant buffoon'.[139] Furbank's assessment matches the recording and while he may have meant it as a criticism (he praises Ralph Richardson's earlier stage performance for its 'music-hall technique'), Ackland's performance seems to simply be a different interpretation of the part, the actor perhaps fitting it to radio where a physical buffoon would be difficult to convey.[140]

Prince Hal was played by Robert Hardy, who at thirty-eight was three years older than Ackland. But Hardy also had a voice that matched his character, lighter and comfortably passing for ten or fifteen years younger than his actual age. Furbank was happier with his performance, stating: 'Hal made a very unpleasantly

---

[133] S. C. Sen Gupta, *Shakespeare's Historical Plays* (London: Oxford University Press, 1964), p. 127. See also John Dover Wilson, 'Introduction', in *The First Part of the History of Henry IV: The Cambridge Dover Wilson Shakespeare*, ed. by Dover Wilson (Cambridge: Cambridge University Press, 2009), pp. vii–xxviii (p. xi); Harold C. Goddard, *The Meaning of Shakespeare, Volume 1* (Chicago: University of Chicago Press, 1951), p. 161. During the history of the BBC, *1 Henry IV* and *2 Henry IV* have usually been performed together, although *1 Henry IV* was produced alone in 1954.

[134] Lefeaux, *Radio Times*, 30 January 1964.

[135] Goddard, *The Meaning of Shakespeare, Vol. 1*, p. 209.

[136] Sen Gupta, p. 127.

[137] Goddard, *The Meaning of Shakespeare, Vol. 1*, p. 179.

[138] P. N. Furbank, 'Radio Drama "Henry IV Part I"', *The Listener*, 13 February 1964, pp. 287–8 (p. 287).

[139] Furbank, *The Listener*, 13 February 1964, p. 288.

[140] Furbank, *The Listener*, 13 February 1964, p. 288.

self-righteous effect, I imagine quite deliberately too.'[141] But he
did not like Sheila Grant as Mistress Quickly, complaining of
her 'throaty stage-Cockney voice'.[142] The issue of the poetry of
Shakespeare also remained in critics' minds. Furbank stated that the
'verse-speaking reached an excellent general level'.[143] But that was
contradicted the following month by Anne Duchene, reviewing the
second play's repeat, saying it was 'admirable, less in the speaking
than in its being so beautifully pitched at a point between the gran-
diloquent, the raucous, and the treacherously modern, and independent of them all'.[144] On listening to the plays, the performances largely
match Duchene's description of 'raucous', creating a buoyant, fun
atmosphere and making the plot easy to follow.

Among the most 'raucous' moments are those in Eastcheap, in
particular the scene where Hal plays his father and Falstaff pretends
to be Hal (*1 Henry IV*, 2.4). Although this scene has much laughter in it, the use of silence underlines the tensions between Hal and
Falstaff that are inherent in the text. When Hal berates Falstaff for
lying about his exploits during the robbery, the rest of the group
are initially quiet (2.4.209; 0:55:49), but as Hal starts throwing
insults they begin to laugh, and by the time Falstaff is cursing Hal
(2.4.224; 0:56:44) all are chuckling. When the Prince reveals he
and Poins have tricked Falstaff, there is an uneasy silence. Falstaff
breaks it by laughing, releasing the tension for all. When Hal acts
out his father (2.4.400; 1:08:16), there is uproarious laughter, until
the Prince begins insulting Falstaff again, when the laughing stops
(2.4.414; 1:09:25). After Falstaff says 'Banish plump Jack, and
banish all the world' (2.4.437; 1:11:00), Hal's response is serious.
Hardy gives a long pause between 'I do; I will' (2.4.438; 1:11:06)
and says the second two words with such conviction it is clear he
means it. There is a brief moment of total silence before Bardolph
enters and the mood is broken. Furbank describes this scene as 'an
excellent piece of production'.[145] It makes clear the uneasy relationship between Hal and Falstaff at times, and foreshadows the end
of the second play, again helping an audience understand what is
happening and preparing them for what is ahead.

Although in many ways this scene conveys the atmosphere well
for radio, there is no indication of how Falstaff feels about Hal's

[141] Furbank, *The Listener*, 13 February 1964, p. 288.
[142] Furbank, *The Listener*, 13 February 1964, p. 288.
[143] Furbank, *The Listener*, 13 February 1964, p. 288.
[144] Anne Duchene, 'Radio', *The Guardian*, 7 March 1964, p. 7.
[145] Furbank, *The Listener*, 13 February 1964, p. 288.

claim he will banish him. The problem arises again when Hal, now King Henry, rejects Falstaff at the end of the second play. Hardy delivers his speech scathingly (5.2.45–69; 2:39:06), but Falstaff has no lines or asides to react to this. Apart from a brief murmur from Ackland near the start of the speech, there is no audible reaction from him and, without this, there is no prompt for the audience to feel sympathy for Falstaff or outrage at his rejection by the new king, both reactions which literary critics expected an audience to feel.[146] This could have been an opportunity to add text or music to assist the audience, but neither is used.

However, another scene from *2 Henry IV* that necessitates some sort of clarification does have two lines of dialogue inserted. At the end of act two, scene two, Poins suggests to Hal that they should 'put on two leathern jerkins and aprons, and wait upon him [Falstaff] at his table as drawers' (2.2.148–9; 0:40:09), so that they might be able to secretly observe him. But it is more than fifteen minutes before this is played out for the radio audience. When Hal and Poins enter, disguised (after 2.4.206), there is no verbal indication of their presence in Shakespeare's text for another twenty lines. Therefore, two short speeches are added after 2.4.208 to enable the audience to understand that Hal and Poins are watching:

> *Music rises then falls.*
> POINS   (*quietly*) Now art thou the very prince of drawers, Hal.
> PRINCE   (*quietly*) Straighten thy apron, Ned. Shh, Shh. Listen.
> 0:57:30

This serves to both indicate their presence and remind listeners that they are not dressed as themselves. It is particularly important that the audience knows they are there but not seen, because Falstaff speaks disparagingly of both in the conversation that follows with Doll (2.4.209–26). It also helps establish that the asides that follow between Hal and Poins (2.4.227–33, 2.4.235–9) are unheard by Doll and Falstaff. The adaptation here makes the text accessible to listeners without requiring them to have prior knowledge of it or to remember an incidental moment from earlier.

These productions of *1 Henry IV* and *2 Henry IV* bring together a number of elements found in previous plays discussed in this chapter: the use of an ensemble to create atmosphere, the need to add to Shakespeare's text in order to make it comprehensible to listeners, and the importance to radio critics of good 'verse-speaking'. As such,

---

[146] Sen Gupta, p. 134; Goddard, *The Meaning of Shakespeare, Vol. 1*, p. 203.

Lefeaux seems to have been aiming to combine poetry and fidelity to the text with performance and storytelling, attempting to democratise Shakespeare while keeping those already familiar with his works happy at the same time.

* * *

The period 1946 to 1966 was a time of expansion and change at the BBC. The introduction of the Third Programme meant that a wider variety of radio programming was possible. It is therefore no surprise that it was during the time of this expanded service that more Shakespeare plays than ever before or since were produced. This in itself had a democratising effect on his work in the sense that the majority of the public could access it. But accessibility also increased in terms of the way Shakespeare was being presented. During this period production techniques developed, creating increasingly engaging and comprehensible productions of his plays, democratising them by generating enjoyment through understanding, as Haley had suggested. However, while drama productions appeared on all three services, it was the Third that became home to Shakespeare, a network that had been 'dismissed in the popular Press as "precious" and "obscure", "an intellectual freak"—the word "elitist" had not yet been invented'.[147] So while many productions were available, some listeners may have been put off by the network where most were to be found. And more change was coming. By the end of this period, the television service had already expanded to two channels and in 1967 the BBC would launch a fourth network radio station. Felton wrote: 'One of these days, radio is going to find that its glasses have been mended by television. When that happens, will it survive?'[148] It did, and so did productions of Shakespeare's plays. They were increasingly marginalised on the new Radio 3. But being almost hidden from much of the BBC's audience did nothing to deter the creativity of producers. In fact, it seems to have led to a more independent breed of producer who, free from the close scrutiny experienced by their predecessors, would be able to take the plays in their own, individual directions.

[147] Briggs, *Volume V*, p. 44
[148] Felton, p. 146.

Chapter 3

Radio Reorganised and Reimagined: 1967–87

The period from 1967 to 1987 saw radio Shakespeare dominated by a small group of male producers with their own, distinct ideas about how to tackle the texts. Steadily declining critical attention outside the BBC, and possibly within, seems to have enabled these men to deliver their own, personal takes on the plays without the pressures of expectation or restrictions of enforced uniformity. This chapter argues that these two decades were the era of the 'radio auteur'. The plays of this period are more a product of individuals than of a collective or institutional BBC, with no clear pattern of production.

The circumstances were conducive to the creation of the 'auteurist' radio Shakespeare producer. Firstly, there does not appear to have been any overarching guidance on which plays should be produced – or how this should be done – giving producers a relatively free rein. Secondly, BBC Radio went through a major reorganisation. At the beginning of this period, in 1967, the BBC added a fourth network: BBC Radio 1. The introduction of the 'all-pop' station led to the rebranding of the existing channels.[1] The Light Programme became Radio 2, the Third, Radio 3, and the Home Service, Radio 4. As a result of the new line-up, the BBC published *Broadcasting in the Seventies*, described as its 'plan for network radio and non-metropolitan broadcasting'.[2] The thirteen-page document set out proposals 'to reshape BBC radio into a pattern which we believe would be more logical, more attractive, and solvent'.[3] It quickly led to Radio 3 losing much of its speech content, but maintaining 'the

---

[1] *Broadcasting in the Seventies* (London: BBC, 1969), p. 3.
[2] *Broadcasting in the Seventies*, cover.
[3] *Broadcasting in the Seventies*, p. 13.

more specialised drama, poetry, and other cultural programmes'.[4] This included Shakespeare. Radio 4, on the other hand, while still airing drama, produced very few Shakespeare plays. During the period 1967 to 1987, Radio 3 broadcast nearly forty, while only half a dozen productions of Shakespeare had their first broadcast on Radio 4, although the network did air the lauded twenty-six-part series *Vivat Rex* (1977), 'a dramatic chronicle of the English Crown through 200 years of its history by the Elizabethan playwrights Shakespeare, Marlowe, and their contemporaries', produced by Martin Jenkins.[5]

Briggs states that in 1969 only two in every hundred BBC listeners were tuned to Radio 3.[6] Radio Shakespeare therefore had a much smaller potential audience than it had had for many decades, and it got much less recognition. Briggs's fifth instalment of his history of British broadcasting, which covers the years 1955 to 1974, barely mentions radio drama, let alone Shakespeare. Similarly, a sixteen-page supplement in *The Times* to mark the BBC's fiftieth birthday in 1972 dedicates half a page to television drama, but nothing to radio drama. In 1976 Sheridan Morley wrote that even 'distinguished radio drama' went 'largely unnoticed by the press':

> Yet upwards of a hundred thousand people listened to the Alec Guinness *Lear* or the Paul Scofield/Nicol Williamson *Othello* on radio, vastly more than will ever get to a production at the Open Space or any of the other smaller theatres regularly reviewed by the national press.[7]

As Morley identifies, the production of Shakespeare's plays on radio was largely ignored by critics outside the BBC, and perhaps even within the corporation, where eyes were firmly fixed on the small screen.

The middle years of this period were the era of the BBC Television Shakespeare project. From 1979 to 1985 the corporation aired productions of the complete canon. The project received 'one of the most elaborate publicity campaigns ever launched for a series of cultural programs'.[8] But it also came in for criticism. Jack Jorgens,

[4] *Broadcasting in the Seventies*, p. 4.
[5] 'Vivat Rex', *Radio Times*, 10 February 1977, p. 27.
[6] Briggs, *Volume V*, p. 771.
[7] Sheridan Morley, 'Preview', *Radio Times*, 15 April 1975, p. 13.
[8] Jack Jorgens, 'The BBC-TV Shakespeare Series', *Shakespeare Quarterly*, 30.3 (1979), 411–15 (411).

writing at the time, stated: 'The verdict is decidedly mixed.'[9] Olwen Terris later summed up many critics' opinions, writing that 'the productions were generally bland and unimaginative'.[10] Such a high-profile, albeit frequently criticised, project may well have distracted from the work on the same texts being done on radio.

With little attention internally or externally on radio Shakespeare, it is unsurprising that its producers were able to shape their productions to their own will, in the same way that cinematic 'auteurs' are able to fashion their films. No longer was there a Farjeon figure complaining about the 'butchering' of the texts. Nor was there pressure to create productions that would be comprehensible to any and all listeners. That does not mean that these were not still issues for producers, but they were no longer front and centre. The use of the term 'auteur' here aims to reflect some of the working practices these men had in common with those in the movies. These 'radio auteurs' are 'the major creative force' in their respective works.[11] They exert 'a high level of control across all aspects' of a play with a 'distinctive style', fulfilling roles including directing and editing.[12] They also convey 'individual perspectives through thematic motifs and stylistic markers'.[13] Producers from the late 1960s to the late 1980s were not constrained by the later 'corporate culture' of the BBC.[14] Tydeman wrote in 1981 that radio production 'has no need to surround itself with a machine of great executive complexity'.[15] Morley reported that Tydeman told him there was 'a greater freedom to explore and to experiment' than there had been previously.[16] And Jeremy Mortimer, who joined the department in the early 1980s, says that at that time it was 'essentially a kind of fiefdom'.[17] In addition, David Hendy suggests that 'something approaching an *auteur*

---

[9] Jorgens, p. 411.

[10] Olwen Terris, 'Shakespeare and British Television Broadcasting 1936–2005', in *Shakespeare on Film, Television and Radio*, pp. 20–39 (p. 31).

[11] 'Auteur Theory', in Britannica, <https://www.britannica.com/art/auteur-theory> [accessed 24 December 2020].

[12] 'What Is an Auteur?', in MasterClass, <https://www.masterclass.com/articles/film-101-what-is-an-auteur> [accessed 24 December 2020].

[13] Rosanna Maule, *Beyond Auteurism: New Directions in Authorial Film Practices in France, Italy and Spain since the 1980s* (Bristol: Intellect Books, 2008), p. 13.

[14] Lloyd Hamilton Peters, 'Media Practice and New Approaches to Mise-En-Scène and "Auteur" Theory in Broadcast Radio' (unpublished doctoral thesis, University of Salford, 2014), p. 37.

[15] Tydeman, 'The Producer and Radio Drama', p. 13.

[16] Sheridan Morley, 'John Tydeman: Lear for the Ear', *The Times*, 14 December 1974, p. 9.

[17] Jeremy Mortimer, private Zoom conversation, 23 February 2021.

tradition of "sound cinema"' was present during the 'early 1970s', partly due to 'inspiration' from 'domestic television' and directors such as 'Ken Loach, Stephen Frears, and Roland Joffe', and partly because of the long-established 'avant-gardist subculture' of the department.[18] Producers had autonomy over their own projects, and four in particular who feature in the case studies below – Raymond Raikes, John Tydeman, Martin Jenkins and Ian Cotterell – used this to execute their own personal takes on Shakespeare's plays.

Lloyd Hamilton Peters states that auteur theory has been described as a 'strategy to increase directorial status', adding that one way of doing this is by 'announcing the director's credit above the title of the film' on posters.[19] Perhaps the equivalent for a radio producer is the listing in the *Radio Times*. Tydeman wrote that 'the addition of the line "Produced by Raymond Raikes" at the end of a *Radio Times* drama billing would create in listeners the anticipation of a spirited production of the highest quality'.[20] Tydeman also highlights Raikes's autonomy within the department: 'The enthusiasm of this one man was trusted and encouraged by successive controllers and two heads of Radio Drama – Val Gielgud (though not without some struggle) and Martin Esslin.'[21] Raikes did things his way, regardless of whether others agreed or not.

Tydeman states that Raikes's background in soap opera and a daily thriller serial stayed with him and 'even with the most obscure works [. . .] he never lost the popular touch'.[22] Tydeman went on to explain how Raikes would rewrite parts of plays by 'absent play-wrights for the sake of clarification', adding that '[a] scholar would note that the hand of Raikes is evident in most of the Shakespeare texts he directed. For the average listener this blasphemy would only make things clearer.'[23] In a similar vein, Margaret Horsfield wrote: 'Raikes believes the texts of all Shakespeare's plays should be carefully reconsidered for radio, to the end that the listener is never at a loss.'[24] Raikes always put his listeners – and their entertainment – first.

In contrast to Tydeman and Jenkins, who both favoured long productions, Raikes was unafraid of cutting a text. His production

[18] Hendy, p. 196.
[19] Peters, p. 36.
[20] John Tydeman, 'Obituary: Raymond Raikes', *The Independent*, 8 October 1998, <https://www.independent.co.uk/arts-entertainment/obituary-raymond-raikes-1176797.html> [accessed 16 November 2020].
[21] Tydeman, *The Independent*, 8 October 1998.
[22] Tydeman, *The Independent*, 8 October 1998.
[23] Tydeman, *The Independent*, 8 October 1998.
[24] Horsfield, p. 33.

of *King John* (1967) runs for less than two hours and was described by reviewer David Wade as having 'a verve and an aptness'.[25] Raikes also produced a two-episode version of the three parts of *Henry VI* (1971), with a total running time of just over four hours. Shortest of all, and the shortest version of any Shakespeare play since the Second World War, was his *Comedy of Errors* (1968), which lasts just eighty minutes.[26] Horsfield states that Raikes created 'a very carefully cut and reworked text of the play, with musical and sound effects incorporated into the script, and with detailed directions about the actors' positions in relation to the stereo microphone'.[27] The reason for this was Raikes's explicit use of stereo in this production. Horsfield explains: 'As the announcer speaks the tolling bell in the east is faded away and the sea wash faded in from the opposite direction. These two sounds mark the perimeters of Ephesus.'[28] Within these, Raikes places 'the sounds of the other locations of the play, such as the Porpentine, the Phoenix and the Centaur Inn. Each of these various locations is given a place in the stereo scene.'[29] In the final act when the two sets of twins meet, Raikes uses stereo to help the listener understand which twin is speaking, by putting one Antipholus and Dromio on the left, and the other pair on the right. There were no reviews of this production, so it is difficult to know whether contemporary audiences were aided by Raikes's use of stereo although, listening to it, the effect is more subtle than the descriptions suggest, and perhaps not as clear as Raikes would have hoped.

Raikes's use of stereo was pioneering. It was something he 'pursued [. . .] with enthusiasm, often in the face of managerial opposition'.[30] His use of sound effects was also extensive compared to his contemporaries. Felton, whose producing career overlapped with the start of Raikes's, wrote that drama producers must not 'lump together' lots of different sounds to convey a setting.[31] And yet this is exactly what Raikes did, particularly in *The Comedy of Errors*. He appears to have ignored advice, and even the wishes of his head of department, to produce plays exactly the way he wanted them. And judging from Tydeman's comments in his obituary, he

---

[25] David Wade, 'Military Memoirs', *The Listener*, 9 March 1967, p. 338.
[26] *The Comedy of Errors*, BBC Radio 3, 20 December 1968, <https://learningonscreen.ac.uk/ondemand/index.php/prog/RT38ABDF?bcast=119002061> [accessed 29 December 2020].
[27] Horsfield, p. 32.
[28] Horsfield, p. 33.
[29] Horsfield, p. 33.
[30] Tydeman, *The Independent*, 8 October 1998.
[31] Felton, p. 42.

was successful. A Raikesian production was one that used radio as a stage, carefully positioning actors within the stereo space. It had a tight script, lots of sound effects and music, and was all about entertaining the audience.

Tydeman's style of production was different in almost every way. He had particular admiration for the likes of Ingmar Bergman and Ken Loach and seems to have seen himself in the same mould as these cinematic auteurs.[32] However, despite his interest in film, he had no intention of trying to replicate the visual for his listeners in the way Raikes did. Wade wrote of his 1971 *Hamlet*: 'As no other medium, radio drives us back onto the text and producers have been known to attempt to compensate for lack of eyes by laying on the music and effects. Mr Tydeman avoids this.'[33] Instead, he put the emphasis on the actors. Tydeman himself wrote: 'The speed at which things happen in a radio studio demands extreme accuracy in casting. In fact the ability to cast well should be one of a radio producer's prime qualities.'[34] Michael Quinn states that Tydeman worked with most of the leading actors of the time including Alec Guinness, Paul Scofield and Peggy Ashcroft.[35] Morley lists them and others alongside their appearances in what Tydeman saw as the 'four great tragedies': *Macbeth* (1966), *Hamlet* (1971), *Othello* (1972) and *King Lear* (1974).[36] Tydeman also produced *Romeo and Juliet* in 1970 with Ian McKellen and Anna Calder-Marshall, and *Antony and Cleopatra* with Robert Stephens and Siân Phillips in 1977, Tydeman's last Shakespeare play for BBC Radio. Some actors, like Ronald Pickup, appear again and again in Tydeman's productions.[37] Tydeman explained that 'because of the brief time allotted for the rehearsal of a radio play, it is of inestimable help to have experience of the qualities and quickness of a particular artist'.[38] It was integral to Tydeman's way of working that his actors did not need to be told what to do or spend a long time rehearsing, and were able to deliver a performance with the minimum of direction.

[32] Morley, *The Times*, 14 December 1974.
[33] Wade, 'Hamlet's Mirror', *The Times*, 30 October 1971, p. 8.
[34] Tydeman, 'The Producer and Radio Drama', p. 15.
[35] Michael Quinn, 'Obituaries: John Tydeman', *The Stage*, 4 June 2020, p. 32.
[36] Morley, *The Times*, 14 December 1974.
[37] Pickup is in *Romeo and Juliet* (1970), *Hamlet* (1971), *King Lear* (1974) and *Antony and Cleopatra* (1977).
[38] Tydeman, 'The Producer and Radio Drama', p. 20.

Tydeman saw himself as the man in charge, describing his role as 'both captain and High Admiral, director and producer both [. . .] he is to a large extent his own script editor'.[39] This desire for control may well have been why he went on to eventually become head of radio drama in 1986. However, his sense that producers should be able to work in their own way was soon challenged. Quinn states that 'two years from retirement, he resigned in 1994 disenchanted with the [director-general] John Birt-led managerial changes that introduced a competitive internal market throughout the BBC'.[40] But Tydeman did not stop producing audio versions of Shakespeare's plays. Instead, to regain his autonomy, he turned to the commercial sector and recorded several unabridged productions for Naxos. Tydeman's distinctive production style included an actor-led approach to performance, casting famous names in leading roles, and using few effects and little music.

Jenkins shares some of Tydeman's attitudes towards Shakespeare's plays and the presentation of them. Horsfield states that 'Jenkins has directed his cast to stick to the text and play what is there before them, without cloying or overly refining issues which may be unfamiliar to twentieth century sensibilities'.[41] Tydeman's attitude to the plays was much the same, as explored in *King Lear* (1974) below. And like Tydeman, Jenkins makes few, if any, cuts to his texts. However, Jenkins had a more interventionist attitude to direction than his colleague, accentuating the theatrical in *Henry V* (1976) and attempting to rein in Denis Quilley as Macbeth (1984). Jenkins also creates a more distinctive soundscape for his productions. Writing about *Henry V*, Horsfield states that he 'sometimes blurs his background noises intentionally, to avoid the intrusion of overly specific sounds'.[42] This is also a feature of his *Macbeth*, with music being suggestive rather than illustrative. Jenkins teamed up with Ilona Sekacz in the early 1980s and, like Raikes before him who frequently worked with Anthony Bernard, the collaboration with a regular composer became an important element of Jenkins's individual style. This is also a common feature of cinema auteurs, as Ruth Doughty and Christine Etherington-Wright point out: 'Many directors work repeatedly with the same composers: Steven Spielberg with John Williams, Sergio Leone with Ennio Morricone,

[39] Tydeman, 'The Producer and Radio Drama', p. 13.
[40] Quinn, *The Stage*, 4 June 2020.
[41] Horsfield, p. 44.
[42] Horsfield, p. 43.

Tim Burton with Danny Elfman.'[43] They add that 'much of the distinctive style associated with these directors is reliant on this collaborative process. The score and soundtrack are once again integral to audience interpretation.'[44] By working consistently with one composer, a radio auteur like Jenkins or Raikes can develop a distinctive sound that goes beyond the actors' delivery of the text or the use of sound effects.

Jenkins's other key distinctive qualities are his depictions of violence and religion. His productions frequently feature visceral scenes of bloodshed, 'bringing the brutality of murder directly to the listener'.[45] No other producer goes as far in their use of audio to do this. Alongside the violence, Jenkins also picks up on the religious references in the plays in a highly personal way, adding Latin texts to develop single lines into full scenes.

Ian Cotterell's production style was influenced by his mentor Raikes, showing many of the same characteristics: lots of sound effects and music, a desire to produce populist entertainment and the use of the audio space in a theatrical way. Because of these similarities, he is not perhaps an auteur in the same way as Raikes, Tydeman and Jenkins. His style is distinctive, but not entirely unique. However, he was still a significant producer during this period, responsible for five Shakespeare plays. In particular he developed Raikes's interest in the use of stereophony by embracing the 1970s technology of quadraphony. Tydeman suggests that this was as a direct result of support given to Cotterell in his amateur days, where 'he experimented with stereophony in its early phases and with quadraphony and surround-sound, experiments which were to continue long after he had "turned professional"'.[46] Horsfield wrote in 1978 that 'three Shakespeare plays have been done in "quad" so far, with mixed success. These include *The Tempest* [1974], *The Merchant of Venice* [1976] and *As You Like It* [1978], all produced by Ian Cotterell.'[47] This 'mixed success' may at least in part have been because listeners were unable to benefit from hearing the plays in 'quad'. Although there were experiments in broadcasting this way, reviewer Gillian

---

[43] Ruth Doughty and Christine Etherington-Wright, *Understanding Film Theory* (London: Palgrave, 2018), p. 8.

[44] Doughty and Etherington-Wright, p. 8.

[45] Jenkins, private email, 1 October 2020.

[46] John Tydeman, 'Obituary: Ian Cotterell', *The Independent*, 2 January 1996, <https://www.independent.co.uk/news/people/obituary-ian-cotterell-1322070.html> [accessed 1 December 2020], para. 4.

[47] Horsfield, p. 20.

Reynolds wrote of *The Tempest*: 'As quadrophony [*sic*] is not yet a part of radio's established service it was transmitted in stereo.'[48] And she went on to confess: 'Having then duly reported on what is a new technical milestone in radio, I must, as usual, humbly admit that I heard it in mono.'[49] Likewise, Derek Parker, reviewing *As You Like It*, admitted he too had only been able to listen in mono.[50] When even reviewers are not using the most up-to-date technology, there is little hope that the wider audience will appreciate the soundscape created.

Cotterell's *The Tempest* was only the second Shakespeare play he ever produced. Horsfield explains: 'It was chosen by Cotterell for "quad" because of its elusive magic which he felt could be effectively evoked if the listener were surrounded by the strange noises of the island on the four speakers of a quadraphonic sound system.'[51] Horsfield herself was able to listen to this production in 'quad' and noted that the voice of Ariel was 'technically manoeuvred to appear to come from nowhere'.[52] She added that '[t]he voice hovers in mid air, and is all the more mystifying because Ronnie Stevens, as Ariel, whispers very quietly into the microphone throughout the play, with a faint echoing reverberation added to his voice'.[53] In conclusion, she observed that '[t]he producer and actor and sound engineer have, in the character of Ariel, combined their efforts to make a very special being who, in the words of Ian Cotterell, "seems to speak from within Prospero's head"'.[54] Horsfield's description of Ariel bears similarity with Raikes's use of the Radiophonic Workshop for *A Midsummer Night's Dream* four years earlier, again suggesting the influence he had on Cotterell. Unfortunately, the BBC only has a stereo version of this production in its archives, and so it cannot be heard in the original 'quad' now.

Cotterell's contribution to radio Shakespeare is not insignificant, with Reynolds stating that his version of *The Tempest* was 'great radio', while Jeremy Rundall in the *Sunday Times* described it as a 'towering production' in which Paul Scofield gave 'an enormous, even terrifying rendering. Not to be missed.'[55] Parker had mixed

---

[48] Gillian Reynolds, 'Tempest over the Air', *The Guardian*, 30 March 1974, p. 12.
[49] Reynolds, *The Guardian*, 30 March 1974.
[50] Derek Parker, 'Radio – Forest Murmurs', *The Listener*, 12 January 1978, p. 55.
[51] Horsfield, p. 39.
[52] Horsfield, p. 40.
[53] Horsfield, p. 40.
[54] Horsfield, p. 40.
[55] Reynolds, *The Guardian*, 30 March 1974; Jeremy Rundall, quoted in 'Radio 3 Drama: The Tempest', *The Listener Supplement*, 26 September 1974, p. iv.

views about *As You Like It* but described the play as 'an enchant-
ment and a delight'.[56] And Cotterell's legacy also continues into the
twenty-first century. The most recent production of *The Tempest*
(2021) uses stereo in a very similar way to Cotterell's use of quad,
giving the listener the sense that Ariel is flying from speaker to
speaker (or headphone to headphone), zipping from left to right and
back again during her speeches. In addition, 'Ariel's songs [are] realised in binaural sound', a successor to quad.[57] While Cotterell did
not have perhaps the individual distinctiveness exhibited by Raikes,
Tydeman and Jenkins, his similarity in style to Raikes's demonstrates
how influential a 'radio auteur' could be on the next generation of
producers, with his own innovations continuing to be felt today.

The following case studies begin with the work of Raikes,
who favoured Shakespeare's comedies, and his production of *A
Midsummer Night's Dream* (1970). They continue with Tydeman,
who made the tragedies his main focus, in this case, *King Lear*
(1974). Attention then turns to Jenkins, whose preference was for
full-text productions of the histories, with realistic and sometimes
disturbing use of sound to portray the violence of battle. He brings
these into full effect in *Henry V* (1976). Next is Cotterell's *The
Merchant of Venice* (1976), which highlights some of the characteristics his work shares with that of his mentor, Raikes. And finally the
chapter returns to Jenkins and his production of *Macbeth* (1984),
which owes much to his engagement with the history plays.

Almost from the moment the BBC began broadcasting, it was
'in direct competition with established theatre drama'.[58] But by the
start of the period covered by this chapter, the National Theatre had
been founded at the Old Vic in London, with plans for a purpose-
built venue on the capital's South Bank. And the former Shakespeare
Memorial Theatre in Stratford-upon-Avon had become home to the
newly formed Royal Shakespeare Company. These were now firmly
established as the premier institutions for Shakespeare. However, in
1970 Raikes had no intention of the latter overshadowing his latest
radio production.

---

[56] Parker, *The Listener*, 12 January 1978.
[57] '*The Tempest*', in *Drama on 3*, <https://www.bbc.co.uk/programmes/m0011cm5>
[accessed 26 February 2022].
[58] Drakakis, 'Introduction', p. 1.

A Midsummer Night's Dream (1970)[59]

Theatre critic John Barber described 1970 as 'simply the year of Brook's "Dream"'.[60] The Stratford-upon-Avon production by Peter Brook has become legendary, a landmark in Shakespearean theatre, famous for its white box setting. Robert Speaight wrote that instead of the traditional 'muslin and Mendelssohn', Brook 'persuaded you to forget a century of theatrical tradition, with its conventions and its clichés; and commanded you into a frame of mind where the very notion of magic, of supernatural agency, had to be created afresh'.[61] However, before he had seen the play, he did have reservations about Brook's 'admiration' for Jan Kott and how that might affect the production.[62] He was not the only one: Raikes must also have feared Kott's influence. The *Radio Times* reported that he was 'glad to be presenting *A Midsummer-Night's Dream* before (as he puts it) Peter Brook and Jan Kott get at it'.[63] Kott had written: 'I imagine Titania's court as consisting of old men and women, toothless and shaking, their mouths wet with saliva, who sniggering procure a monster for their mistress.'[64] According to the *Radio Times*, 'this is not Raymond Raikes's idea at all'.[65] Raikes himself wrote that his production 'may be one of the last chances to hear Shakespeare's fairy-comedy before it is *reinterpreted* by Kott and Brook' (added emphasis).[66] The prepublicity would suggest that what Raikes really meant was 'ruined'. This is all the more surprising, given that Raikes's immediate boss, head of drama Martin Esslin, was a friend of Kott, having written the introduction to the latter's influential book *Shakespeare our Contemporary*, first published six years earlier. Raikes was evidently not restricted by this and was able to create his own interpretation of the play and even publicise it in direct competition to Brook and Kott.

---

[59] *A Midsummer Night's Dream*, BBC Radio 3, 21 June 1970, <https://learningonscreen.ac.uk/ondemand/index.php/prog/RT395517?bcast=119087070> [accessed 10 September 2020].

[60] John Barber, 'A Dream, a Queen and a Shylock', *Daily Telegraph*, 28 December 1970, p. 8.

[61] Robert Speaight, 'Shakespeare in Britain', *Shakespeare Quarterly*, 21.4 (1970), 439–49 (448).

[62] Speaight, p. 448.

[63] D. A. N. Jones, 'The Storyteller in the Market-place', *Radio Times*, 18 June 1970, p. 14.

[64] Jan Kott, *Shakespeare our Contemporary*, trans. by Boleslaw Taborski (New York: Norton, 1974), p. 227.

[65] Jones, *Radio Times*, 18 June 1970.

[66] 'A Midsummer-Night's Dream', *Radio Times*, 18 June 1970, p. 26.

The message from Raikes was clear: conservative lovers of Shakespeare would prefer his production to Brook's. And on the face of it, a conservative production was what Raikes was giving them. The play opens with a pastoral tune evoking a bygone era and an announcement that it was composed by Anthony Bernard 'for productions of the play at Stratford-upon-Avon in the 1930s', with the *Radio Times* listing adding that there would also be an Elizabethan melody, 'Heartsease' and 'an old English folk tune'.[67] Bernard's style sits in the genre of British Light Music, which 'grew from the indulgent and sentimental music of the nineteenth century' and featured 'harmonically unchallenging, smooth and entertaining melodic lines'.[68] Bernard was also a regular collaborator of Raikes's, the pair having met at the Stratford Memorial Theatre more than thirty years earlier. Raikes's choice sets the radio production up in contrast with what was expected from the new Stratford production, where Richard Peaslee's music would include 'the coil spring from a car suspension unit, and a new instrument from America [. . .] a "Free-ka"'.[69] However, while Raikes's production was superficially much more conservative than Brook's, he was not averse to experimentation.

Raikes had long championed the use of stereo as a way to help listeners picture the action in his plays. D. A. N. Jones reported that Raikes believed it gave 'extra depth', allowing 'the listener to know the position and movement of the characters'.[70] In *A Midsummer Night's Dream* he particularly employs it in act three, scene two. In the conversation between Puck and Oberon, Puck is solely on the right, Oberon on the left (1:13:50). Here, it does not seem to be used to distinguish who is who, but to indicate Puck's arrival (3.2.110). In this case it is the audio equivalent of having two actors enter from opposite sides of the stage. Then, when the confusion between the Athenian lovers is at its height, he employs it again. Helena is placed to the left, while Hermia is on the right; Demetrius is on the left, and Lysander on the right (1:17:20 onwards). It is more subtly used this time; no character is purely on one side or the other. When using headphones, one can discern who is standing where, but only with attentive listening. But again, it places them in the scene. Using stereo

---

[67] 'A Midsummer-Night's Dream', *Radio Times*, 18 June 1970.
[68] 'British Light Music', in Naxos, <https://www.naxos.com/series/british_light_music. htm> [accessed 17 September 2020].
[69] T. S. Ferguson, 'What's Happening – Swinging Music', *Sunday Telegraph*, 30 August 1970, p. 11.
[70] Jones, *Radio Times*, 18 June 1970.

in such a way is peculiar to Raikes at this time. While other producers were making stereo productions, only Raikes actively uses sound to mimic the position of actors on a stage.

Raikes also employed the BBC's Radiophonic Workshop, which provided music, sound effects and vocal distortion for this production. Oberon and Titania's voices are treated with a strange echoey, whispery sound (2.1.60; 0:23:51), which is used throughout on the fairy king and queen. Puck's voice is also distorted immediately after Bottom is 'translated' (3.1.94; 0:53:19), and when the fairies are waiting on Bottom (3.1.145; 0:56:46). But the solo fairy standing 'sentinel' to watch over Titania is not (2.2.25–6; 0:38:01). Raikes uses the technique only when it is essential to identify a character as being from the fairy realm, or invisible to the humans. Radiophonic music is used sparingly, such as when Oberon sends Puck to look for Helena (3.2.100; 1:13:09). It is very simple and is combined with an effect on Puck's voice, which repeats 'Swifter than arrow from the Tartar's bow' (3.2.101), each time getting higher and more distorted. While this might seem exactly the sort of non-traditional treatment a conservative audience would dislike, listeners' comments printed alongside the repeat listing in September 1970 suggest otherwise: 'The stereo effects and unfamiliar music made the fairy-haunted woodland very real indeed, and the fairies quite other-worldly.'[71] Despite Raikes's outward conservatism, his use of stereo and radiophonics demonstrates his desire to embrace all the techniques available to him and a more radical style of production than his contemporaries.

Textually, little is cut from the script: generally just the odd line or couplet. However, there are many insertions, especially in the scenes with the mechanicals. All are male with similar voices so, to aid recognition for listeners, they repeatedly address each other by name. Raikes also frequently inserts their jobs after their names. While Peter Quince does initially do this in Shakespeare's text (e.g. 'Nick Bottom, the weaver', 'Francis Flute, the bellows-mender', 1.2.14 and 34), their jobs are not continually referenced. It is likely Raikes was again trying to make the characters distinct for his listeners. He also adds lines that emphasise the connection between the characters' jobs and what they say. After Quince has cast the play-within-a-play, *Pyramus and Thisbe*, he says 'and I hope, *speaking as a carpenter*, here is a play fitted' (1.2.54; 0:17:43), suggesting the importance of well-fitted timber in carpentry and the irony of the ill-suited players.

[71] 'A Midsummer-Night's Dream', *Radio Times*, 24 September 1970, p. 25.

A few lines later in Bottom's speech about which beard he will wear as Pyramus (1.2.77–9), Raikes inserts at the beginning: 'Then, using my weaver's dyes' (0:18:54). Whether he wanted to explain why Bottom would have so many coloured beards, or perhaps felt the original, sexual joke in the exchange with Quince (whose response, 'Some of your French crowns have no hair at all', is a reference to venereal disease) would be lost on the audience, is unclear. Raikes's relationship with the text is highly personal, with additions not heard in productions by his colleagues before or since.

Raikes also exaggerates the mechanicals' ineptitude by inserting additional lines and repetitions. In perhaps the most Raikesian scene, the performance of *Pyramus and Thisbe* in act five, he creates in sound a sense of the visual 'business' of a stage production. When 'Pyramus' is on stage, there is a clanking noise, as if he is wearing an ill-fitting sword (1:58:21). 'Wall' stomps across the 'stage' in heavy boots (2:00:35). Shakespeare's text has Bottom repeat his mistake from the rehearsal in referring to 'Ninny's tomb' (5.1.200), but Raikes adds Quince hissing from the side 'Ninus, Ninus', and Bottom correcting himself (2:00:24). Quince's frustration as director is also illustrated when part of one of Bottom's lines is given to him: rather than Bottom correcting himself 'Which is—no, no was—the fairest dame' (5.1.282), Quince corrects him (2:04:25). In all his plays, Raikes seems to be trying to capture the atmosphere and storytelling of theatre but in sound, as well as finding ways to make the comedy work for a radio audience.

While the versions of the play produced by Raikes and Brook in 1970 may have been superficially very different, both were influenced by the glamour of the commercial theatre. Tydeman described Raikes as 'a scion of show business who always referred to a production as "the show"'.[72] Brook has stated that his production of *The Dream* was greatly influenced by Broadway.[73] This perhaps suggests they had more in common than might be expected, not least their respective desires to produce something individual and distinctive, as well as entertaining. Tydeman himself was more influenced by 'serious' theatre, making it his mission to bring his interpretations of Shakespeare's tragedies to the radio, often with the most highly regarded Shakespearean actors in leading roles. However, while this undoubtedly brought his productions publicity, the reasoning behind it seems to have had more to do with his hands-off approach

[72] Tydeman, *The Independent*, 8 October 1998.
[73] Peter Brook, *Playing by Ear* (London: Nick Hern Books, 2019), pp. 81–2.

to directing and his preference for actors who already understood the texts they were working with.

King Lear (1974)[74]

When Tydeman came to *King Lear* he had a decade of radio Shakespeare plays behind him, starring some of the most highly regarded actors of their generation. Miriam Margolyes, who worked with Tydeman at the BBC from the mid-1960s onwards, described him as 'impossibly grand and magisterial even then'.[75] It is therefore perhaps unsurprising that, as a producer unafraid to work with famous names, he should approach a film star for his production of *King Lear*.

Alec Guinness had performed Shakespeare on radio several times between 1939 and 1947. But after a gap of nearly thirty years, he wanted to know there was 'a measure of agreement' between Tydeman and himself before agreeing to take on Lear.[76] Tydeman's attitude was very straightforward: 'I don't believe in this clarification of Shakespeare. You just say to the actor: "You just bloody say it!"'[77] This is in keeping with Guinness's comment in an interview that 'I just do it'.[78] It is indicative of Tydeman's style of production and one of the key elements of his particular auteurist qualities. He relied on his casting skills more than detailed direction in order to get the performances he required and, to this end, chose star names to populate his plays. This attitude of non-interference seems also to have extended to Tydeman's scripts. He sometimes cuts but makes fewer changes or additions than either Raikes or Jenkins. A Tydeman production guaranteed star names, a 'straight' rendering of Shakespeare's text and little in the way of sound effects and music.

Tydeman's attitude to Shakespeare production won plaudits but did not always produce the results he himself desired. This was

---

[74] *King Lear*, BBC Radio 3, 12 December 1974, <https://learningonscreen.ac.uk/onde mand/index.php/prog/RT3B4BD1?bcast=119299260> and <https://learningonscreen. ac.uk/ondemand/index.php/prog/buf4f55b7?bcast=123962349> [in two parts, accessed 6 November 2020].

[75] Ned Chaillet, 'John Tydeman Obituary', *The Guardian*, 4 May 2020, <https:// www.theguardian.com/tv-and-radio/2020/may/04/john-tydeman-obituary> [accessed 4 January 2021].

[76] Peter Martin, 'Sir Alec Guinness Talking ... But So Discreetly He's Hardly There', *Radio Times*, 12 December 1974, p. 17, p. 19.

[77] Tydeman, private phone conversation, 18 February 2020.

[78] Martin, *Radio Times*, 12 December 1974.

particularly the case with *King Lear*. While Tydeman and Guinness may have seemed in agreement, Guinness's attitude to radio acting was not quite as straightforward as he made it sound. Two anecdotes about the recording give an indication of this. The *Radio Times* reported that Tydeman had asked his cast to imagine what their costumes might be like for their roles: 'When Guinness came to do the mad scene, he remarked, "I must remember I'm wearing my nightshirt and the pretty hat with wild flowers on it!"'[79] Tydeman recalled another incident in the studio: 'Alec brought an immaculate pair of slippers to wear. Cyril [Cusack, who played Gloucester] noticed this and the next day he brought out his rotten old carpet slippers!'[80] Both suggest Guinness was precise and careful in his performance, something that disappointed Tydeman. More than four decades after the recording, Tydeman described Guinness as 'too polite. I couldn't get the animal out of him. Although he had the capability of doing it, he was afraid.'[81] Tydeman's feelings may have been evident to the actor, who wrote in his diary that he felt he had 'failed hopelessly in the storm sequence' although may have been 'rather good in the last scenes'.[82] Tydeman's hands-off approach appears to have backfired, at least in his own mind.

However, radio critics felt that Guinness and the 'stellar cast' did bring something out of the text.[83] Val Arnold-Forster wrote that it was a 'production that made one very conscious of the fact that the play is about family relationships'.[84] She added: 'What we got was Lear the father even more than Lear the King. But, since Alec Guinness is a very great actor, the tragedy was in no way diminished.'[85] Tydeman saw the 'spine' of the play as 'a political one', but Arnold-Forster's suggestion that this version is more family focused seems apt.[86] Guinness's voice is not unlike that which he uses for Obi-Wan Kenobi in the *Star Wars* franchise two years later. He is a dignified and controlled Lear at the start, becoming bewildered, endearing and gently comic during the mad scenes. His lack of the 'animal' means he is never overly wrathful with his daughters, and therefore it is easier to empathise with him as the play goes on. In the storm

[79] 'This Week', *Radio Times*, 12 December 1974, p. 3.
[80] Tydeman, private phone conversation.
[81] Tydeman, private phone conversation.
[82] Alec Guinness quoted in Piers Paul Read, *Alec Guinness: The Authorised Biography* (London: Simon & Schuster, 2003), p. 488.
[83] Martin, *Radio Times*, 12 December 1974.
[84] Val Arnold-Forster, 'Radio', *The Guardian*, 21 December 1974, p. 8.
[85] Arnold-Forster, *The Guardian*, 21 December 1974.
[86] Morley, *The Times*, 14 December 1974.

scene (3.2.1 onwards; 1:23:50), Guinness's delivery is less dramatic than that of his predecessors. For example, John Gielgud in his 1951 performance bellows the speech as if he is playing to a huge auditorium. Guinness's performance is more intimate. His voice is angry, but he does not shout. He is not competing with the storm but challenging it. In the play's final scene, Guinness's Lear is sad, almost wistful, and has an air of childishness about him, particularly when he thinks Cordelia may still be alive. As he delivers the five nevers, his voice is very soft, sad and with a sing-song tone that accentuates the childlike quality (5.3.284; 2:55:24). Sigurd Burckhardt, writing six years before this production, states that Lear's final words are 'the cry of the man who cares for nothing more except the hope that truth has breath and voice and that from it issues visible realities'.[87] But Guinness's interpretation suggests that his Lear cares little about truth. Instead, as observed by Arnold-Forster, the combination of his delivery and the text emphasises the importance of family as he dies. His voice almost fades away as he looks at Cordelia (5.3.286–7; 2:55:41), leaving the audience in no doubt that his daughter, rather than the crown or succession, is the most important thing to Lear at the end.

Likewise, Goneril, Regan and Cordelia are played with subtlety. Arnold-Forster praised the performances of Jill Bennett, Eileen Atkins and Sarah Badel respectively as the sisters for 'exceptional acting', adding 'none of your stereotyped two baddies and a goodie here'.[88] Guinness also praised Atkins and Badel in his diary, describing them as 'excellent'.[89] Badel in particular creates a nuanced Cordelia that contrasts with the way the character was more often portrayed on radio and in contemporary literary scholarship. Harold C. Goddard describes Cordelia as 'a spirit', while Maynard Mack suggests she is a symbol of 'human virtue' and L. C. Knights describes her 'serenity'.[90] In the opening scene, the reaction of Badel's Cordelia to Lear's demands is much more human. She finds her sisters' comments ridiculous; there is almost a chuckle in her voice during her

---

[87] Sigurd Burckhardt, *Shakespearean Meanings* (Princeton: Princeton University Press, 1968), p. 258.

[88] Arnold-Forster, *The Guardian*, 21 December 1974.

[89] Guinness quoted in Read, p. 488.

[90] Harold C. Goddard, *The Meaning of Shakespeare, Volume 2* (Chicago: University of Chicago Press, 1951), p. 156; Maynard Mack, '"We came crying hither": An Essay on Some Characteristics of King Lear', in *Essays on Shakespeare*, ed. by Gerald Wester Chapman (Princeton: Princeton University Press, 1965), pp. 138–76 (p. 162); L. C. Knights, *Some Shakespearean Themes* (London: Chatto & Windus, 1959), p. 130.

asides after they give their declarations of love (1.1.60; 0:04:40 and 1.1.74–6; 0:05:35). When she answers her father, her responses suggest she finds the whole situation rather silly. She speaks plainly and honestly when she declares 'I love your majesty / according to my bond' (1.1.90–1; 0:06:28), unaware that this will be insufficient for her father. And her delivery of 'Why have my sisters husbands if they say / they love you all?' (1.1.97–8; 0:06:45) gives the impression of a woman anticipating a loving, rather than dutiful, relationship with her future husband. Badel's Cordelia is not unable to 'heave her heart unto her mouth' (1.1.89–90) but sees no point in it: her mistake is to assume her father is as mature as her. There is nothing in any of Tydeman's comments on the play to suggest this interpretation comes from him, perhaps indicating that his reluctance to explain Shakespeare enabled Badel to determine her own reading of the character.

Ronald Pickup as the Fool also gives a different interpretation to many of his radio predecessors. Recordings from the 1940s to the 1960s feature Fools with light, almost childlike voices who sing many of their lines and seem timid around their respective Lears. Pickup plays the Fool with a tone that suggests he is superior to all the other characters, including Lear. When he addresses Lear as 'my boy' he is not reverential or affectionate but patronising (1.4.125; 0:34:23). When Kent says: 'This is not altogether fool, my lord' (1.4.127.12), Pickup's confident and knowing delivery of the response suggests he views himself as less of a fool than those around him (1.4.127.13–16; 0:34:58). This has echoes of Feste's initial exchange in *Twelfth Night*, where he uses logic to prove Olivia is the fool, rather than him (1.5.50–64). Pickup pointedly delivers the lines with the assuredness of someone who knows what is going on and what the future holds. Tydeman had previously cast Pickup as 'the best Hamlet' he had ever heard, adding that Pickup 'sounded as if he had a mind'.[91] This may explain Pickup's interpretation of the Fool, thoughtful and observant rather than subservient. Tydeman's familiarity with Pickup's acting style would suggest he was expecting Pickup to portray the Fool in this way without necessarily specifically giving him that direction.

In Tydeman's productions, the interpretations of the actors are to the fore, rather than his own directorial hand. His expectation that his cast would just instinctively deliver the lines allowed them to give their own, individual responses to the roles they played, based on the

[91] Tydeman, private phone conversation.

text rather than theatrical or literary convention. Tydeman's auteurism is rooted in his commitment to enabling his actors to use their skills to develop roles, rather than in strong, prescriptive direction.

Like Tydeman, Jenkins makes few cuts to the texts and often casts well-known actors, though rarely as famous as those used by Tydeman. However, Jenkins's use of sound effects is more prominent than his colleagues' and is used to a specific end: to convey the brutalities of war. While Tydeman focused on the tragedies, Jenkins favoured the history plays, beginning with *Henry IV Part One* and *Two* in 1973, and returning to the second tetralogy three years later with *Henry V*, which shows a keen interest in evoking the sounds of battle, as well as emphasising the Christian context of the plays.

Henry V (1976)[92]

By 1976, there had been more than a dozen productions of *Henry V* on BBC radio. However, reviewers did not compare Jenkins's version to any of these, but to a contemporary stage version and a film. Morley suggested: 'Jenkins is intent on displaying *Henry V* as a war poem, an interpretation which should afford an enthralling contrast with the "reluctant hero" King recently offered by Alan Howard for the RSC at Stratford.'[93] Derek Parker, on the other hand, made a connection between Jenkins's production and perhaps the most famous twentieth-century version, stating it was 'substantially cast in the same mould' as Laurence Olivier's 1944 film.[94] However, Jenkins suggests that neither were direct influences, stating: 'I think I am most influenced by the demands of the text.'[95]

Parker's observation does have some merit, however, as there are elements of the production that seem to echo its cinematic predecessor. Like the film, it opens in a theatre, although more in the style of a West End venue than the outdoor Globe. Jenkins begins with the sound of an audience muttering, then a 'theatre manager' (rather than a standard BBC announcer) proclaims: 'Ladies and gentlemen. Henry the Fifth by William Shakespeare' (0:00:05). He goes on to

---

[92] *Henry V*, BBC Radio 3, 18 April 1976, <https://learningonscreen.ac.uk/ondemand/index.php/prog/RT3BDE91?bcast=119360665> and <https://learningonscreen.ac.uk/ondemand/index.php/prog/buf4f55ba?bcast=123962352> [in two parts, accessed 12 October 2020].
[93] Morley, *Radio Times*, 15 April 1975.
[94] Derek Parker, 'Radio: The Words Rule – OK?', *The Listener*, 29 April 1976, p. 543.
[95] Martin Jenkins, private email correspondence, 1 October 2020.

list sixteen cast members, which was an unusually high number for the opening credits. A hush descends over the 'audience' as he reads, and by the time he comes to the last name there is a moment's pause before he speaks in a quiet, slightly reverential voice: 'With John Gielgud as Chorus' (0:00:49). There is then a brief silence before Gielgud launches into 'Oh, for a muse of fire' in highly dramatic tones. Jenkins's setting is theatrical and echoes Olivier's film, yet does so in a way that takes a text written for the stage and transforms it into something comprehensible on radio.

Gielgud's casting seems to have been a deliberate attempt to emphasise the theatrical nature of the Chorus, rather than create a radio narrator. Although the 'theatre audience' never returns, Gielgud's delivery of the Chorus's speeches always sounds as if he is projecting to an auditorium, with a slight echo added to his voice accentuating this (e.g. 0:00:55, 0:25:21, 2:34:22). This fits with the literary criticism of Goddard, who saw the Chorus as a combination of 'History filling in the gaps of the story' and 'stage manager apologizing for [. . .] the general inadequacy of the stage'.[96] Parker stated that the right note was struck 'at the beginning by John Gielgud's noble Chorus' who 'again gift[ed] us all his intelligence and vocal command'.[97] Unlike Tydeman, it seems likely that Jenkins took an active role in directing his performers. Gielgud provided more intimate, radio-friendly performances in other productions around this time, so the decision to present the Chorus in a theatrical manner is likely to have come from Jenkins, especially as other aspects of the production also reflect this style.

Henry was played by John Rowe, who Parker suggested was 'of the same stuff' as Henry Ainley, renowned for his loud and theatrical radio performances.[98] Rowe does give a performance that seems rooted in the theatre, which is perhaps surprising as he was a member of the BBC Drama Rep and would therefore have been an experienced radio actor.[99] This would again suggest a deliberate decision on the part of Jenkins to accentuate the consciously theatrical nature of the play. However, his presentation of the battles is in contrast to this. While aspects of the production do seem to be non-naturalistic, his use of sound effects to create the sounds of combat and death are realistic. In the text, the battles never happen

[96] Goddard, *The Meaning of Shakespeare, Vol. 1*, p. 217.
[97] Parker, *The Listener*, 29 April 1976.
[98] Parker, *The Listener*, 29 April 1976. See also Chapter 1.
[99] Morley, *Radio Times*, 15 April 1975.

on stage. By choosing to present them on radio, Jenkins ensures his audience cannot forget the consequences of war, a key aspect of his presentation of the history plays.

Jenkins developed his techniques for the audio representation of war throughout his career at the BBC, but even by 1976 he was creating some of the most violent soundscapes heard on radio. In this production, between scenes two and three of act four, there is a comprehensive sound mix of many voices shouting from a distance, the faint sound of neighing horses and the noise of arrows being fired. This builds with trumpets, the sound of hooves on earth, getting nearer, louder shouting and the occasional cries of pain (2:09:04). The killing of the boys by the French is symbolised by the murder of 'Boy', who is heard crying out in pain at the end of 4.4.69 (2:13:19), and then gurgling as if blood is in his throat. The killing of the French prisoners is also portrayed, with French voices calling in fear, while the English repeatedly shout 'Kill the prisoners' (2:16:48). When Montjoy describes the scene after the battle, of princes 'drowned and soaked in mercenary blood' and horses 'fetlock-deep in gore' (4.7.68, 71), Jenkins has ensured the listener already has these images in their mind. However, this makes the Chorus's prior apology for having 'four or five most vile and ragged foils' (4.0.50) seem not only unnecessary but contradictory. Contemporary literary critic Robert Ornstein believed the use of the Chorus in the play to keep 'the battle offstage' was Shakespeare deliberately sparing the audience 'the horror of war'.[100] In any theatre production, a director wanting to bring that violence on to the stage would find it difficult to do so realistically. Jenkins uses radio to create the impression of hundreds of men involved in battle, and places it at the heart of his production, sparing his audience nothing. While not as realistic as later radio plays of the canon which feature battle scenes, including Jenkins's own versions, this production of *Henry V* does give a sense of the violence of war, something Jenkins was keen to emphasise.

Jenkins's portrayal of war was also successful in the play's less dramatic moments. These received the greatest praise from Parker, who stated that 'Jenkins's major contribution was, perhaps, in the quieter scenes, realising the tensions in both camps before the battles. The Englishmen might have been waiting to go over the top on the Somme on 1 July 1916.'[101] Jenkins also uses religious observance to

[100] Robert Ornstein, *A Kingdom for a Stage: The Achievement of Shakespeare's History Plays* (Cambridge, MA: Harvard University Press, 1972), p. 192.
[101] Parker, *The Listener*, 29 April 1976.

accentuate the impact of war. At the end of act four, Henry says: 'Do we all holy rites. / Let there be sung *Non nobis* and *Te Deum*' (4.8.116–17; 2:32:54). There is no suggestion in the text that this would be staged; however, Jenkins chooses to add this at the end of the scene, initially with a single, unaccompanied English voice singing *Non nobis*, before the rest of the English soldiers join in. This is then cross-faded with the sound of church bells (2:33:12–2:34:22). By doing this, Jenkins creates a greater sense of mourning for the dead, taking the audience from the violence of the battlefield through to the impact on those left behind.

By contrast to Jenkins's powerful handling of the battles and their aftermath, Parker was unimpressed with the comedy in the play, stating 'there were aural over-gesticulations on the part of the clowns' which he believed were due to 'desperation' in having no visuals to fall back on.[102] This, he concluded, 'raises the whole question of totally uncut productions of Shakespeare, and whether they are really justified'.[103] The comic characters in the play, such as Bardolph, Pistol and Nym, are played very broadly, with Michael Aldridge as Pistol particularly unsympathetic. During the description of Falstaff's death, Elizabeth Spriggs as Mistress Quickly sounds genuinely emotional (2.3.9; 0:48:00). However, Aldridge's Pistol remains unsympathetically comic throughout, finally demanding 'give me thy lips' and making an exaggerated kissing sound (2.3.39; 0:50:36). Likewise, the group of soldiers from across the British Isles are played broadly for comedy. The actors portraying Fluellen, Gower, Macmorris and Jamy (a Welshman, Englishman, Irishman and Scot respectively) all use exaggerated and unconvincing national accents. Ornstein viewed the characters as a distraction from the horrors of war, and it appears Jenkins felt that exaggerating them for comic effect would emphasise that contrast and increase the potency of the scenes of violence.

Jenkins's trademarks of visceral, sometimes disturbing violence, and the use of religion as a counterpoint to that, were not copied by other producers for many years. Likewise there is no obvious successor to Tydeman. However, Raikes's treatment of the comedies was influential on another producer. By this point in the mid-1970s, Raikes had retired from the BBC, and with Tydeman and Jenkins concentrating on the tragedies and histories respectively, the lighter plays in Shakespeare's canon needed a new champion on radio.

[102] Parker, *The Listener*, 29 April 1976.
[103] Parker, *The Listener*, 29 April 1976.

Cotterell, a protégé of Raikes, had joined the radio drama department and was clearly influenced by his mentor's work, bringing Shakespeare's comedies to the airwaves with a Raikesian use of effects, comedy and audio technology.

The Merchant of Venice (1976)[104]

Cotterell's first experience of producing radio drama was as part of the Studio Managers Amateur Dramatic Group, 'under the guidance of the doyen director Raymond Raikes'.[105] Unlike most radio drama producers, then and now, Cotterell did not have a university education and prior to joining the radio drama department had been a BBC filing clerk and then a production assistant. Raikes had guided him when he was still an amateur and his influence is evident in Cotterell's productions, which combine a greater use of sound effects, music and sound manipulation than most of those by Tydeman or Jenkins. Like Raikes, Cotterell also worked primarily on the comedies and in 1976 turned to *The Merchant of Venice*, the play which had been Raikes's first foray into producing Shakespeare on radio in 1949.

With the growth of television, radio was attracting less and less attention in the press. In previewing this production Arnold-Forster wrote: 'Good things turn up on radio which only constant readers of the smallest print can expect to hear about in advance. Tomorrow evening, for example, Radio 3 is presenting an interestingly cast Merchant of Venice.'[106] Her comment highlights the hidden nature of many productions of Shakespeare's plays on radio at this time. Previews and reviews were becoming less frequent and listings were getting smaller. In 1956, the *Radio Times* dedicated four pages per day to radio; in 1976 it was two. Newspaper listings were also increasingly cramped, making more space for television.

The casting was also commented on by *The Listener*, which reported that the play would feature 'father and daughter playing father and daughter': Alan and Sarah Badel playing Shylock and Jessica.[107] In this way, Cotterell drew attention to the Jewish characters, in particular Jessica, a relatively small part in the play.

---

[104] *The Merchant of Venice*, BBC Third Programme, 3 October 1976 (unpublished, BBC Sound Archive).

[105] Tydeman, *The Independent*, 2 January 1996, para. 4.

[106] Val Arnold-Forster, '30 Years Snore', *The Guardian*, 2 October 1976, p. 8.

[107] 'Drama – Radio 3', *The Listener*, 2 September 1976, p. iv.

This might have been an opportunity to look at the treatment of these characters. Seven years earlier, Herbert Bronstein wrote that the 'anti-Jewish stereotype' of Shylock 'makes many uncomfortable with *The Merchant of Venice*, not only Jews, but directors, actors, and critics, as well'.[108] Instead, Arnold-Forster's review makes clear that this production gave a stereotypical portrayal of Jewishness, with an unsympathetic Shylock whose 'lisping Jewish accent [. . .] sounded from time to time like a comic send-up of an East End tailor so that the essential dignity of the character was lost'.[109] His daughter also adopts this style of speech but more subtly, creating a more sympathetic and integrated persona, perhaps because this is the trajectory of the character. But it is impossible to ignore the fact that both father and daughter could be said to be continuing Bronstein's 'anti-Jewish stereotype'. From Bronstein's comments, it seems likely that Cotterell would have been aware of the possible concerns around the portrayal of Shylock, suggesting the choice was deliberate. However, it was not without precedent. Both Michael Redgrave a generation earlier in 1953 and David Suchet more than a decade later in 1987 adopt a similar vocal style for the character. Cotterell, perhaps influenced by Raikes's desire for clearly defined characters, appears to have perpetuated an existing stereotype without considering the implications.

Badel's Shylock may be a caricature, ranting in an exaggerated fashion at the end of the trial scene and making a somewhat comic sound when Antonio says 'He presently become a Christian' (4.1.385; 2:03:39). However, the audio image of Shylock is not just down to Badel's performance, as Cotterell uses sound effects to heighten the caricature. Throughout Shylock's first meeting with Antonio (act one, scene three) there is the noise of coins clattering on a table, presumably being counted (from 0:17:13 onwards). And in the trial scene, the sound of a knife being sharpened can be heard prominently (1:49:36–53), as well as emphatic tapping when Shylock says 'Nearest his heart' (4.1.252; 1:56:43). Similarly, Jessica's Jewishness is augmented with sound, even after she has converted to Christianity. At the start of act five (2:09:19) when Jessica and Lorenzo are alone, a solo violin plays a klezmer-style melody and there is also the twanging of a Jew's harp. Cotterell's use of music and sound effects, especially to reflect lines in the text

---

[108] Herbert Bronstein, 'Shakespeare, the Jews, and *The Merchant of Venice*', *Shakespeare Quarterly*, 20.1 (1969), 3–10 (3).
[109] Val Arnold-Forster, 'European Merchandise', *The Guardian*, 9 October 1976, p. 8.

(such as the knife sharpening), are in keeping with Raikes's style of production, which always aims at textual clarity through sound.

The heightened 'Jewishness' of Shylock and Jessica is in contrast to the Christian characters. If any excuse for the accents can be justified, it is in differentiating this divide. The greatest contrast is with Antonio. Bertrand Evans writes that the 'centre of Antonio's character is his goodness'.[110] In this production he is played with an avuncular English warmth by Patrick Barr. When Antonio and Shylock first meet, Alexander Leggatt suggests their 'apparently casual conversation crackles with suppressed animosity'.[111] However, in Cotterell's interpretation it seems one-sided. Badel adopts an exaggeratedly friendly tone, which together with the long aside immediately beforehand indicates his falseness to the audience (1.3.53; 0:20:06). Barr's Antonio is initially cool but not unkind to Shylock. Although he briefly comes close to losing his temper after Shylock's long speech complaining of his mistreatment (1.3.100–22), Barr quickly calms down. Once they have agreed to their 'merry bond' (1.3.166), he gives a friendly chuckle and sounds sincere as he says 'Hie thee, gentle Jew. / The Hebrew will turn Christian: he grows kind' (1.3.170–1; 0:26:41). Antonio is portrayed as Bronstein's 'hero', while Shylock is the 'villain'.[112] This is not dissimilar to Raikes's interpretations of characters, which are often drawn as 'goodies' and 'baddies'. Cotterell's portrayal of Antonio and Shylock as hero and villain respectively mirrors this and, like Raikes, it appears to be used as an aid to storytelling.

This idea of good and bad is also evident in the contrast between Shylock and Portia. Anna Massey's precise and clear-cut RP voice fits well with Leggatt's description of Portia as one with a 'cool ironic wit' who is no 'romantic heiress'.[113] Arnold-Forster felt Massey was 'an excellent choice', adding that 'we were in no doubt about the good sense of the lady'.[114] In the courtroom scene (act four, scene one) Arnold-Forster states that 'she treated the quality of mercy speech as an explanatory exercise; it became a lecture on sentencing policy rather than the evocation of a God-given virtue'.[115] Leggatt states that 'Portia and Shylock speak with utterly opposing

---

[110] Bertrand Evans, *Shakespeare's Comedies* (Oxford: Clarendon Press, 1960), p. 56.
[111] Alexander Leggatt, *Shakespeare's Comedy of Love* (Abingdon: Routledge, 2004), p. 120.
[112] Bronstein, p. 4.
[113] Leggatt, p. 129.
[114] Arnold-Forster, *The Guardian*, 9 October 1976.
[115] Arnold-Forster, *The Guardian*, 9 October 1976.

voices'.[116] Massey's contained, courtroom drama-style delivery is in contrast to Badel's melodramatic Shylock: restrained RP versus exaggerated emotion and accent. Although this fits with Leggatt's literary criticism, it is more likely Cotterell's choices come from a desire to clearly define the two characters and to steer the audience's view of them.

Cotterell left the text of the play uncut, meaning characters that often appear peripheral, like the 'clown' Launcelot, seem more prominent. Leggatt suggests that the scene where Launcelot is 'joking with Old Gobbo' (act two, scene two) 'does not allow the detachment of farce'.[117] However, Steve Hodson, as Launcelot, and Richard Goolden as his father play the scene in a knockabout way. When Old Gobbo enters, there is the sound of the pair colliding, both grumbling, and then the tapping of a stick, indicating the old man's blindness (0:32:16). Goolden uses an exaggerated old man voice, indistinct as if he had missing teeth. Throughout the scene he coughs, wails, 'ooh's and 'ah's, and the tapping continues. Just as Raikes had done with the mechanicals in *A Midsummer Night's Dream* (1970), Cotterell is creating a theatrical representation of the scene in audio.

Cotterell also uses a lavish sound mix. Arnold-Forster stated that 'the various scene-setting was done firmly and rather noisily—plenty of trumpets, splashy gondolas, and vociferous bird-song'.[118] Cotterell's production style owes much to his mentor in the way it uses sound and presentation of character to help the audience understand what is happening; in the extensive use of sound effects and music; in its concentration on comedy; and in its placement of actors within the sound space in a similar way to their positioning on a stage. While it would be wrong to say Cotterell is copying Raikes, the older producer's influence can be felt and Cotterell does not seem to be doing anything distinctively different from his mentor. In his obituary for Cotterell, Tydeman was a little reserved in his praise for his former colleague, writing that he 'was not an interventionist director but one who provided the right ingredients and created the right atmosphere for it all to happen'.[119] This is not unlike Arnold-Forster's assessment of this production: 'Ian Cotterell's *Merchant of Venice* was a firm, clear reading of the play [. . .] All in all, a rational,

---

[116] Leggatt, pp. 137–8.
[117] Leggatt, p. 128.
[118] Arnold-Forster, *The Guardian*, 9 October 1976.
[119] Tydeman, *The Independent*, 2 January 1996, para. 6.

intelligent production.'[120] In both cases, while there is praise, it is not effusive.

Raikes had started his career working on serials and moved into long form drama. Cotterell went the other way, leaving Shakespeare behind in 1979 to produce popular adaptations of the Sherlock Holmes stories and the critically acclaimed series *Barnes' People* (1981–87). Tydeman had also stopped producing Shakespeare, becoming assistant head of radio drama. However, Jenkins continued to work on the canon into the 1990s. In 1984 he tackled the tragedy *Macbeth* but brought to bear all his experience with the history plays, developing further his depiction of war, and again bringing a religious overtone to his production.

Macbeth (1984)[121]

Jenkins had produced six Shakespeare plays for BBC radio by the mid-1980s, largely the histories and Roman plays, as well as the epic *Vivat Rex*. In his 1973 production of *Titus Andronicus*, the actors playing Chiron and Demetrius make sounds almost as if they are gargling as their throats are 'cut', something he developed further in *Vivat Rex*.[122] By the time he produced *Macbeth*, he was skilled at depicting scenes of violence and creating disturbing audio images, some of which he later admitted 'still retain their gruesome impact', even in the twenty-first century.[123]

The killing of Banquo is a case in point. It is preceded by the sounds of dull stabbing and much exertion from the actors. Just before his final words, Nigel Terry as Banquo makes a gurgling sound, as if his lungs are full of blood (3.3.21; 1:00:48). His murder is portrayed as brutal and difficult. Macbeth's death, something that does not take place on stage in Shakespeare's text, is even more visceral. A prolonged fight is interspersed with the dialogue that precedes the killing (5.7.38–64; 2:02:35). Movement is slow and laboured; there is no quick clash of swords as other producers used in earlier productions, but heavy clangs and sounds of extreme exertion from John Rowe and Denis Quilley as Macduff and

[120] Arnold-Forster, *The Guardian*, 9 October 1976.
[121] *Macbeth*, BBC Radio 4, 23 April 1984, <https://learningonscreen.ac.uk/ondemand/index.php/prog/RT3F7EF1?bcast=119706073> [accessed 30 September 2020].
[122] *Titus Andronicus*, BBC Radio 3, 28 October 1973, 2:26:23.
[123] 'Vivat Rex', in *Radio 4 and 4 Extra Blog*, <https://www.bbc.co.uk/blogs/radio4/2012/04/radio_4extra_vivat_rex.html> [accessed 3 January 2021], para. 7.

Macbeth respectively. The sound of the final two stabs suggests great force and is accompanied by painful, guttural noises from Quilley (2:05:05). The violence of the deaths was a deliberate decision by Jenkins: 'Horror and brutality are two of the key themes of the play. As Macbeth sinks ever deeper into the bloodbath of his own making it seems to me essential that the audience should experience the sheer horror of his actions.'[124] He added that 'Radio is a great medium for bringing the brutality of murder directly to the listener. We devised ways to make this as shocking as possible.'[125] The depictions of these deaths are in keeping with Kott's comment that 'blood in Macbeth is not just a metaphor; it is real blood flowing out of murdered bodies'.[126] Jenkins, as with his *Henry V*, uses his skill with sound to convey this palpably to the listener.

The killings in the play are heightened not only by the performances of the actors and the sound effects, but also by the use of music. The closing credits state it 'was improvised and played by Ilona Sekacz'. Her background was in *musique concrète*, a 'type of quasi-musical organization of sound'.[127] Prior to this production she had worked at the RSC as well as on a number of Jenkins's other radio productions. He describes her as having 'a great ear for mood and atmosphere'.[128] Her score for *Macbeth* is sparse, featuring instruments that are not readily identifiable and often using abstract, percussive sounds. Reviewer Peter Davalle described it as 'unearthly' and 'creepy', exerting 'maximum impact in terms of atmosphere'.[129] Jenkins uses Sekacz's music to create a soundscape for his production in a non-literal way. For example, the opening scene with the witches has just an occasional metallic tone and a single string plucked once. At other points smooth tones are replaced with spiky ones (0:15:46), a very low xylophone sound underscores Lady Macbeth (1.5.38; 0:18:30), a dull throb plays under 'Is this a dagger which I see before me' (2.1.33; 0:29:34). Towards the end of the play, the music becomes more like a throbbing heartbeat, as Macbeth's situation becomes more desperate (5.4 onwards; 1:53:58). All the music is seamlessly blended and, although it is sometimes very

---

[124] Jenkins, private email, 1 October 2020.
[125] Jenkins, private email, 1 October 2020.
[126] Kott, p. 87.
[127] Arthur Jacobs, 'Concrete Music', in *A New Dictionary of Music* (Harmondsworth: Penguin Books, 1967), p. 83.
[128] Jenkins, private email, 1 October 2020.
[129] Peter Davalle, 'Today's Television and Radio Programmes – Choice', *The Times*, 28 November 1984, p. 27; Peter Davalle, 'Today's Television and Radio Programmes – Choice', *The Times*, 23 April 1984, p. 19.

quiet, it is rarely absent, enabling Jenkins to create atmosphere in an almost subliminal way. However, he does still use some of the same sound effects as his predecessors. Thunder punctuates the production throughout, including just before Macbeth's death (2:04:50), and there is even a brief cawing of crows prior to Banquo's murder (0:59:35). This suggests that in certain scenes Jenkins felt additional sounds were needed to have greater impact.

Arnold-Forster described the cast as 'formidable' but there were conflicting opinions on Quilley and his Lady Macbeth, Hannah Gordon.[130] Davalle described Quilley's performance as 'masterly', adding that 'with a voice like his, he was born to play Macbeth'.[131] Davalle also praised Gordon, writing that 'she tackles a symphony-size character with chamber music technique and the result is unforgettably chilling'.[132] However, not everyone agreed. John Wain complained that 'realism is all very well, but it is carrying realism too far to make Lady Macbeth utter her first great soliloquy [. . .] in a whisper because she happens to be alone'.[133] Wain continued that 'if we can believe that the woman is speaking immortal verse, it is surely not too much to go on and believe that she is doing so out loud'.[134] This seems to be not only negating the nature of and possibilities offered by radio performance, but perhaps also suggesting something about his attitude to female performers, an attitude some literary critics felt was inherent in the text of *Macbeth*. Peter Stallybrass suggested the play 'mobilizes the patriarchal fear of unsubordinated woman'.[135] Gordon's often naturalistic interpretation of the character creates a Lady Macbeth who is not just strong but real, and ultimately vulnerable. By contrast, Quilley's performance is noticeably more theatrical than Gordon's, although Wain makes no comment on his delivery. Quilley himself acknowledged: 'I had to be forever reminded to tone the voice down.'[136] This suggests Jenkins took an active role as director, although perhaps not quite containing Quilley. Gordon, on the other hand, must have given Jenkins what he was looking for, as he used her in other productions before and after *Macbeth*.

---

[130] Arnold-Forster, 'Pick of the Week's Television and Radio', *The Guardian*, 24 November 1984, p. 10.

[131] Davalle, *The Times*, 28 November 1984.

[132] Davalle, *The Times*, 28 November 1984.

[133] John Wain, 'Radio – Birthday Bard', *The Listener*, 3 May 1984, p. 28.

[134] Wain, *The Listener*, 3 May 1984.

[135] Peter Stallybrass, 'Macbeth and Witchcraft', in *Focus on Macbeth*, ed. by John Russell Brown (London: Routledge, 2005), pp. 189–209 (p. 205).

[136] 'A Real King – That's Quilley's Macbeth', *Radio Times*, 19 April 1984, p. 18.

Wain's long review repeatedly harks back to the sort of comments being made half a century earlier about voice and poetry. In the 1930s, Henry Ainley's performance as Othello was praised for being 'most musical', while a production of *Antony and Cleopatra* was criticised for a lack of 'word-music'.[137] In 1984, Gordon's initial speech was described by Wain as 'unmusical'. He also felt that 'there were many passages where the actors seemed to be speaking the verse in too much of a hurry, conveying nothing of its haunting music'.[138] Once again there was a critical desire for Shakespeare to only be spoken in a certain way. However, Jenkins believed the most important thing was to cast actors he felt would 'give strong, truthful performances', adding that 'these have to be real people the listener can believe in'.[139] Like his presentation of violence and bloodshed, Jenkins wanted his characters to be as realistic as possible.

Jenkins leaves the text of the play virtually untouched. He does not make any edits, even keeping the traditionally cut Hecate passage, and adds just the occasional name or 'My lord' to indicate an entrance. However, he does add one line at the start of act three, scene six, which again suggests a desire to reflect a Christian context for Shakespeare's plays. The play text gives no indication of location, but Jenkins opens the scene with simple organ music evoking a chapel. The character of the Lord then says: '*In nomine Patris, et Filii, et Spiritus Sancti. Amen*' (1:12:03). Jenkins says that he believes the scene to be 'very important' and points to the mention towards the end of a 'holy angel' (3.6.46) as a reference to its religious overtones. The scene also ends with the Lord saying 'I'll send my prayers with him' (3.6.50). Jenkins adds: 'I have always felt that within the play there is a clash between the pagan/witchcraft and inherent Christianity.'[140] This chimes with several earlier literary critics, including Jane H. Jack, who wrote that the play had an 'explicitly Christian quality'.[141] Jenkins himself says he was not consciously reflecting literary criticism: 'I had been in the play at University and had read a great deal about it. However, I always try to come to every production unburdened by the past.'[142] Like his version of *Henry V* he takes a single line and develops it into a religious

---

[137] 'Review of Broadcasting: Mr Henry Ainley as Othello', *Manchester Guardian*, 6 December 1939; Maine, p. 103.
[138] Wain, *The Listener*, 3 May 1984.
[139] Jenkins, private email, 1 October 2020.
[140] Jenkins, private email, 1 October 2020.
[141] Jane H. Jack, 'Macbeth, King James, and the Bible', *ELH*, 22.3 (1955), 173–93 (180).
[142] Jenkins, private email, 1 October 2020.

moment in the play. In both cases the scenes not only accentuate the Christian element, but also provide a counterpoint to the violence.

The four producers featured in these case studies were not the only ones working on radio productions of Shakespeare's plays at the time, but between them they were responsible for more than half of those broadcast.[143] Their colleagues usually only did one or two, concentrating on other radio drama, and did not demonstrate a unique style of their own. While their predecessors may also have had their own, distinct ideas about how to present Shakespeare, the circumstances in which Raikes, Tydeman, Jenkins and Cotterell were working gave them greater opportunity than ever before to present these plays in their own style, enabling them to develop into 'radio auteurs'.

* * *

The production of Shakespeare's plays on BBC radio seems to have been almost exclusively the preserve of men at this time; of the approximately fifty productions during this twenty-year period, only two were produced by a woman: Jane Morgan. However, this was about to change. From the 1990s onwards an increasing number of female producers were responsible for Shakespeare on radio, with the majority of twenty-first-century plays produced by women. Other – less welcome – changes were coming too. In 1978, Horsfield wrote that 'deciding on the production techniques to be used in putting Shakespeare's plays on radio is now much more of an aesthetic choice than it was in the early days of radio'.[144] And that choice was down to the producer. However, as the 1980s drew to a close, the conditions that enabled producers to act with autonomy were about to end. Crook explains: 'The pressures which liquidated the new dramatist's television studio play in favour of filmed series and serials have been visited on Radio Drama.'[145] The BBC's director-general, John Birt, 'imported' his 'economic ideology' and 'multi-million pound surveys produced by outside management

---

[143] Of the forty-three main Shakespeare productions during this twenty-year period (ignoring those for schools and works of 'Shakespeare Apocrypha'), twenty-six were produced by these four producers: Cotterell and Tydeman produced five each, Raikes did seven and Jenkins nine.

[144] Horsfield, p. 50.

[145] Tim Crook, 'International Radio Drama – Social, Economic and Literary Contexts', in *Independent Radio Drama Productions*, <http://www.irdp.co.uk/radiodrama. htm> [accessed 4 January 2021], para. 27.

consultants' which 'marginalised talented and experienced editors and producers'.[146] The autonomy of the past was being severely eroded. In the 1990s, producers would find their work much more restricted, something that was enough to make Tydeman leave the BBC. But before he did, he led the department as another auteur, this time from the cinema, made his contribution to radio Shakespeare: Kenneth Branagh. His productions of *Hamlet* and *Romeo and Juliet* for Radio 3 put Shakespeare back on the front cover of the *Radio Times*, and were followed a few years later by the 'Shakespeare for the Millennium' series on the network, 'a magnificent new project' originally intended to broadcast seventeen of the plays with introductions by Richard Eyre, who had just left the National Theatre.[147] One of the selling points of this series was that it would be available to buy on cassette or compact disc immediately after broadcast. It was the logical progression of a decision taken in 1988 to make Jenkins's *Macbeth* the first Shakespeare play to be released as part of the BBC Radio Collection, and for the first time made BBC productions available to the public to listen to anytime, anywhere.

[146] Crook, 'International Radio Drama', para. 27.
[147] Sue Gaisford, 'Man of the Millennium', *Radio Times*, 9 September 1999, pp. 32–3 (p. 32).

Chapter 4

Man of the Millennium: 1988–2001

By 1988, the BBC had been producing versions of Shakespeare's plays for sixty-five years. Yet in many ways the majority had moved on little from Reith's concept in the 1920s of performances that rely chiefly on 'the conviction of the speakers'.[1] While there was no prescribed house style, basic conventions had been established that might be described as 'traditional' radio Shakespeare production. Only limited changes were made to the text; some cuts and simple additions, such as names, were acceptable, but little else. Sound effects and music were usually kept to a minimum; soundscaping and detailed musical underscoring were rare. Actors usually had RP voices and were frequently recruited from Shakespearean plays in the theatre. While not all producers adhered to this formula, most did, especially during the period between the late 1980s and the turn of the millennium. Despite the innovations of producers like Raikes and Jenkins, techniques at this time almost seem to have gone backwards, with productions more akin in style to those from the 1950s. The idea expounded in 1924 by Cecil Lewis that Shakespeare's 'amazing beauty lies almost entirely in the spoken word as a means of presenting character and situation', without adornment, seems to have typified production at this time.[2] Coinciding with this was a period of change, both inside and outside the BBC, as well as an era which saw the growth of the concept of 'heritage' or 'cultural tourism' relating to Shakespeare, including the opening of Shakespeare's Globe on London's South Bank in 1997. This chapter argues that the majority of the plays produced during this period both fit within what had

[1] Reith, p. 168.
[2] Lewis, *Broadcasting from Within*, pp. 61–2.

been established as 'traditional' BBC radio Shakespeare production and were part of a growing move towards 'manufacturing heritage' in 'cultural institutions'.[3]

As the year 2000 approached, feelings about Shakespeare were mixed. Sue Gaisford reported: 'Some people worry that we are moving too far from the currency of Shakespeare's vocabulary, that soon his work will seem impossibly obscure, too difficult to understand.'[4] However, she disputed this: 'The truth is that Shakespeare has never been so popular. He has been granted the supreme accolade of being voted man of the millennium by listeners to Radio 4's *Today* programme.'[5] It is in this atmosphere of both reverent popularity and the fear of being obscure that the BBC radio drama department had to chart its course. As such it seems to have sought reassurance in past success and attempted to build on both the BBC's and Shakespeare's heritage.

Productions of Shakespeare on BBC radio at this time were described by newspaper reviewers using terms and phrases such as 'straightforward', 'plays it along straight, classical lines', 'springs no surprises' and even 'all too "official" a version' of Shakespeare's text.[6] At least one producer describes their own work from this period as 'traditional'.[7] They were 'clear, straight down-the-line' versions of the plays.[8] Few productions took risks: many seemed to be looking to build on the heritage status both of the BBC and of Shakespeare. Perhaps those most explicitly falling into this category were the three co-directed by and starring Kenneth Branagh: *Hamlet* (1992), *Romeo and Juliet* (1993) and *King Lear* (1994). His film work of this period has subsequently been described as 'heritage Shakespeare' and his radio productions could also be described in this way.[9] In previewing *Romeo and Juliet*, Morley describes Branagh as being

---

[3] Robert Hewison, '*The Heritage Industry: Britain in a Climate of Decline*' [extract], in *Art and its Histories: A Reader*, ed. by Steve Edwards (New Haven and London: Yale University Press, 1999), pp. 319–25 (p. 320).

[4] Gaisford, *Radio Times*, 9 September 1999, p. 32.

[5] Gaisford, *Radio Times*, 9 September 1999, p. 32.

[6] Linda O'Callaghan, 'Sunday Radio – Pick of the Day', *Daily Telegraph*, 16 February 1992, p. xxviii; Sheridan Morley, 'Renaissance Romeo', *Radio Times*, 22 April 1993, p. 29; Val Arnold-Forster, 'Prince Charming', *The Guardian*, 1 May 1992, p. 32; Tom Lubbock, 'Audio Nasty? The Eyes Have It', *The Observer*, 17 April 1994, p. 25.

[7] Mortimer, private Zoom conversation, 23 February 2021.

[8] Charles Spencer, 'A Mind's-Eye Vision of Elsinore', *Daily Telegraph*, 27 April 1992, p. 15.

[9] Pascale Aebischer, *Screening Early Modern Drama: Beyond Shakespeare* (Cambridge: Cambridge University Press, 2013), p. 221.

'in the direct tradition of the Shakespearean romantics'.[10] Morley states that Branagh's full-text productions are 'light on any single thesis about the play' with 'an uncomplicated readiness to celebrate rather than analyse the text'.[11] This is very much in keeping with the post-war period where the poetry was often prioritised above story-telling. Morley's descriptions could also be applied to many other productions from this era.

Academic writing at this time was examining the 'Shakespeare myth' and how it 'functions in contemporary culture as an ideological framework for containing consensus and for sustaining myths of unity, integration and harmony in the cultural superstructures of a divided and fractured society'.[12] In a similar way, the BBC was described as a national institution that 'consistently promotes the illusion of a unified and integrated political region with a system of common values and beliefs. It is [*sic*] very existence perpetuates this myth.'[13] The concept of 'traditional' radio Shakespeare production seems to fit with this conservative view of both Shakespeare and the BBC: these productions do not challenge or upset the perceived way of presenting Shakespeare's plays but conform to established norms.

There was also an eye on preserving the output for the future. In 1959 McWhinnie wrote that radio is 'ephemeral; sound comes out of the air, vanishes; most radio works get no more than two or three broadcasts at most'.[14] But radio Shakespeare was no longer ephemeral. All the BBC's productions were now archived and from 1988 onwards cassettes of some were available for listeners to buy. Producers were no longer making productions that would only be broadcast once or twice; often they were crafting versions that would be listened to over and over again by fans of Shakespeare's plays or those studying them. There were also two attempts to launch something akin to a radio version of the BBC Television Shakespeare, firstly by Kenneth Branagh and then on the run-up to the year 2000. Branagh's ended after just three plays; 'Shakespeare for the Millennium' ended after fifteen. Neither expressly stated that they were attempting the complete works, but both were seen as having

---

[10] Morley, *Radio Times*, 22 April 1993.

[11] Morley, *Radio Times*, 22 April 1993.

[12] Graham Holderness, 'Preface: "All this"', in *The Shakespeare Myth*, ed. by Holderness (Manchester: Manchester University Press, 1988), pp. xi–xvi (p. xiii).

[13] William Maley, 'Centralisation and Censorship', in *The BBC and Public Service Broadcasting*, ed. by Colin MacCabe and Olivia Stewart (Manchester: Manchester University Press, 1986), pp. 32–45 (p. 37).

[14] McWhinnie, p. 99.

the potential to create productions that would do for radio what the BBC Television Shakespeare had done for that visual medium: 'form a permanent, definitive canon'.[15] This sense of reflecting the heritage of Shakespeare on radio and attempting to create a legacy seems to have come at a moment when changes at the BBC were creating uncertainty and Shakespeare provided an anchor for the department.

Peter Lewis states that the period from 'the mid-1980s' onwards was 'characterized by [. . .] a weight of tradition' and that 'these conditions produced much outstanding and much run-of-the-mill work'.[16] This might have contributed to the fact that during this period, more than any other, there was a lack of variety in the choice of plays. Several plays received two productions in little more than a decade; *Julius Caesar* and *Macbeth* were produced three times each between 1990 and 2000. Meanwhile, a dozen plays were not performed at all although, with the exception of *Henry V*, most would be considered Shakespeare's lesser-known texts. This suggests there was a conscious favouring of the more popular plays, possibly in a bid to secure listeners.

The political world outside the BBC was also beginning to encroach on the corporation at this time, perhaps making it a more cautious institution. During the late 1980s, John Birt joined the BBC, going on to become director-general in 1992. Peter Lewis states that 'Birt's mission was to save the BBC from privatization by the Thatcher government'.[17] John Cain notes that 'the years from 1987 to 1992 witnessed the most radical changes ever seen in broadcasting in the United Kingdom'.[18] The BBC 'was seen as wasteful, arrogant and unaccountable'.[19] 'Producer Choice' was introduced in the early 1990s, ostensibly putting the finances in the producers' hands to ensure that departments provided 'the best value for money'.[20] However, there were also budget cuts. During this period it was announced that 'Radio 3's drama output is to be halved'.[21] Tydeman, then head of department, stated: 'We have lost up to 50 slots, opportunities for new plays.'[22] However, Shakespeare was left untouched, with an average output of two or three productions a

---

[15] Terris, 'Shakespeare and British Television Broadcasting 1936–2005', p. 32.

[16] Peter Lewis, 'Opening and Closing Doors: Radio Drama in the BBC', *Radio Journal*, 1.3 (2003), 161–76 (174).

[17] Peter Lewis, p. 164.

[18] John Cain, *The BBC: 70 Years of Broadcasting* (London: BBC, 1992), p. 133.

[19] Peter Lewis, p. 164.

[20] Cain, p. 141.

[21] Russell Twisk, 'Making a Crisis out of Drama', *The Observer*, 19 April 1992, p. 65.

[22] John Tydeman quoted in Twisk, *The Observer*, 19 April 1992.

year every year between 1988 and 2001. This suggests that while 'radio drama is expensive' and 'sucks up resources and employs an army of staff', Shakespeare was among the writers still deemed important enough to be broadcast.[23]

Simultaneously the audiences for radio drama were declining. Nick Higham wrote: 'The controller of Radio 3, John Drummond, is worried that nobody listens to his plays. They cost him a lot of money, they are the product of much dedicated work, and yet the audience is negligible.'[24] Writing about the 1988 *The Taming of the Shrew*, Gillian Reynolds claimed: 'I bet there were fewer than 10,000 people listening.'[25] She went on to complain that 'Radio 4 has long since ceased to be a National Theatre of the Air' and to question whether Radio 3 was the right place for Shakespeare, adding that his works are part of a 'culture, part of a heritage which BBC Radio has, in the past, made available to everyone'.[26] She also felt Radio 3 was facing an 'acute' dilemma about 'who it is serving and at what cost'.[27] Coinciding with this drop in listenership was the demise of the BBC's magazine about radio, *The Listener*, which had frequently championed BBC radio Shakespeare productions. It ceased publication at the end of 1991.

Outside the BBC during the late 1980s and 1990s there was a 'Shakespeare boom'.[28] The marketplace was exploiting Shakespeare's 'star-quality'.[29] Dennis Kennedy describes the 'Bardification of culture' as 'the latest capitulation in cultural affairs to the unstoppable march of a consumerist economy'.[30] At a time when money and audiences were in the spotlight at the BBC, it made good commercial sense to jump on this particular bandwagon, especially when it came to the potentially lucrative audiobook market. The first cassettes of BBC radio Shakespeare were released in 1988. James Green lists them as '*King Lear* with Sir Alec Guinness, *Othello* with Paul Scofield, *Macbeth* with Denis Quilley and Hannah Gordon, and *Hamlet* with Ronald Pickup'.[31] With the exception of *Macbeth*, these were all produced by Tydeman. It seems the initial impetus for

---

[23] Twisk, *The Observer*, 19 April 1992.
[24] Nick Higham, 'Listen Out – Forthcoming Radio', *The Listener*, 19 May 1988, p. 37.
[25] Gillian Reynolds, 'When Drama Is a Duty', *Daily Telegraph*, 24 May 1988, p. 16.
[26] Reynolds, *Daily Telegraph*, 24 May 1988.
[27] Reynolds, *Daily Telegraph*, 24 May 1988.
[28] Dennis Kennedy, 'Shakespeare and Cultural Tourism', *Theatre Journal*, 50.2 (1998), 175–88 (187).
[29] Kennedy, p. 181.
[30] Kennedy, p. 187.
[31] James Green, 'Taping Up Nicely', *The Stage*, 22 September 1988, p. 18.

doing this came from the 'increasing number of people listen[ing] on cassette – not always legally taped, no doubt'.[32] David Hatch, the then managing director of BBC Network Radio and vice-chairman of BBC Enterprises, stated at the launch of the BBC Radio Collection: 'We are going into the market place aggressively. We know there has been lots of illegal taping but now we can provide listeners with good quality tapes.'[33] Nigel Andrew describes it as 'the big event of recent months in the world of spoken-word tapes'.[34] Green states that the BBC expected to 'gross £2 million during the coming year' not only from the sale of Shakespeare plays but also from comedy and other archive recordings released on double cassettes.[35] A year later, Cheryl Markosky stated the BBC 'will be declaring profits exceeding £10 million'.[36] This gave BBC Enterprises, and later its successor, BBC Worldwide, considerable power, including over the radio output. This was not good news for producers like Jeremy Mortimer: 'They kept on reissuing those cassettes or CDs and it was so irritating, because just when you thought someone might have forgotten them, they got reissued and then it was: "Oh, you can't do another one because they're still selling these ones."'[37] Even when new productions were made they got little attention, as the previously issued versions on cassette and CD continued to sell. Mortimer says: 'It was quite difficult. You felt you were in competition with BBC Worldwide sometimes.'[38] With such a successful money-spinner, it is perhaps not surprising there was a conservatism in production, and a desire to cash-in on the BBC's heritage.

The BBC Radio Collection released archive recordings, but at two points during this period there was an attempt to create a series of productions specifically aimed at being broadcast and then immediately available for purchase. The first came from Branagh and producer Glyn Dearman. Both Russell Twisk and Anne Karpf reported that the pair had 'plans to do Shakespeare's complete works'.[39] However, the BBC, perhaps because of the Radio Collection, did

---

[32] Val Arnold-Forster, 'Bloody Sundays', *The Guardian*, 3 September 1988, p. 17.
[33] David Hatch quoted in Green, *The Stage*, 22 September 1988.
[34] Nigel Andrew, 'A Good Listen', *The Listener*, 20 October 1988, p. 36.
[35] Green, *The Stage*, 22 September 1988.
[36] Cheryl Markosky, 'Aunty Joins the High-Tech Age', *Daily Telegraph*, 28 June 1989, p. 26.
[37] Mortimer, private Zoom conversation, 7 April 2021.
[38] Mortimer, private Zoom conversation, 7 April 2021.
[39] Russell Twisk, 'A Renaissance for Shakespeare', *The Observer*, 25 April 1993, p. 69. See also Anne Karpf, 'Radio: New Voice for an Old Love', *The Guardian*, 1 May 1993, p. 30.

not support the idea. Karpf reported that 'BBC Enterprises turned down *Hamlet*', their first collaboration, adding that instead Branagh and Dearman would 'do the entire Shakespeare canon for Random House'.[40] However, the project ended after the third production, *King Lear* (1994). Five years later, the idea of a co-ordinated Shakespeare project appeared again, this time from within the BBC. 'Shakespeare for the Millennium' was described by the controller of Radio 3, Roger Wright, as 'a shining example of the kind of editorially distinctive, collaborative project that only the BBC could mount. It gives Radio 3 listeners the chance to hear fresh and contemporary, yet authoritative performances of these great plays.'[41] Head of drama Kate Rowland hoped the series would 'burst through the schedule'.[42] It was initially intended to include 'new radio productions of 17 Shakespeare plays over four years'.[43] It eventually only ran for three years, with two fewer plays. All were preceded by introductions from Sir Richard Eyre, who had recently stepped down from running the National Theatre. They were also all released for listeners to buy 'on CD and cassette, with helpful notes and introductions, from the BBC Radio Collection'.[44] These notes included an introduction from Eyre and a synopsis of the play. However, the series quickly suffered a similar fate to the BBC Television Shakespeare series. Ian Johns wrote: 'Radio 3 and the BBC Collection's on-going attempts to avoid the usual doublet-and-hose approach (ie radio ham) to the Bard have produced some mixed results so far.'[45] He singled out a 'tricksy and confusing' *Romeo and Juliet* (1999) for particular criticism, although he felt the 'all-Scots *Macbeth*' (2000) was one of the best. This was the first time a Scottish Macbeth had been heard on BBC radio, other than perhaps on the Scottish regional stations in the 1920s.[46]

Rowland said that her producers were 'given a relatively free hand' and that it was not a 'BBC approach' but 'something more daring'.[47] The productions were supposedly given 'a comparatively

[40] Karpf, *The Guardian*, 1 May 1993.
[41] Dalya Alberge, 'Radio 3 Plans Four Years of Shakespeare', *The Times*, 16 July 1999, p. 8.
[42] Kate Rowland, private Zoom conversation, 12 April 2021.
[43] Alberge, *The Times*, 16 July 1999.
[44] Gaisford, *Radio Times*, 9 September 1999, p. 32.
[45] Ian Johns, 'Bend your Ear', *The Times*, 13 December 2000, p. 22.
[46] *Macbeth* was produced in Aberdeen (1924) and Glasgow (1927 and 1928) but it is unclear whether Scottish accents were used. The 1928 production starred Robert Donat.
[47] Kate Rowland quoted in Gaisford, *Radio Times*, 9 September 1999, p. 32.

modern setting'.[48] However, in many cases it is difficult to tell. For example, an announcement at the start of *Julius Caesar* (1999) establishes the setting as being Mussolini's Rome, but after the initial sound effects there is very little to indicate this.[49] *Hamlet* (1999) was set in the 'early years of the century' but only 'sharp-eared listeners' would hear 'Polonius dictating to a typist, Laertes departing from a naval dockyard, Fortinbras arriving with tanks'.[50] In fact, the dock-yard sounds quite sixteenth century, with what appears to be the sound effect of a horse and wooden cart passing through (0:29:55).[51] The plays' introductions from Eyre may have increased the sense of heritage around them, but there is no indication that he had heard the productions and his short talks do little to encourage listeners. As Mortimer, who directed three of the plays for the series, says, Eyre sounds 'so depressed. He just sounds miserable. I think it's very off-putting. He's quite eloquent, but that's not really the point, is it?'[52] At least one listener described themselves as 'satisfied' although, writing to the *Radio Times*, Alison Hull was disappointed that only seventeen of Shakespeare's plays were due to be produced, and felt it would have been better if they had been made for television, as 'if you don't know a text well, following it on radio is tricky'.[53]

The casting of many of the plays of this period often seems to hark back to an earlier era, with actors returning who had had a long or distant association with BBC radio Shakespeare. Laurence Payne, who had appeared as Laertes in the corporation's 1946 production of *Hamlet* as well as several other plays in the 1940s and 1950s, features as Baptista in *The Taming of the Shrew* (1988). He had also 'been with Gielgud at Stratford in the 50s' and Mortimer states 'there was a wonderful tradition' in having him as part of the cast.[54] Other actors also returned. Maurice Denham, who had appeared in Shakespeare plays on radio as far back as 1959, returned for the first time in twenty years for *Macbeth* (1992), *Romeo and Juliet* (1993) and *King Lear* (1994). Robert Hardy, who had played Prince Hal in the 1964 *Henry IV* plays, returned in 1995 to play Falstaff in new productions of them. Judi Dench, Juliet in a schools' production

[48] Gaisford, *Radio Times*, 9 September 1999, p. 32.
[49] *Julius Caesar*, BBC Radio 3, 26 September 1999, <https://learningonscreen.ac.uk/on demand/index.php/prog/RT4819FB?bcast=120454060> [accessed 29 April 2021].
[50] Gaisford, *Radio Times*, 9 September 1999, p. 33.
[51] *Hamlet*, BBC Radio 3, 12 September 1999, <https://learningonscreen.ac.uk/ondema nd/index.php/prog/RT48135F?bcast=120452036> [accessed 29 April 2021].
[52] Mortimer, private Zoom conversation, 7 April 2021.
[53] Alison Hull, 'Letters – The Play's the Thing', *Radio Times*, 30 September 1999, p. 5.
[54] Mortimer, private Zoom conversation, 7 April 2021.

of *Romeo and Juliet* in 1962, played the Nurse in the 1993 version. While John Gielgud was never far away from BBC radio Shakespeare, he had not appeared for ten years when he returned to play the Ghost to Branagh's Hamlet in 1992, more than four decades after he last played the lead for the BBC in his celebrated 1948 performance. The *Radio Times* not only gave over its front cover to a picture of Gielgud and Branagh, there was also a three-page article inside: something unheard of for radio drama at this time. Gielgud also played Lear on radio for his fourth and final time in 1994, at the age of ninety. In addition, this period saw the sons of actors who had appeared in Shakespeare plays on radio coming to prominence. Toby Stephens played Orlando in *As You Like It* (1997), twenty years after his father, Robert, starred in *Antony and Cleopatra* (1977). Michael Redgrave's son, Corin, played Lear in 2001, almost half a century after his father had played the part. In the same production, David Troughton appeared as Kent; his father, Patrick, had played Edmund to Gielgud's Lear in 1951, as well as half a dozen other roles from the 1950s to the 1980s.

This harking back to actors from previous generations, as well as the sons of actors from the past, contributed to the very RP sound of many of those appearing in plays of this period. Much as in previous eras, it is sometimes difficult to tell characters apart. This can also be the case with productions which on the face of it are expanding their casting choices. The 1995 *Richard III* was a co-production with the Northern Broadsides theatre company, which is known for using actors with northern accents. However, this production suffers from the same problems that RP productions do: the voices are very similar, making it difficult to tell characters apart.[55] As such, it seems to follow the tradition of BBC radio Shakespeare, requiring the audience to have prior knowledge of the play.

Casting also started to include non-white actors more frequently. As late as 1988, BBC Radio 3 was still repeating the 1972 production of *Othello* with Paul Scofield in the title role. Radio finally heard its first black Othello in 2001.[56] Other black actors were also being cast, including Sophie Okonedo in *Richard II* (2000) and Chiwetel Ejiofor in *Much Ado About Nothing* (2001). Both are British born and their characters' ethnicity is never explicit. However, some actors were asked to provide more stereotypical

[55] *Richard III*, BBC Radio 3, 24 September 1995, <https://learningonscreen.ac.uk/ondemand/index.php/prog/RT4581F4?bcast=120246226> [accessed 29 April 2021].
[56] See Chapter 5.

performances. In Nigel Bryant's 1993 *Twelfth Night*, Adjoa Andoh as Maria and Jason Yates as the Sea Captain, also both British born, adopt Caribbean voices. Alongside Rudolph Walker as Feste, who is from Trinidad and Tobago, this gives the production a colonial feel, although there is nothing else in it to suggest this was the intention of the producer.[57]

There was also change on the technical side. Quarter-inch tape began to be phased out and digital recording came in, making it much easier and more cost effective to record multiple takes. Similarly, the first digital editing systems were available, enabling producers to create more complex sound mixes. While the majority of productions in this period seem to have taken little advantage of this and fit comfortably within the label of 'heritage' or 'traditional', Clive Brill's do not. He produced just two Shakespeare plays for the department at this time, but both are unlike those of any of his contemporaries. He described his *King John* (1990) as 'the first modern dress Shakespeare on radio. I got this idea in my head that the Bastard would arrive on a Harley Davidson and once I'd got that in my head, everything else followed.'[58] Brill uses an intercom and telephone in the opening scene (0:02:42).[59] In the middle of act two, scene one, there is the sound effect of a siren (0:26:21). There are also effects of a megaphone, rockets being set off and a radio being tuned in (0:27:44). The music is by Einstürzende Neubauten, who Brill describes as a 'mad German band. All their albums were simply industrial equipment – it's crazy stuff. I was definitely trying to push the boundaries.'[60] The production uses regional accents but not specifically to denote class. For example, both the Dauphin (Scott Cherry) and Hubert (Brian Glover) have regional accents. Brill says: 'I just knew that I wanted to introduce other voices but I was also experimenting with the idea of class.'[61] Brill's production clearly sets the play in the twentieth century in a way that the later 'Shakespeare for the Millennium' productions attempt with less success.

Brill's second production a year later, *A Midsummer Night's Dream*, combines his skilled use of sound effects with a multi-racial

---

[57] *Twelfth Night*, BBC Radio 3, 3 January 1993, <https://learningonscreen.ac.uk/ondemand/index.php/prog/RT43DDDB?bcast=120101172> [accessed 29 April 2021].

[58] Clive Brill, private Zoom conversation, 2 March 2021.

[59] *King John*, BBC Radio 3, 22 June 1990, <https://learningonscreen.ac.uk/ondemand/index.php/prog/RT427CED?bcast=119975915> [accessed 29 April 2021].

[60] Brill, private Zoom conversation, 2 March 2021.

[61] Brill, private Zoom conversation, 2 March 2021.

cast.[62] This production could be described as the first truly modern production of a Shakespeare play on radio, having much more in common with plays produced in the second decade of the twenty-first century than anything aired during the twentieth. Brill himself says: 'I knew I wanted a big musical content. [. . .] And then I had this idea of musical mechanicals. [. . .] I knew it was Tony Armatrading playing Bottom. I knew I wanted him to be basically Louis Armstrong. So that was amazing.'[63] In addition, Brill now had access to twenty-four-track digital editing: 'We recorded it conventionally but we edited it unconventionally. I remember doing two or three all-nighters because we couldn't edit it the way we wanted it on normal tape. So that again felt very exciting to me.'[64] Brill did not record any further Shakespeare productions for the BBC for thirty years, but did go on to create the Arkangel Shakespeare: thirty-eight plays (*Pericles* and *The Two Noble Kinsmen* as well as the thirty-six in the *First Folio*) recorded as a single audio collection for the educational market.

This was an era in which the BBC in general, and radio drama in particular, faced much change: it was no longer the 'fiefdom' of previous years.[65] There is no evidence of a deliberate decision to create 'traditional' or 'heritage' plays that would satisfy the BBC's more conservative critics, but Shakespeare does seem to have been prioritised over new plays. Unlike the 1960s, when playwrights like Joe Orton, Harold Pinter and Tom Stoppard were making their debuts on radio, no comparable writer was 'discovered' by producers at the end of the twentieth century. It was also a time of considerable change in management. Peter Lewis states that 'in the mid-1980s only four people had held the post of Head of Radio Drama since broadcasting began'.[66] But there were another four during the era covered by this chapter: Tydeman, Caroline Raphael, Rowland and finally Gordon House in 2001. It appears 'traditional' Shakespeare may have been a reaction to change and a way of creating stability in an organisation and a department where there was much uncertainty.

The following case studies all fit the idea of 'traditional' BBC radio Shakespeare outlined above. In each case the plays make

---

[62] *A Midsummer Night's Dream*, BBC Radio 3, 23 June 1991, <https://learningonscreen. ac.uk/ondemand/index.php/prog/RT430950?bcast=120031234> [accessed 29 April 2021].

[63] Brill, private Zoom conversation, 2 March 2021.

[64] Brill, private Zoom conversation, 2 March 2021.

[65] Mortimer, private Zoom conversation, 23 February 2021.

[66] Peter Lewis, p. 174.

limited changes to the text, use unsophisticated sound effects and music, the majority of the actors use RP voices, and many had already established themselves as theatrical Shakespeareans; in some cases they were appearing in Shakespeare plays on stage concurrently with the broadcasts. Jeremy Mortimer's 1988 *The Taming of the Shrew* does make some changes to the text, but mainly to accommodate material from another early modern version of the play, thereby accentuating the 'heritage' nature of the production. In 1992 Nigel Bryant produced *Macbeth*, attempting to add period authenticity by bringing battle re-enactors into the studio alongside the cast. The following year, Kenneth Branagh appeared as Romeo opposite his stage Juliet with a cast of some of the most famous names in theatrical Shakespeare. Mortimer's 2000 *Richard II* was part of 'Shakespeare for the Millennium' as well as being created for academic use, indicating it was intended as a production with a long afterlife. Finally, Sally Avens's *Much Ado About Nothing* (2001) reflects contemporary literary criticism in its portrayal of the play's four lovers. However, her use of sound is more sophisticated than many of her predecessors and her involvement in Shakespeare production bridges the gap between the 'traditional' and more innovative twenty-first-century work, including a far greater presence of female producers.

The Taming of the Shrew (1988)[67]

Although Mortimer had joined the BBC radio drama department several years earlier, *The Taming of the Shrew* was his first Shakespeare play. He says: 'I definitely felt I was on probation doing that.'[68] However, within the corporation it was received well: 'the then Director-General came up and said: "yes, I heard your *Taming of the Shrew*, very good, very good."'[69] Radio critics were generally pleased: Reynolds also used the words 'very good' to describe it, adding it was 'thoughtful and animated', while David Gillard told his readers: 'You may expect the sparks to fly – even on radio.'[70]

---

[67] *The Taming of the Shrew*, BBC Radio 3, 20 May 1988, <https://learningonscreen.ac.uk/ondemand/index.php/prog/RT416E2D?bcast=119882285> [accessed 5 April 2021].

[68] Mortimer, private Zoom conversation, 23 February 2021.

[69] Mortimer, private Zoom conversation, 23 February 2021.

[70] Reynolds, *Daily Telegraph*, 24 May 1988; David Gillard, 'Hear This! – Shrew Story', *Radio Times*, 12 May 1988, p. 24.

Reviews, like much contemporary literary criticism, focused on the relationship between Petruchio and Katherina. Publicity material also concentrated on this. A photograph in the *Radio Times* shows the lead actors, Bob Peck and Cheryl Campbell, dressed in their normal clothes with Peck standing behind Campbell, holding her wrists as she claws towards the camera.[71] The accompanying copy states that Peck has been 'grappling' with 'Miss Campbell's talents'.[72] This suggests a lack of subtlety, but both actors spoke about the thought that went into the production. Peck told the magazine that 'we came to the conclusion that Shakespeare had not intended it as an anti-feminine play. It's about the recognition of wills after a lot of testing.'[73] Campbell added: 'It's an old fashioned play but I don't believe it's about the subjugation of women.'[74] Mortimer himself says that he 'definitely wanted [his] Katherina to be feisty and spirited and not entirely broken by the events of the play', adding that by the end of her final speech 'she is now in charge'.[75] Andrew stated that Campbell's delivery of the speech was 'detached, weary and, one could almost believe, undefeated. Almost.'[76] Davalle described Campbell as 'the quintessential Katharina [sic]'.[77] The concept that there could be such a thing, and that the BBC had found it, identifies the production as one in keeping with Shakespearean heritage.

However, among contemporary literary critics there was no consensus as to what the 'quintessential Katharina' might be. John C. Bean suggests there were 'two camps, the revisionists and the anti-revisionists'.[78] The revisionists, he claims, 'have argued that Kate's notorious last speech is delivered ironically' while the anti-revisionists insist 'on historical accuracy' and have argued that Katherina's taming is through 'old-fashioned farce'.[79] Bean himself rejects both, suggesting instead 'that Kate is tamed not in the automatic manner of behavioral psychology but in the spontaneous manner of the later romantic comedies where characters lose themselves in chaos and

[71] Gillard, *Radio Times*, 12 May 1988.
[72] Gillard, *Radio Times*, 12 May 1988.
[73] Bob Peck quoted in Gillard, *Radio Times*, 12 May 1988.
[74] Cheryl Campbell quoted in Gillard, *Radio Times*, 12 May 1988.
[75] Mortimer, private Zoom conversation, 7 April 2021.
[76] Nigel Andrew, 'Nasty, Brutish, and Not Very Long', *The Listener*, 26 May 1988, p. 47.
[77] Peter Davalle, 'Radio Choice', *The Times*, 20 May 1988, p. 23.
[78] John C. Bean, 'Comic Structure and the Humanizing of Kate in *The Taming of the Shrew*', in *The Woman's Part*, ed. by Carolyn Ruth Swift Lenz, Gayle Greene and Carol Thomas Neely (London: University of Illinois Press, 1980), pp. 65–78 (p. 65).
[79] Bean, p. 65.

emerge, as if from a dream, liberated into the bonds of love'.[80] This is closest to Mortimer's take on the play. He wanted to make it 'more of a fable' and felt that by keeping the Induction, 'the contextualisation of the Christopher Sly story' helped to do that.[81] Again, by retaining the Induction, an element often cut on stage and radio, Mortimer was creating a production that reflected the whole play, and its heritage, rather than a simplified edit for modern audiences.

Literary critics also felt Sly was a key element to 'frame and fictionalise the story' and 'create some detachment', thereby mitigating Petruchio's behaviour.[82] In Shakespeare's text, Sly only appears in the Induction and at the end of act one, scene one. However, Mortimer brings the character back throughout the play. In some cases, this is to help convey visual episodes, such as 'Lucentio in disguise' (0:27:20) and 'Say where he has the lute about his ears' (0:40:27). However, elsewhere the insertions are close to those in the earlier, anonymous play *The Taming of a Shrew*; Mortimer says he was probably aware of it from his university days.[83] This section, added by Mortimer to act three of Shakespeare's play, bears a strong resemblance to a section in act one, scene one of *A Shrew*:

SLY   Oh, madam. When will the fool Petruchio come again?
PAGE   He'll come again, my lord, anon.
SLY   Not if he's gone to church with a shrew. That'll keep his coming more. Give us some more drink here! Oh, zounds, where's the tapster? Here, madam. I drink to thee.
PAGE   My lord. Here come the players again. Tranio and Lucentio.
SLY   Oh, brave. Here's two fine gentlemen who've kept out of church.

1:04:50

The comparable section in *A Shrew* is:

SLY   Sim, when will the fool come again?
LORD   He'll come again, my Lord, anon.
SLY   Gi's some more drink here; souns, where's the Tapster? [. . .] Here, Sim, I drink to thee.
LORD   My lord, here comes the players again.
SLY   O brave, here's two fine gentlemen.[84]

---

[80] Bean, p. 66.
[81] Mortimer, private Zoom conversation, 7 April 2021.
[82] Carol Rutter, *Clamorous Voices: Shakespeare's Women Today* (London: Women's Press, 1988), p. 2; Leggatt, p. 56.
[83] Mortimer, private Zoom conversation, 7 April 2021.
[84] Anon., *The Taming of a Shrew*, ed. by F. S. Boas (London: Chatto and Windus, 1908), 1.1.324–331.

Similarly, at the end of Shakespeare's text, Mortimer adds the final Sly episode from *A Shrew* with a few minor changes.[85] By including excerpts from another early modern play, Mortimer is accentuating the canonicity of the text and its historical status.

Radio critics approved of Mortimer's choice, with Andrew suggesting that it 'kept the ugly core of the play at a distance by emphasising the tranced artificiality of the play-within-a-play'.[86] The decision to repeatedly return to Sly also echoed modern theatrical productions, where 'it is usual for Sly to remain on stage, constantly reminding us that the Shrew play is a theatrical illusion and keeping us at some distance from it'.[87] The idea of adding Sly's final scene from *The Taming of a Shrew* to the end of Shakespeare's play had also been done before, both at the RSC and in Stratford, Ontario.[88] However, the use of the Induction was relatively unusual on radio. It was cut from both the 1973 and 2000 productions, although it was included in 1954.

While the majority of the cast speak in RP or close to it, the actors playing Lucentio and Tranio, Stephen Tompkinson and Robert Glenister respectively, use northern English accents, differentiating them from the rest and indicating they are from elsewhere. In addition, when Glenister as Tranio is pretending to be Lucentio, he drops the northern accent and assumes an RP voice. He uses this to particular effect in Tranio's asides, delivering them in a northern accent and switching back to RP when talking to other characters (e.g. 2.1.361; 0:50:48 and 4.4.67–8; 1:37:02). Mortimer also makes changes to the text to assist the listening audience, moving chunks of it around. In act one, he delays the entrance of Lucentio and Tranio, who enter first in Shakespeare's play and observe the commotion between Baptista, his daughters and Bianca's suitors. Instead, they appear part-way through the scene (1.1.1–47 to after 1.1.67; 0:12:02). This enables the audience to establish the main action and characters first, before being introduced to the new arrivals. Mortimer does this again shortly afterwards (1.1.68–73 to after 1.1.79; 0:13:36). In this case it serves to remind listeners that Lucentio and Tranio are still watching. In both cases the interjections from Lucentio and Tranio play out over a hubbub of people, suggesting that the action is continuing. Similarly, Mortimer moves two lines near the beginning of act three, scene two (3.2.12–13 to after 3.1.20; 1:00:22). This creates

---

[85] For a comparison, see 2:01:18 of this production and 4.2.45–53 of *The Taming of a Shrew*.
[86] Andrew, *The Listener*, 26 May 1988.
[87] Leggatt, p. 44.
[88] Leggatt, p. 44n.

the illusion that Katherina is talking to herself, or the radio audience, rather than the many people listed in the stage directions for this scene. By moving 'I told you, I, he was a frantic fool, / Hiding his bitter jests in blunt behavior', Katherina only addresses the rest of the gathering at the end of the speech, drawing them in for what follows.

While Mortimer does make subtle textual changes to *The Taming of the Shrew*, his only major change is the addition of Sly throughout. In this way, he situates the play as a fable, diminishing the sting of the treatment of Katherina at a time when criticism, both literary and theatrical, was starting to question this. The additions from *A Shrew* can be seen as both a heritage addition and an echo of previous stage performances. This sense of heritage is conjured up in a different way by Bryant with his production of *Macbeth*: instead of seeking early modern textual additions, Bryant increases his heritage content through the use of historical enthusiasts.

Macbeth (1992)[89]

The preview for this production in the *Radio Times* noted that it 'sets the play firmly in its period – a time when witchcraft was taken very seriously, not least by King James himself'.[90] Meanwhile the *Daily Mail* reported that the production would include 'military hardware supplied by the Sealed Knot'.[91] Both these statements suggest a desire for the play to be presented in a 'traditional' fashion, but they also highlight the problem of trying to set it in the 'correct' period. The real Macbeth lived in the eleventh century, but Shakespeare was writing in the early seventeenth century, when James VI of Scotland became king of England. The Sealed Knot re-enact the mid-seventeenth-century English Civil War, which took place long after Shakespeare and King James had died. Both the *Radio Times* previewer and Geoffrey Hobbs in the *Daily Mail* seem to conflate all three. In fact, Bryant consciously set the play during the Civil War with 'witch-hunts and witch-hangings, and armies singing psalms to psych themselves up for battle'.[92] However, like most other radio

---

[89] *Macbeth*, BBC Radio 3, 16 February 1992, <https://learningonscreen.ac.uk/onde mand/index.php/prog/RT436257?bcast=120062080> [accessed 16 February 2021].

[90] 'R3', *Radio Times*, 13 February 1992, p. 83.

[91] Geoffrey Hobbs, 'Pick of the Radio Week – Wild Piper Recalls his Tunes', *Daily Mail*, 15 February 1992, p. 35.

[92] Nigel Bryant, private email correspondence, 25 February 2021.

productions made at the end of the twentieth century, while the sound of this production is atmospheric, it would be difficult for the average listener to pinpoint its exact setting, although it does create a general sense of the distant past.

Bryant went to considerable trouble to create the sound and atmosphere he wanted. His use of the Sealed Knot went far beyond what the preview implied. Members of the group came into the studio 'to be in the background with their noisy period gear, and so that the actors could borrow some of their armour'.[93] This was not just to provide a general clanking sound, but to enhance the actors' performances: 'Wearing appropriate costume and equipment in radio drama can sometimes be surprisingly important, not only because (especially in the case of armour) you can hear it, and not only because it helps actors get into the mood of a period, but because it affects movement, which is subtly relayed in the voice.'[94] In addition the Sealed Knot also brought period military drums and taught the cast authentic period battle cries. Bryant used unaccompanied singing by the soldiers to add to this, although reviewer David Sexton was unimpressed with what he heard, complaining that the play 'opened with several minutes of a football crowd — or so it sounded: shouts of "Move it!", thuds, grunts, screams, distant explosions and tuneless team chants'.[95] In fact the men are singing Psalm 68:

> Let God arise, and then his foes
> Will turn themselves to flight,
> His enemies for fear shall run,
> And scatter out of sight.

The choice was not made by Bryant but by the play's composer, Vic Gammon, who has a background researching popular religious music. Gammon says that Bryant 'wanted something martial that he could use in the battle scenes' and Gammon suggested Psalm 68 because there is 'a whole mythology' which suggests that 'Cromwell's troops went into battle singing that'.[96] He admits 'it's totally wrong for the period' but says 'it's music for effect; in no way is it attempting any historical accuracy'.[97]

The use of the psalm is much more than a 'team chant', as it is setting up the conflict between good and evil associated with the play.

[93] Bryant, private email, 25 February 2021.
[94] Bryant, private email, 25 February 2021.
[95] David Sexton, 'Sound Effects and Fury', *Sunday Telegraph*, 23 February 1992, p. xvi.
[96] Vic Gammon, private Zoom conversation, 23 February 2021.
[97] Gammon, private Zoom conversation, 23 February 2021.

Bryant returns to this motif several times: just before Macbeth meets the witches for the first time (unidentifiable song heard very quietly underneath 1.3.30 onwards; 0:08:18), and again later, towards the end of the play, when the two sides are preparing for battle ('The Almost Christian' sung at the start of 5.2; 1:49:03). Bryant finally returns to Psalm 68 at the very end of the play, finishing with the men singing the second verse:

And as wax melts before the fire,
And wind blows smoke away,
So in the presence of the Lord
The wicked shall decay.

These are not the only uses of religious texts in the play, which Bryant describes as one where 'religion hangs heavy'.[98] At the start of act one, scene two, he inserts a priest reciting part of the Eucharistic Prayer I in Latin (0:02:47), apparently blessing Duncan and Malcolm. Like the use of song, this has the effect of signalling the good and the bad characters within the play along religious lines, something that could be seen as conservative if not strictly traditional.

Bryant also increases the use of the witches and Hecate, extending the supernatural overtones present in the text to scenes where there would not normally be any. The messenger who visits Lady Macduff, advising her to 'be not found here' (4.2.65; 1:30:30), sounds very like the voice used for Hecate three scenes earlier (3.5.2; 1:14:42). Both are gruff and distorted, suggesting a supernatural presence. The witches also make additional appearances, including after Macbeth's final speech while he is fighting Macduff, repeating lines from earlier in the play:

FIRST WITCH   Macbeth, Macbeth, Macbeth. Beware Macduff.
                Beware the Thane of Fife.
SECOND WITCH   None of woman born shall harm Macbeth.

Macbeth cries out tormentedly, continues under.

ALL WITCHES   All hail Macbeth . . .
THIRD WITCH   . . . that shalt be king hereafter.
ALL WITCHES   Hail! Hail! Hail! Hail! Hail! (*continues and fades*)
MACBETH   (*long cry*)
    FX – *violent stabbing sound. Silence.*

                                            2:05:39

[98] Bryant, private email, 25 February 2021.

These lines originate in 4.1.70–2, 4.1.79–80 and 1.3.51. Using them here ties in with comments made by literary critic Alan Sinfield, who suggests 'the fall of Macbeth seems to result more from (super) natural than human agency'.[99]

At the very end of the play, after Malcolm's final speech, Macduff shouts 'God save the King', with the rest of the men repeating this. As singing resumes, the witches reappear, speaking the opening lines in unison: 'When shall we three meet again / In thunder, lightning, or in rain?' (1.1.1–2; 2:09:08). The psalm is then faded up and ends. As well as exaggerating the supernatural presence already within the play, this also suggests that the cycle of violence might begin again. This is in keeping with Sinfield's opinion that 'Macduff at the end stands in the same relation to Malcolm as Macbeth did to Duncan in the beginning. He is now the kingmaker on whom the legitimate monarch depends.'[100] Sinfield also suggests that 'the recurrence of the whole sequence may be anticipated (in production this might be suggested by a final meeting of Macduff and the Witches)'.[101] Whether Bryant was directly influenced by Sinfield or not, it is an ending that reflects modern literary critical thought in a production that handles the play overall in a more traditional manner.

Unlike previous productions, where the witches sound very similar, or the 1995 radio production *Berkoff's Macbeth*, where Cleo Laine plays all three, the actors in this production (Mary Wimbush, Tamsin Greig and Steven Granville) sound distinctly different from each other. Marilyn French states that 'the Witches themselves incarnate ambiguity of gender'.[102] Bryant's casting enables this, but also makes clear that they are a trio, rather than a single entity. He makes particular use of their different voices in act four, scene one, when the witches are chanting their incantation. Instead of each witch having their own verse, Bryant divides up the lines, alternating just a few words at a time (1:19:34). The three distinct vocal tones create a sense of movement in a scene that might otherwise seem static on radio.

In addition to enlarging the role of the witches, Bryant makes several subtle textual changes. However, Sexton was unhappy about

[99] Alan Sinfield, 'Macbeth: History, Ideology and Intellectuals', *Critical Quarterly*, 28.1–2 (1986), 63–77 (67).

[100] Sinfield, p. 70.

[101] Sinfield, p. 70.

[102] Marilyn French, *Shakespeare's Division of Experience* (New York: Summit Books, 1981), p. 242.

this: '"They were suborned" became the rather flat job description, "they were hired". When Macbeth did the deed, his miserable comment, "This is a sorry sight. (*Looking on his hands*)" was converted into "Look at these hands, they're a sorry sight".'[103] Bryant makes many substitutions in Shakespeare's text including: 'kerns and gallowglasses' (1.2.13), which becomes 'mercenary kerns'; 'as a promise' is substituted for 'for an earnest' (1.3.105); 'suspicions' for 'jealousies' (4.3.29). Also in act four, scene three, the following is changed: 'Scotland hath foisons to fill up your will. / Of your mere own: all these are portable' (4.3.88–9) becomes 'Scotland hath *treasures* to fill up your will. / Of your mere own: all *this is bearable*' (added emphasis). All these changes turn words and phrases that might be unfamiliar or even incomprehensible to a modern ear into something more immediately understandable. While this is a departure from more traditional ways of presenting Shakespeare's texts on radio, and Sexton was clearly unconvinced by them, Reynolds does not mention them at all, suggesting that even if she had noticed them, they did not offend her, thereby retaining the production's status as one that does not largely diverge from the expected.

Bryant's leading actors were Tim McInnerny, at the time 'the RSC's current Mercutio and Sir Andrew Aguecheek', and Harriet Walter, who had been appearing in leading roles for the RSC since 1981.[104] But while McInnerny and Walter were established and respected in their field, Kenneth Branagh sought much more famous actors for his productions. His first, *Hamlet*, was in the same year as *Macbeth*. The following year he returned with another major tragedy: *Romeo and Juliet*.

Romeo and Juliet (1993)[105]

Branagh worked with Dearman on all three of the Shakespeare plays he appeared in for the BBC in the 1990s. Branagh's reputation for Shakespearean stage and film work was already well established, including a production of *Romeo and Juliet* seven years earlier at the Lyric Studio, Hammersmith. His Juliet then was Samantha Bond and she reprised her role for this radio production. The rest of the

[103] Sexton, *Sunday Telegraph*, 23 February 1992.
[104] Gillian Reynolds, 'Macbeth Shrink-Wrapped', *Daily Telegraph*, 18 February 1992, p. 14.
[105] *Romeo and Juliet*, BBC Radio 3, 25 April 1993, <https://learningonscreen.ac.uk/ondemand/index.php/prog/RT44104D?bcast=120118097> [accessed 18 March 2021].

cast was described as one 'the RSC and National would die for' and included Judi Dench, John Gielgud, Derek Jacobi and Simon Callow.[106] In her review for *The Guardian*, Karpf observed: 'There are those who believe that if William Shakespeare made contact with earth today, he would do it through the medium of Radio 3.'[107] And she felt the production reflected many preoccupations about both Shakespeare and the BBC: 'These people regard Radio 3 as a gloriously uncorroded conduit for the words of the Bard, one which gives us the *echt* Shakespeare, free of directorial whim. And the BBC, which sees itself as a purveyor of cultural continuity, has done little to discourage it.'[108] In particular she noted that '[t]heir press release points out that Sir John Gielgud was a radio Romeo in March 1925 and now returns to star as Friar Laurence — as if there were an unbroken line from Shakespeare via Gielgud to Kenneth Branagh'.[109] As well as highlighting the cultural heritage of the BBC and of Shakespeare, the production was also a distinctly conservative take on the play. Morley praised it for not being 'vulnerable to fashionable or directorial whims of taste'.[110] Twisk described it as 'a straight, carefully crafted version'.[111] Both the publicity around the production and its critical reception suggest Karpf was correct in pointing to a conscious link between two cultural institutions.

That publicity led to an unusually high number of reviews for radio Shakespeare at this time. However, despite the starry cast and cultural cachet of the play, reviewers were not impressed. Twisk writes that 'each actor milks lines for all they're worth; a little directional discipline might have helped'.[112] Reynolds describes Callow's Benvolio and Jacobi's Mercutio as 'waving so much from their speeches it was quite easy to feel the scenes drowning'.[113] Karpf adds: 'As for Gielgud, to my mind the fabled sonority of his verse-speaking here often obscures rather than enhances its actual meaning.'[114] Morley, however, disagrees, stating that Gielgud gives

---

[106] Karpf, *The Guardian*, 1 May 1993.
[107] Karpf, *The Guardian*, 1 May 1993.
[108] Karpf, *The Guardian*, 1 May 1993.
[109] Karpf, *The Guardian*, 1 May 1993. Gielgud's early appearance as a radio Romeo was not in a full production, but as part of 'Popular Excerpts from Shakespeare', *Radio Times*, 27 February 1925, p. 441.
[110] Morley, *Radio Times*, 22 April 1993.
[111] Twisk, *The Observer*, 25 April 1993.
[112] Twisk, *The Observer*, 25 April 1993.
[113] Gillian Reynolds, 'Romeo's Irritating Habit', *Daily Telegraph*, 27 April 1993, p. 16.
[114] Karpf, *The Guardian*, 1 May 1993.

'a master-class in Shakespearian verse-speaking'.[115] But the leading actors come in for the most criticism. Karpf complains that 'Branagh hasn't the voice of a romantic hero — it's not his fault if he's forever doomed to sound bloke-ish'.[116] She is also unimpressed with Bond, 'a talented and versatile actress' who 'starts off with a wooden reading of Juliet which doesn't soar', concluding that Bond and Branagh 'feel too studied for the most part to be counted among the great Romeo and Juliets'.[117] Derwent May bemoans that 'the love story is the weakest part of the production', stating that Bond 'plays the part in a voice that at first makes you think of a modern girl in a fruity sit-com, then turns thin and shrewish'.[118] He adds: 'Branagh, as Romeo, plays with his voice, dropping suddenly from soprano to bass; he fills the lines with meaningless pauses, or else stresses too many words in a line for it to have any clear meaning.'[119] Reynolds also criticises Branagh's delivery, writing that it was like 'politicians and sports commentators' who 'signal the sense of what they are about to say by changing the tune in their voice', adding that 'there were times when "Goal!" would not have sounded out of place' at the ends of his lines.[120] Branagh also appears to be trying to sound younger than he is, particularly during the balcony scene (2.1.91; 0:50:45) and when Romeo visits Friar Laurence after he is banished (3.3.42; 1:50:43). Writing about the text, Coppélia Kahn describes that scene as leaving Romeo 'unmanned' as he 'hurls himself to the floor in tears and petulantly refuses to rise'.[121] This description fits Branagh's portrayal perfectly. His histrionics may sound over the top but fit in with what was felt to be the way the character is presented in the text.

In preparing for the production, Branagh consulted academic Russell Jackson. He states that they worked out a 'quasi-visual conception of the play'.[122] This is evident in the sound directions from the script:

[115] Morley, *Radio Times*, 22 April 1993.

[116] Karpf, *The Guardian*, 1 May 1993.

[117] Karpf, *The Guardian*, 1 May 1993.

[118] Derwent May, 'Radio Review – Hits and Misses in Vocal Range', *The Times*, 28 April 1993, p. 31.

[119] May, *The Times*, 28 April 1993.

[120] Reynolds, *Daily Telegraph*, 27 April 1993.

[121] Coppélia Kahn, 'Coming of Age in Verona', *Modern Language Studies*, 8.1 (1977–78), 5–22 (11).

[122] Russell Jackson, 'Two Radio Shakespeares: Staging and Text', *Actes des congrès de la Société française Shakespeare*, 12 (1994), 195–204 (198).

> Crossfade music to square in Verona. In background sounds of busy life, most particularly from a tavern. After a moment the door flies open and Samson and Gregory burst out somewhat the worse for drink. They wear swords and bucklers. During the course of the following they walk. Sounds of tavern recede.[123]

The idea of creating a visual identity to scenes is carried through the use of sound effects in the play. Whenever the scene is Juliet's balcony or bedroom, there is a constant sound of running water (e.g. 2.1.43; 0:47:24 and 3.5.1; 2:13:00). Similarly, street scenes are accompanied by a continual hum of people, horses' hooves and wooden carts (e.g. 2.3.1; 1:09:23 and 3.1.1; 1:26:12). Thirty years earlier, McWhinnie wrote that a sound effect that 'serves no dramatic purpose' can 'drive the listener to distraction'.[124] This seems a particularly apt description of the water effects, which are not rooted in the text and appear only to be used to indicate location. While this production uses more effects than many of this era, it does not always use them to best advantage and they are repetitious rather than true soundscaping, adding little to the essential spoken word simplicity of traditional production.

Morley also points out that the production is 'heavy on music'.[125] It was composed by Branagh's regular collaborator Patrick Doyle, and is at times reminiscent of Doyle's score for Branagh's film version of *Much Ado About Nothing*, which was released the same year. However, the BBC's budget did not stretch as far as that of the cinema and, while the music is often grand, it is created using synthesised instruments rather than an orchestra. Almost every scene break features a short piece of music (e.g. 0:15:28, 0:21:04 and 0:27:03). This is something that was much more common in the immediate post-war era, although McWhinnie described it as 'a fairly primitive function' for music.[126] Doyle's music is also used in two long sections during the production, dividing the play roughly into thirds (after act two, scene one; 0:58:37 and after act three, scene five; 2:14:27). In each case the music runs for about five minutes, although it is not one single piece but three separate pieces joined together, as if this was a decision made in the edit rather than planned for in advance. This is similar to Raikes's *A Midsummer Night's Dream* (1970) which also uses music from the play during

[123] Quoted in Jackson, p. 195.
[124] McWhinnie, p. 82.
[125] Morley, *Radio Times*, 22 April 1993.
[126] McWhinnie, p. 69.

the interval, although in the case of *Romeo and Juliet* these musical breaks are not signalled in advance to the audience, making them less effective as mini intervals.

Twisk suggests that Branagh and Dearman had 'plans to do Shakespeare's complete works'.[127] However, this did not happen. Why not is unclear, but there appears to have been some tension over the commercial potential of these productions. Karpf noted that 'the first Renaissance/Radio 3 co-production — last year's *Hamlet* — has sold over 10,000 copies and went straight into the bestseller lists for the spoken word'.[128] She added: 'The question which John Birt should be asking the BBC is why it hasn't issued the cassette of the production itself [. . .] The answer is because BBC Enterprises turned down the *Hamlet* cassette, and never got a second chance.'[129] The idea of presenting a series of plays was revived again a few years later with the 'Shakespeare for the Millennium' series. Like Branagh's plays, it began with a production of *Hamlet* (1999), produced by Mortimer, and in the year 2000 he went on to tackle *Richard II*, which was not only part of the millennium series, but also linked to another cultural institution: the Open University.

Richard II (2000)[130]

Mortimer has described his production of *Richard II* as being 'traditional' in 'many ways'.[131] Like productions going back generations, Mortimer employs many well-known actors in his cast and uses music and sound effects discreetly. Like all the plays in the 'Shakespeare for the Millennium' project, it features an audio introduction by Eyre, who talks about the deposition scene (act four, scene one) and the fact that it was 'censored out of the early printed editions of the play'. He also mentions the special performance commissioned by the Earl of Essex on the eve of his attempted coup against Elizabeth I. In addition, the play was used by the Open University as part of its 'Shakespeare text and performance' module. This combination of 'traditional' production, an introduction by an esteemed theatre director talking about the play's history, and its creation, in part, for educational

---

[127] Twisk, *The Observer*, 25 April 1993.
[128] Karpf, *The Guardian*, 1 May 1993.
[129] Karpf, *The Guardian*, 1 May 1993.
[130] *Richard II*, BBC Radio 3, 30 April 2000, <https://learningonscreen.ac.uk/ondemand/index.php/prog/RT48829B?bcast=120489457> [accessed 25 February 2021].
[131] Mortimer, private Zoom conversation, 23 February 2021.

purposes gives the sense that this is a production primarily celebrating Shakespeare's heritage and academic importance.

The idea of a heritage production is carried through with the casting of the older actors. Stephen Regan, who gives a fourteen-minute introduction to the Open University recording of the play, highlights the decision by Mortimer to 'rearrange the opening two scenes', pointing out that this 'gives prominence to the seasoned voices of two highly experienced actors, Janet Suzman as the Duchess of Gloucester and Joss Ackland as John of Gaunt'.[132] Suzman's credits with the RSC go back to the 1960s, while Ackland first worked at Stratford-upon-Avon in 1947, and had played Falstaff, Macbeth and Sir Toby Belch on BBC radio. This production also features Ronald Pickup as York, another actor with a long pedigree in radio Shakespeare, as well as Timothy Bateson as the Gardener, who had appeared in ten Shakespeare productions for BBC radio from 1950 onwards, mainly in comic parts.

However, the main characters, Richard and Bolingbroke, were played by actors who were less well known at the time. Samuel West, as Richard, had regularly appeared on radio and television, but had yet to work for the RSC when this production was recorded, although by the time it aired he was playing Richard II at Stratford.[133] Bolingbroke was played by Damian Lewis, who had just a few radio and television appearances to his credit. Mortimer says he was par-ticularly keen to use actors who were 'the right age' for the parts, as there had been 'a resistance' against this in the drama department, especially for Shakespeare's plays.[134] Jean E. Howard and Phyllis Rackin suggest that both characters are theatrical, with Richard presenting 'a powerful expression of personal subjectivity' while Bolingbroke offers 'an effective political strategy'.[135] This description fits with West's and Lewis's portrayals. Regan praised the casting of West in particular, commenting that his voice 'has the range and flexibility to do justice to both the shallow, calculating temperament and the strange, elusive depths suggested by the text. He gives us a Richard who is by turns impetuous and reflexive, callous and tender,

---

[132] *AA306 Shakespeare: Text and Performance – CD3 Richard II* [with introduction by Stephen Regan], dir. Jeremy Mortimer (Open University, CDA5029, 2007), 02:43, 03:35.

[133] *Richard II* opened at The Other Place at the start of April 2000. The radio production was broadcast on 30 April.

[134] Mortimer, private Zoom conversation, 23 February 2021.

[135] Jean E. Howard and Phyllis Rackin, *Engendering a Nation: A Feminist Account of Shakespeare's English Histories* (London: Routledge, 1997), p. 153.

flippant and earnest, cruel and gentle.'[136] Howard and Rackin state that 'Richard is characterized as "effeminate," but this does not mean that he is "homosexual"'.[137] This concurs with West's interpretation. It is particularly evident in the scenes between West and Okonedo as the Queen, where there is genuine affection; it is a relationship which Mortimer felt 'worked really well'.[138] Reviewer Moira Petty also liked West's performance, describing him as 'liv[ing] up to the demands of a role upon which the whole production stands or falls [. . .] he used his technique to give us the king in all his guises, each manifestation being credible'.[139] She also praised Lewis for 'a persuasive sweetness' as Bolingbroke.[140]

Like *Macbeth* (1992), issues around the exact time setting of the play were elided in this production. Petty comments: 'the music by Sylvia Hallett played a huge role not just in setting the atmosphere of the scenes but in anchoring the play in two time frames: the medieval era and all times.'[141] This is reflected in Mortimer's instructions to Hallett, which stated: 'I don't want anything that sounds as if it's trying to be medieval. On the other hand, there might be some useful hints in the harmonies of medieval church music and ballads. I'm not looking to create an authentic late fourteenth-century setting.'[142] He added: 'We do need something that can create a sense of occasion and which can be used to punctuate the action where necessary.'[143] Hallett used a wide range of unusual instruments to create the music, including 'the khen, a tied bamboo mouthorgan used for the fanfares; the zarb, which is an Iranian goblet drum; the waterphone, a modern instrument from California, used to create shrieking and wailing sounds; and also the musical saw'.[144] The effect is to create music that often feels slightly spooky or unsettling and, as Mortimer had requested, sounds neither medieval nor entirely modern. In turn this follows traditional radio production techniques, where music is rarely contemporary and usually conjures up a vague idea of the past rather than specifically recreates it.

Mortimer says he believes 'Shakespeare really demands movement and that's very difficult on the radio because it's a lot of people

---

[136] *AA306 Shakespeare* [CD], 07:56.
[137] Howard and Rackin, p. 143.
[138] Mortimer, private Zoom conversation, 23 February 2021.
[139] Moira Petty, 'Radio Review', *The Stage*, 11 May 2000, p. 21.
[140] Petty, *The Stage*, 11 May 2000.
[141] Petty, *The Stage*, 11 May 2000.
[142] Mortimer, private Zoom conversation, 23 February 2021.
[143] Mortimer, private Zoom conversation, 23 February 2021.
[144] *AA306 Shakespeare* [CD], 12:09.

standing at a microphone'.[145] To help achieve the effect of movement, he frequently uses the sound of footsteps and shuffling of feet
on a stone floor (e.g. 0:03:41; 0:13:49, 0:56:58). Mortimer recorded
a lot of 'wild tracks' to play behind the speeches in order to do
this.[146] Regan also picks up on the way Mortimer uses sound effects,
stating that they are 'neatly cued-in to verbal patterns in the text'.[147]
In particular he notes that John of Gaunt is breathless after York
says "tis breath thou lackst and that breath wilt thou lose' (2.1.30;
0:40:12). He subsequently comments on Mortimer's use of the line
'small showers last long but sudden showers are short' (2.1.35) as
a cue for more effects: 'Rain and thunder accompany his [Gaunt's]
great speech in praise of England [2.1.40–68; 0:40:55]. This, and
Gaunt's breathlessness, give that speech a much more pensive and
circumspect mood than we might expect.'[148] Regan adds: 'Rather
than offering us an indulgently patriotic eulogy, Joss Ackland gives
us a troubled, low-key performance, and the speech is all the more
effective for that.'[149] Petty notes that Ackland 'quivered with wisdom
and his "this sceptred isle" speech had added beauty due to the
unsilken grittiness of his voice'.[150] Unlike earlier Shakespearean
actors, Ackland is praised for *not* sounding beautiful – something
McWhinnie had noted as being important forty years earlier.

By the year 2000, Mortimer was well established in the BBC radio
drama department, which was no longer dominated by male producers. The department's head was a woman and an increasing number
of female producers were taking the reins of Shakespeare plays.
Among them was Avens, who had produced a number of comic
dramas for BBC Radio 4. She put these skills to good use in her first
Shakespeare play.

Much Ado About Nothing (2001)[151]

Much Ado About Nothing was the tenth in the 'Shakespeare for the
Millennium' series. Although it does not appear to have been reviewed

[145] Mortimer, private Zoom conversation, 23 February 2021.
[146] Mortimer, private Zoom conversation, 23 February 2021.
[147] *AA306 Shakespeare* [CD], 06:46.
[148] *AA306 Shakespeare* [CD], 07:04.
[149] *AA306 Shakespeare* [CD], 07:13.
[150] Petty, *The Stage*, 11 May 2000.
[151] *Much Ado About Nothing*, BBC Radio 3, 23 September 2001, <https://learningo
nscreen.ac.uk/ondemand/index.php/prog/0014663A?bcast=387677> [accessed 30
March 2021].

at the time, Andrew Dickson later selected it as 'the best and most interesting adaptation' of the play available in audio format.[152] Dickson states that 'on tape as much as on stage, it's the casting of Beatrice and Benedick that decides whether *Much Ado* sinks or swims. This version emphatically does the latter.'[153] Avens herself talks about her choices in the booklet that accompanied the cassette release of the play: 'I found my perfect casting in Samantha Spiro and David Tennant — David had just finished playing Romeo for the RSC and Samantha had won an Olivier Award for her work in Sondheim's *Merrily We Roll Along*.'[154] As well as the fact they were successful actors, Avens points out that '[w]hat they both had in common was brilliant comic timing, essential for the quickfire dialogue that they had to interpret, and an understanding of the necessity that Beatrice should never appear shrewish and Benedick never turn into a misogynist'.[155] Writing about the characters, Penny Gay describes the 'profoundly-held fantasy' of 'late twentieth-century audiences' of a Benedick who 'reveals his sensitivity as well as releasing his sexuality from the confines of male bonhomie' and a Beatrice who is 'witty and independent' and 'whose libido is high but whose emotions run deep'.[156] This description could apply to Tennant and Spiro, and Avens was conscious of ensuring there was chemistry between her actors as the characters go on a 'journey from sparring partners to wedded bliss'.[157]

Literary critics were divided as to whether the characters were genuinely in love from the start, with Howard suggesting that there was no 'pre-existent love' and that 'Don Pedro works hard to create it'.[158] However, both Harold Bloom and Stanley Wells believed the pair were 'reluctant lovers' on a 'journey of self-discovery'.[159]

---

[152] Andrew Dickson, *The Rough Guide to Shakespeare* (London: Rough Guides, 2005), p. ix.

[153] Dickson, p. 257.

[154] Sally Avens, 'This Production', in booklet included with *BBC Radio Collection: Much Ado About Nothing* (BBC Worldwide, ISBN 0563 535334, 2001 [Cassette]), pp. 12–13 (p. 12).

[155] Avens, p. 12.

[156] Penny Gay, *As She Likes It: Shakespeare's Unruly Women* (London: Routledge, 1994), pp. 175–6.

[157] Avens, p. 12.

[158] Jean E. Howard, 'Renaissance Antitheatricality and the Politics of Gender and Rank in *Much Ado about Nothing*', in *Shakespeare Reproduced: The Text in History and Ideology*, ed. by Howard and Marion F. O'Connor (New York: Routledge, 1987), pp. 177–8.

[159] Harold Bloom, *Shakespeare: The Invention of the Human* (New York: Riverhead Books, 1998), p. 195; Stanley Wells, *Shakespeare: The Poet and his Plays* (London: Methuen, 1997), p. 166.

This latter concept is the one presented by Avens. From the moment that Beatrice and Benedick first talk, there is great animosity between them, suggesting they know each other well (1.1.92; 0:06:56). Avens also sets them apart from the rest of the group by having the sound of conversation between the others continue under Beatrice and Benedick's exchange. Spiro delivers Beatrice's line 'I know you of old' (1.1.118–19; 0:08:10) quietly and sadly, hinting that she may still hold some feelings for Benedick. When Benedick is alone with Claudio and states that Beatrice exceeds Hero in beauty (1.1.156–8; 0:09:47), Tennant's voice suggests genuine sadness at Beatrice's 'fury' and admiration for her appearance. In doing so, Avens's production sets up from the start that, despite outward appearances, Beatrice and Benedick are already in love, ensuring the romance is to the fore.

Tennant and Spiro play their respective gulling scenes both for laughs and for sentiment and are aided by Avens's production technique. In both scenes (act two, scene three and act three, scene one) the text indicates that the lovers do not think they can be seen by their friends while they are eavesdropping. However, this can be difficult to convey on radio. Avens uses two solutions. Firstly, in Benedick's scene, she takes advantage of a moment at the start. In Shakespeare's text, Benedick asks 'Boy' to get a book for him (2.3.1–7), but the boy never returns. Avens chooses to bring back the boy, just at the moment when Benedick is trying to hide. Amid the rustling of leaves and the indistinct sound of conversation between Don Pedro, Claudio and Leonato, the following is inserted:

BOY	(*off, distant*) Signor, your book.
BENEDICK	Shhh!
BOY	(*off, distant*) Your book, Signor.
BENEDICK	(*gritted teeth, whisper*) Go away!
BOY	(*off, distant*) Signor!
BENEDICK	(*gritted teeth, whisper*) Go away!

0:38:22

When the conversation between the trio becomes audible and moves on to the subject of Beatrice (2.3.82), there is another rustle of leaves, as if Benedick is falling out of a tree, and a mumbled 'Oh my go—' from Tennant (0:42:00). Both moments indicate that Benedick does not want to be seen, but they do not immediately convey the sense of distance between Benedick and his friends. Avens does this by manipulating the sound.

As Leonato, played by David Swift, says 'that she should so dote on Signor Benedick' (2.3.87–8; 0:42:12), the voices of everyone but

Benedick are faded down and continue quietly, as if at a distance, while Benedick's breathing and verbal and vocal reactions (such as whimpers and the occasional 'oh') are heard at the front of the sound mix, giving the audience his perspective on what is happening. This lasts for about thirty seconds before the listener is returned to the perspective of the whole scene. Avens repeats this trick a short while later (2.3.157; 0:45:27). The effect of these changes in sound perspective is to keep the scene focused on Benedick and his reactions, with little additional dialogue. A similar procedure takes place when Hero and Ursula trick Beatrice. Sound effects, and puffs and panting from Spiro, give the impression that Beatrice has climbed into a tree. Again, the voice of Hero is faded down but not out (3.1.49; 0:53:30) and Beatrice's reactions are placed in the audio foreground. Beatrice also attempts to cover up her reactions by following her exclamations of 'oh' with poorly executed bird noises (0:53:54). Dickson states that 'the gulling scenes come across surprisingly well with some adept sound balance'.[160] In both, the manipulation of sound helps the audience focus on the effect the gulling is having on Beatrice and Benedick, as well as conveying the emotional changes in both. This is a more sophisticated use of sound than preceding productions of this era, signalling the way forward for other twenty-first-century interpretations of Shakespeare's plays.

Avens was conscious not to focus on Benedick and Beatrice to the detriment of the play's other couple, Hero and Claudio, stating that it was 'as important' in her mind 'to ensure we were as moved' by them.[161] She explains that this was 'a difficult task as Hero is horribly underwritten, especially for radio'.[162] Like most radio producers, Avens adds character names into speeches, or alters a family relationship to a name (such as 'Beatrice' for 'niece' in 2.1.48). But she does this more than ever for Hero, who is frequently name-checked and is also given lines of acknowledgement to indicate her presence (e.g. 'My lord' after 1.1.91 and 'Yes, Father' after 2.1.57). Avens noted that there are two opportunities in performance to show Hero as 'more than just an obedient child'.[163] The first is 'in the enjoyment she takes in gulling Beatrice into believing that Benedick is in love with her (Emilia Fox, who plays Hero, was allowed to give full rein to the more playful side of Hero here)'.[164] The second is the

[160] Dickson, p. 257.
[161] Avens, p. 12.
[162] Avens, p. 12.
[163] Avens, p. 12.
[164] Avens, p. 12.

church scene 'where Claudio wrongly accuses her of being intimate with another man, where Hero's distress and Leonato's denial of his daughter move the play towards tragedy'.[165] Avens does not invent extra speeches for the character in these scenes but, like Tennant and Spiro in the gulling scenes, Fox uses non-verbal communication, in particular sobbing during act four, scene one, to indicate Hero's reaction to what is happening. This seems to be in line with A. R. Humphreys's observation that Hero is 'almost imperceptible in most traditional representations' but by the later twentieth century 'has been encouraged to make a more noticeable impact'.[166] Contemporary critical opinion on Claudio suggests the character is 'tiresome and empty', 'immature' and affected by 'the faults of his milieu'.[167] Avens seems to have been aware of this, writing that she cast Ejiofor in the part because he invested it with 'a romantic sensibility that ensured we never lost our sympathy for the character'.[168] Ejiofor had recently played the male lead in the National Theatre's *Romeo and Juliet*, for which he was nominated for several awards. His casting here was also a success, with Dickson commenting that Ejiofor 'brings a sombre sympathy to Claudio – a character who might not seem to deserve it'.[169] Again, Avens places the romantic elements of the play to the fore, sympathetically interpreting the text in a way that traditionalists would be happy with while subtly enhancing the smaller roles in the play.

The year after *Much Ado*, 'Shakespeare for the Millennium' ended and Rowland says that there was never any intention to do the full canon as 'it was occupying a lot of the drama money' and after 'three to four years you just think – enough'.[170] The year after it finished the department made no new Shakespeare productions for the first time in its history. Producing the full canon could have been the ultimate 'heritage' project for BBC Radio Drama. However, attitudes to Shakespeare and radio drama were changing once again.

* * *

[165] Avens, p. 12.
[166] A. R. Humphreys, 'Introduction', in William Shakespeare, *Much Ado About Nothing*, ed. by Humphreys (London: Methuen, 1981), pp. 1–84 (p. 47).
[167] Bloom, p. 200; Gay, p. 144; Humphreys, p. 48.
[168] Avens, p. 13.
[169] Dickson, p. 257.
[170] Rowland, private Zoom conversation, 12 April 2021.

Between 1988 and 2001 there were many changes both within the BBC and outside. Commercial pressures were being felt with the BBC's internal market and from BBC Enterprises and Worldwide. All productions were now being archived and many were made available for sale, meaning that a once ephemeral production would no longer be heard and forgotten. Instead it might be repeated multiple times and released and re-released for sale. Unlike Brill's Arkangel collection, these were aimed at the domestic market. A production might also get more scrutiny because of its availability to be relistened to, and therefore face more criticism. In 1988 the 'fiefdom' of the BBC radio drama department was still in place, with Tydeman as its head. Tydeman's own preference for long yet simple productions with famous names in leading roles may have set the tone for productions made under his management. This was slow to change. Even by 2001, when the department was run by Rowland, its second female head, that conservatism largely remained, despite an expressed desire to create productions that were 'daring'. It was only in the new millennium that production really did begin to change, with a greater proportion of female producers, many more black and Asian actors, and the regular use of digital editing, enabling a manipulation and complexity of sound that had previously been impossible.

Chapter 5

Digital Developments and Diversity: 2002–23

The twenty-first century saw the biggest changes in radio production since the inception of broadcasting. New ways of listening to BBC programmes were introduced, both in the UK and across the world. Audiences could listen online, not just at the scheduled broadcast time, but also at any time convenient to them in the coming days. Soon listeners were able to download their Shakespeare and take it with them almost anywhere. The wider availability of digital audio recording and editing gave producers an opportunity for more flexibility to record on location as well as the ability to layer many more sound elements, creating more complex and expansive sound mixes. Playback was no longer on tape, or rather a series of tapes, making it easier to create a cohesive sound running throughout a production. Attitudes were also finally changing over which voices were suitable for Shakespeare on radio; regional and international voices became less rare and were no longer confined to comic or servant roles. In addition, Shakespeare was no longer a heritage product, to be treated as sacrosanct. Instead, his works could be adapted to new locations and people, from productions including languages other than English, to those bringing the plays into the twenty-first century, using sound to relocate them from their original settings. This chapter shows that the combination of these developments has led to a reframing of Shakespeare on BBC radio, creating productions with more imaginative settings and more inclusive casts, as well as giving a wider range of people the opportunity to listen to them.

In their book *Locating Shakespeare in the Twenty-First Century*, Kelli Marshall and Gabrielle Malcolm write that, prior to this era, popularising Shakespeare 'was fine as long as it was true to the text'.[1] They explain: 'In other words, integrity was encouraged and there was very little that was considered liminal or cutting edge about most versions of nineteenth- and (much) twentieth-century Shakespeare.'[2] While they do not mention radio, this generalisation holds true for the majority of productions prior to the turn of the millennium. Reviews such as Wyndham Goldie's for *Othello* in 1939 or May's for the 1993 *Romeo and Juliet* made clear that modernising Shakespeare was not acceptable.[3] These attitudes prevailed for decades. However, from the start of the period covered by this chapter, producers were increasingly creating versions of Shakespeare's plays that reflect modernity in a variety of ways.

This coincided with a shift in the gender balance of producers. Up until the end of the twentieth century, the radio drama department, and radio Shakespeare in particular, had been male dominated. Now, there were more Shakespeare plays produced by women than men and more women producing them. There was also a change in the sort of plays being produced and the way they were treated. As well as stories led by women, such as comedies with strong female characters like *Twelfth Night* (2012) and *As You Like It* (2015), both produced by Sally Avens, more complex stories about women were not only produced, but were told in different ways to previous generations. *Measure for Measure* (2004), produced by Claire Grove, leaves open to interpretation the outcome of the play, but certainly does not present an exuberantly happy ending for Isabella. The 2018 production by Gaynor Macfarlane goes further, with Isabella sobbing at the end. And Desdemona in Emma Harding's *Othello* (2020) has more agency than her predecessors, with Othello's actions presented less sympathetically. In *King Lear* (2016), also produced by Macfarlane, when Goneril and Regan are discussing Lear's actions in banishing Kent and Cordelia, there is anxiety in the voices of Madeleine Worrall and Frances Grey who play the sisters (1.1.281–302; 0:14:42). Lear's comment that Goneril is 'too much of late i'th'frown'(1.4.159) is interpreted as her being very unhappy, rather than angry or condemnatory. And when she complains of the behaviour of Lear's knights, Worrall's voice is unsteady, almost tearful (1.4.169–217; 0:31:19).

---

[1] Kelli Marshall and Gabrielle Malcolm, *Locating Shakespeare in the Twenty-First Century* (Newcastle upon Tyne: Cambridge Scholars, 2012), pp. 1–2.

[2] Marshall and Malcolm, p. 2.

[3] For more, see Chapter 1 and Chapter 4 respectively.

The suffering of male characters is also sometimes brought to the fore. In Harding's *The Merchant of Venice* (2018), the play ends with Shylock reciting the Nicene Creed over the sound of a church organ (1:56:16), emphasising the impact of his forced change of faith.[4] Writing about female theatre directors of Shakespeare, Elizabeth Schafer suggests that 'gender is an influential factor in how a play is read'.[5] However, Kim Solga states that 'women directors have for decades sought to protect their careers by minimizing their feminist politics when they speak in the broader public sphere, especially when their productions of canonical texts constitute the material at issue'.[6] Schafer's comment might well apply to radio, although the recent style of production suggests the reverse of the situation posited by Solga, perhaps indicating that radio is less in the public sphere (certainly it is less reviewed) than mainstream theatre, or that managers and commissioners are more supportive of feminist interpretations of the plays.

The choice of plays also became less mainstream. While popular texts were still performed, there was only one each of *Hamlet* (2014), *Romeo and Juliet* (2012) and *A Midsummer Night's Dream* (2011) in the twenty-one years covered here. However, there were two productions of *The Two Gentlemen of Verona* (2007 and 2019), two of *Measure for Measure* (2004 and 2018) and even two of the anonymous *Arden of Faversham* (2004 and 2019), although only the earlier one alludes to a possible Shakespeare connection.[7] This does not seem to have been a conscious decentring of the canon by producers and executives. Instead, producers speak of feeling the need to take on plays that have not been done recently or prominently. There is also a sense that the lesser-known texts might allow producers to take a more creative approach to them without the risk of being accused of tampering, as critics would be less familiar with them and less likely to be aware of what has been changed or removed.

In terms of relocating productions, some have specifically shifted the action, such as the 2018 *Merchant of Venice* which was billed

---

[4] *The Merchant of Venice*, BBC Radio 3, 22 April 2018, <https://learningonscreen. ac.uk/ondemand/index.php/prog/110B64D1?bcast=126559776> [accessed 14 June 2021].

[5] Elizabeth Schafer, *Ms-Directing Shakespeare* (New York: St. Martin's Press, 2000), p. 4.

[6] Kim Solga, 'Shakespeare's Property Ladder: Women Directors and the Politics of Ownership', in *The Oxford Handbook of Shakespeare and Performance*, ed. by James C. Bulman (Oxford: Oxford University Press, 2017), pp. 104–21 (p. 104).

[7] 'Arden of Faversham', *Radio Times*, 3 June 2004, p. 118.

as 'transposed to the City of London and the 2008 financial crisis'.[8] Or *The Two Gentlemen of Valasna* (2007), a retitled version of *The Two Gentlemen of Verona* which shifts the time and location of the play to Victorian India. However, others have been less specific, instead using regional or international accents to suggest new locations or at least differences in nationality. In *Coriolanus* (2002), the Romans speak with English accents while the Volscians are Irish.[9] And in 2005's *Troilus and Cressida*, the Trojans are African while the Greeks use a variety of UK accents, including Yorkshire and Welsh.[10] Most of these accents had rarely been heard previously and, if they had, they were likely to have been in minor roles. Accent was no longer a signifier of class but an aid to a producer in distinguishing different characters and their political allegiances.

During this period there has also been a black Antony to a white Cleopatra (David Harewood and Frances Barber in 2002) and an Irish Shylock (Andrew Scott in the 2018 *Merchant of Venice*).[11] But perhaps most striking is the casting of Othello. Between 1972 and the turn of the millennium, the only production to be broadcast (and repeated three times) starred Paul Scofield as the title character. In 2001, Ray Fearon became the first black actor to play Othello on BBC radio.[12] In the two decades covered by this chapter, two more black actors took the part: Chiwetel Ejiofor in 2008 and Lenny Henry in 2010.[13] Then, after a ten-year gap, Khalid Abdalla became the first actor of Arab heritage to play Othello on the BBC. Attitudes towards casting the play have changed substantially in the last century, with the end of a practice which could be considered the vocal equivalent of blacking-up. There has also finally been a shift away from casting theatre actors (all three black Othellos had already successfully played the part on stage) and even a

---

[8] 'The Merchant of Venice', *Drama on 3*, <https://www.bbc.co.uk/programmes/b09zm vmp> [accessed 14 June 2021].
[9] *Coriolanus*, BBC Radio 3, 20 October 2002, <https://learningonscreen.ac.uk/onde mand/index.php/prog/001B26CF?bcast=1637833> [accessed 14 June 2021].
[10] *Troilus and Cressida*, BBC Radio 3, 30 October 2005, <https://learningonscreen.ac.uk/ ondemand/index.php/prog/0054FCE3?bcast=12640901> [accessed 29 April 2021].
[11] *Antony and Cleopatra*, BBC Radio 3, 27 October 2002, <https://learningonscreen.ac. uk/ondemand/index.php/prog/001B42D4?bcast=1657151> [accessed 14 June 2021].
[12] *Othello*, BBC Radio 3, 30 September 2001, <https://learningonscreen.ac.uk/ondema nd/index.php/prog/00148EA5?bcast=411815> [accessed 14 June 2021].
[13] *Othello*, BBC Radio 3, 4 May 2008, <https://learningonscreen.ac.uk/ondemand/in dex.php/prog/008F3991?bcast=29238524> [accessed 14 June 2021]; *Othello*, BBC Radio 4, 27 February 2010, <https://learningonscreen.ac.uk/ondemand/index.php/pr og/014380F6?bcast=84590077> [accessed 14 June 2021].

conscious re-examination as to what the ethnicity of the character might be.

Diversity of casting has improved but remains limited, although productions do increasingly choose a wider range of actors than in previous generations. Women are now more regularly being cast in male roles, including Maureen Beattie as Escalus in *Measure for Measure* (2018) and Jessica Turner as the Duke of Venice in *Othello* (2020). There have also been, on occasions, signs of consciously casting non-British characters with actors of the appropriate heritage: Queen Katherine in *Henry VIII* (2009) was played by the Spanish actor Yolanda Vazquez, and Peter Polycarpou, who is of Greek Cypriot heritage, was Montano, the Governor of Cyprus, in *Othello* (2020).[14] However, this does not always apply. The 2015 *Macbeth* featured many northern English actors, but no Scots. Meanwhile *King Lear* (2016) had an almost entirely Scottish cast, even though Lear was an English king. Casting purely for voice, something advocated by producers from the very earliest days of radio, also seems to have finally come into its own. The use of Willard White as Gower in *Pericles* (2017) takes advantage of his sonorous vocal quality, mixing it with gongs, abstract strings and sound effects, to increase the impact of the character's speeches.[15]

In the 1940s Felton wrote that 'if you want to establish, let us say, a seaside background, it is no good collecting all the different noises—the waves, children, rock-sellers, pierrots and the rest—and lumping them all on together: the result is confusion'.[16] He was firmly opposed to what would now be described as 'soundscaping'. But in an era when the generation, control and mixing of sounds was limited, it is perhaps not surprising he urged caution. Now, as independent radio producer Dirk Maggs states: 'It's perfectly possible for the medium to build a world around you [. . .] to create a very full and layered picture.'[17] The combination of editing software, enabling many tracks to be mixed relatively simply, with the increased quality of broadcast audio means producers can combine many sounds, almost without limit, as well as varying the levels from near silence to very loud, without loss of clarity. All the most recent

---

[14] *Henry VIII*, BBC Radio 3, 19 April 2009, <https://learningonscreen.ac.uk/ondemand/index.php/prog/00EC7EC8?bcast=122385470> [accessed 25 August 2021].

[15] *Pericles*, BBC Radio 3, 2 April 2017, <https://learningonscreen.ac.uk/ondemand/index.php/prog/0EA3A9E7?bcast=129488388> [accessed 25 August 2021].

[16] Felton, p. 42.

[17] Dirk Maggs in Nicholas Barber, 'He Flies through the Airwaves', *The Independent (Sunday Review)*, 5 February 1995, p. 27.

productions take advantage of this; some, such as *Othello* (2020), go further, using sound to create something akin to Maggs's audio 'movies', competing with films 'on their own ground soundwise'.[18] Others, like *Macbeth* (2015), manipulate audio to take the audience inside the heads of their protagonists.

Producers have also had an opportunity to create 'filmic radio' in other ways.[19] Again, thanks to advances in technology, more location recording has been possible. As well as the relatively simple, such as the location work for *Cymbeline* (2006) detailed below, and the highly complex, as discussed in the case study of *The Two Gentlemen of Valasna* (2007), there has also been a production of *A Midsummer Night's Dream* (2011) recorded 'in 22 acres of Sussex woodland'.[20] David Thomas was the sound engineer on the production and explains that although they were not far from home, they still had problems as they were recording 'at midnight in midsummer in the woods. The idea was that we would have scripts and head torches, [but] all the insects wake up and come straight to your face! So it was definitely iPads after that.'[21] He also says they had to abandon recording altogether one night as a rave started up in a nearby field. However, like others who have recorded on location, he believes it can make a 'huge difference' to the performances given, compared to those in a studio.[22]

Another form of recording also made a brief reappearance in 2017: surround sound. After Cotterell's experiments with quad in the 1970s, radio producers had stuck to stereo. But when Alison Hindell came to produce *Richard II*, she decided it was the right play to reinvestigate a technology with a similar effect to quad for the listener: binaural sound. She says she wanted to do this because the play 'can be a very subjective piece'.[23] She explains: 'I wanted to make it Richard's experience and not a kind of pageant seen from the outside. So I wanted it to be a very personal experience for the

---

[18] Maggs in Barber, *The Independent (Sunday Review)*, 5 February 1995.

[19] Willi Richards, 'Introduction', in *The Two Gentlemen of Valasna*, BBC Radio 3, 29 July 2007.

[20] 'A Midsummer Night's Dream', *Drama on 3*, <https://www.bbc.co.uk/programmes/b014fb7x> [accessed 26 August 2021]; *A Midsummer Night's Dream*, BBC Radio 3, 11 September 2011, <https://learningonscreen.ac.uk/ondemand/index.php/prog/01F345EF?bcast=126919189> [accessed 25 August 2021].

[21] Thomas, private Zoom conversation, 22 April 2021.

[22] Thomas, private Zoom conversation, 22 April 2021.

[23] Hindell, private Zoom conversation, 17 June 2021; *Richard II*, BBC Radio 3, 16 April 2017, <https://learningonscreen.ac.uk/ondemand/index.php/prog/0EB81D73?bcast=123946157> [accessed 25 August 2021].

listener of this character's fall from grace.'[24] It also helped get the play commissioned: 'Radio 3 was very interested in finding reasons for revisiting the classics, because the temptation is just to do it again because it's a good play or because you got some nice actor that wants to play it.'[25] This is a recurring theme from producers: not that a gimmick, as such, was required, but that there needed to be an impetus to do a particular play. Another common response is that a certain amount of time must have elapsed before a play can be produced again. Harding says: 'There's a general rule about not repeating productions within at least ten years.'[26] This probably explains why many of the better-known works are not performed more than once during this period, as they were part of the 'Shakespeare for the Millennium' series, and in the case of *Hamlet*, *Romeo and Juliet* and *King Lear* had also been produced as part of the short Kenneth Branagh series.

However, that is not to say that the well-known plays were off limits, although they did often feature famous actors. Celia de Wolff's *A Midsummer Night's Dream* (2011) has a cast list that would delight most television producers, including Lesley Sharp, Toby Stephens, Roger Allam, Freddie Fox, Nicholas Farrell and Emma Fielding. Thomas says: 'Celia knows all the actors because of Rob [her husband, Robert Glenister], she moves in those circles, so people that you may not normally get, Celia can get because she knows them.'[27] There was also a star cast for 2014's *Antony and Cleopatra*, with Kenneth Branagh and Alex Kingston.[28] This was the first time Branagh had played Shakespeare on radio for twenty years and the idea to return was his. He had originally approached Hindell with the idea of doing *Macbeth* using Laurence Olivier's unfilmed screenplay. But then he was offered the opportunity to do the play at the Manchester International Festival. As neither Manchester nor Radio 3 wanted the play second-hand, the radio *Macbeth* was dropped and replaced with *Antony and Cleopatra*. Reviews were somewhat mixed, with Paul Donovan proclaiming that the pair 'do full justice to the title roles [. . .] in an authoritative new production'.[29] By contrast, Martin Hoyle felt that it was

[24] Hindell, private Zoom conversation, 17 June 2021.
[25] Hindell, private Zoom conversation, 17 June 2021.
[26] Emma Harding, private Zoom conversation, 27 May 2021.
[27] Thomas, private Zoom conversation, 22 April 2021.
[28] *Antony and Cleopatra*, BBC Radio 3, 20 April 2014, <https://learningonscreen.ac.uk/ondemand/index.php/prog/06E37EE0?bcast=114780900> [accessed 9 July 2020].
[29] Paul Donovan, 'Pick of the Day', *Sunday Times*, 20 April 2014, p. 47.

'worthy, though the Nile remains un-aflame'.[30] The star names also enabled the BBC to use the broadcast 'to mark the 450th anniversary of William Shakespeare's birth', broadcast as it was on 20 April.[31]

Until the new millennium, radio was mainly broadcast on FM, long and medium wave. The BBC had been experimenting with DAB since the late 1990s, but it was not until 2002 that it finally launched regular, digital services.[32] These have been hugely success-ful: in 2023, three-quarters of the population were now tuning in digitally.[33] This development coincided with improvements in audio recording and editing afforded by digital technologies. Together these meant that listeners within range of a DAB transmitter could now hear higher-quality sound productions via a higher-quality broadcast medium, without the hiss of analogue radio. Digital broadcasting has not only provided a better platform for the BBC's existing network stations, but the corporation also introduced a number of new ones, including what was initially called BBC 7, now BBC Radio 4 Extra: an all-speech station of archive material, largely from Radio 4. A select few repeats of Shakespeare's plays have been aired here, including Paul Scofield's *Macbeth* (1966, repeated 2007) and the 1988 *Taming of the Shrew* (repeated 2005), as well as two series of combined plays, *Noble Romans* (*Julius Caesar* and *Antony and Cleopatra*) and *Cry God for Harry* (*1 Henry IV, 2 Henry IV* and *Henry V*) from the World Service. And new produc-tions occasionally took on new formats. Marc Beeby produced two plays as daily serials for Radio 4, broadcast immediately after *The Archers* (1951–) in the afternoon drama slot: *Hamlet* (2014) across five days and *Julius Caesar* (2016) across three.[34] *Hamlet* seems

---

[30] Martin Hoyle, 'Radio Choice', *Financial Times Weekend Supplement*, 19 April 2014, p. 17.

[31] 'Dylan Thomas unaired screenplay to get Radio 3 premiere', *BBC News*, <https://www.bbc.co.uk/news/entertainment-arts-25942059> [accessed 27 August 2021].

[32] Alex Pryde, 'Happy Birthday, radio', *BBC Blogs*, <https://www.bbc.co.uk/blogs/about thebbc/entries/786bf13c-cf7d-3577-8507-f3b404fc83a6> [accessed 14 June 2021].

[33] 'Data Release Infographic Q2 2023', *RAJAR*, <https://www.rajar.co.uk/docs/news/RAJAR_DataRelease_InfographicQ22023.pdf> [accessed 12 September 2023].

[34] *Hamlet* [parts 1–5], BBC Radio 3, 24–28 March 2014, <https://learningonscreen.ac.uk/ondemand/index.php/prog/06B030E4?bcast=128821207> <https://learningonscreen.ac.uk/ondemand/index.php/prog/06C0A4E7?bcast=128829543> <https://learningonscreen.ac.uk/ondemand/index.php/prog/06C0ADCF?bcast=128835608> <https://learningonscreen.ac.uk/ondemand/index.php/prog/06C16F89?bcast=128841209> <https://learningonscreen.ac.uk/ondemand/index.php/prog/06C19FE3?bcast=128847 330> [all accessed 25 August 2021]; *Julius Caesar* [parts 1–3], BBC Radio 4, 3–5 May 2016, <https://learningonscreen.ac.uk/ondemand/index.php/prog/0C6FE468?bc

particularly prescient, as it foreshadowed the current popularity of podcasts at a time before the BBC was enabling downloads of its productions.

Online radio streaming and 'on demand' also came to the BBC in 2002.[35] The ability to listen online created opportunities for the audience to decide for themselves when it was most convenient to hear their chosen programme, as well as the possibility of listening wherever there was an internet connection, rather than just where there was a radio signal. Initially, 'on demand' was only available for seven days after broadcast.[36] However, this was later extended to twenty-eight days, or longer in some cases. In 2015 it also became possible to download programmes, including whole Shakespeare plays.[37] And from 2018 onwards some productions have been available to download permanently for free via the BBC's Shakespeare Sessions website, which bills itself as 'Your one-stop shop for all things Shakespeare. Catch A-List casts in brand new audio versions of Shakespeare's greatest plays.'[38] While it is not well publicised, the description of productions on this site as 'podcasts' suggests it is aiming at a new generation of potential listeners, although it seems to have been mothballed, with no new content since 2020. Instead, listeners can find some recent archive productions on the BBC Sounds app. However, the corporation has not followed Beeby's *Hamlet* and *Julius Caesar* with more podcast-style productions. The nearest they have come has been *Macbeth* (2022) and *Twelfth Night* (2023), both of which were produced as two, hour-long episodes. Despite the growing popularity of podcast drama, the BBC has yet to embrace a shorter, serial format for its Shakespeare productions akin to programmes such as its 'eco-thriller' *Forest 404*.[39]

ast=126750960> <https://learningonscreen.ac.uk/ondemand/index.php/prog/0C706EA 4?bcast=126760304> <https://learningonscreen.ac.uk/ondemand/index.php/prog/0C7 079E7?bcast=126765458> [all accessed 25 August 2021].

[35] Steve Bowbrick, 'Radioplayer – all of UK radio in one place', *BBC Blogs*, <https://www.bbc.co.uk/blogs/radio/entries/09f09e32-48b2-339d-b8b4-6ef4d78b81e0> [accessed 14 June 2021].

[36] 'BBC re-launches internet radio – everything in one place', *BBC Press Office*, <http://www.bbc.co.uk/pressoffice/pressreleases/stories/2005/01_january/24/player.shtml> [accessed 14 June 2021].

[37] 'Mobile downloads launches on BBC iPlayer Radio for the start of the BBC Proms', *BBC Media Centre*, <https://www.bbc.co.uk/mediacentre/latestnews/2015/mobile-downloads-radio> [accessed 23 August 2021].

[38] *BBC Shakespeare Sessions*, <https://www.bbc.co.uk/programmes/p0655br3> [accessed 14 June 2021].

[39] *Forest 404*, BBC Radio 4, <https://www.bbc.co.uk/programmes/p06tqsg3> [accessed 15 July 2024].

The period covered by this chapter also includes the time of the Covid-19 pandemic. It was the biggest challenge to face radio drama since the Second World War and production was temporarily halted, meaning a planned version of *2 Henry IV* to follow 2020's *1 Henry IV* did not happen for three years. While radio production in general moved online, new Shakespeare plays did not. However, the pandemic did bring surprising parallels, not with wartime broadcasting but with early radio Shakespeare. When Macfarlane produced *The Tempest* (2021) with each actor performing in a separate booth at a voice-over studio, it was reminiscent of the way plays were first performed when the BBC moved into Broadcasting House in 1932.[40] And while in 1923, actors were 'applauded by telegram', Zoom theatre productions of Shakespeare's plays on YouTube were receiving their applause by emoji.[41]

The case studies in this chapter reflect the technical developments and the presentation of Shakespeare on the BBC during the early twenty-first century, both of which contribute to a reframing of the playwright's work. The 2004 *Measure for Measure* has a majority black cast and uses accents and music to suggest a location far removed from the play's original setting of Vienna. *Cymbeline* (2006) showcases regional accents, in this case Welsh, as well as taking advantage of digital recording to go on location to an ancient underground chamber. *The Two Gentlemen of Valasna* (2007) takes location recording even further – quite literally. Not only did the producer transpose Shakespeare's play to India, it was recorded there with an Indian cast, on location: something that only modern recording equipment makes practical. *Macbeth* (2015) sees Neil Dudgeon take the lead, an actor best known for his northern accent and warm television persona as John Barnaby in *Midsomer Murders* (1997–), rather than as a famous Shakespearean. The production also uses digital sound technology to great effect, especially for the appearance of Banquo's ghost. And 2020's *Othello* brings together innovative casting with a setting of 'an imagined near future', created with a complex sound mix in a production that unites many of the key elements of this period.[42] These productions frequently reframe Shakespeare on radio in terms of location for the text, performers and performance, and use of the medium. Grove's *Measure for Measure* not only does this, but also

---

[40] Macfarlane, private Zoom conversation, 3 February 2022.
[41] 'Shakespeare by Wireless', *Belfast Telegraph*, 29 May 1923.
[42] 'Othello', *Drama on 3*, <https://www.bbc.co.uk/programmes/m000hgqz> [accessed 14 June 2021].

reflects contemporary literary criticism of the play and in particular its focus on sex.

Measure for Measure (2004)[43]

Bloom states that *Measure for Measure* conjures up 'unsurpassable visions [. . .] of sexual malaise'.[44] Whether or not Grove was familiar with this when she produced her version, the opening of this production seems rooted in the same sense of the play. It begins with rhythmic drumming on bongos, quickly joined by the throbbing pulse of an electric bass guitar and finally a violin playing a Middle Eastern-style melody. Simultaneously there is the sound of a couple kissing, then groans of pleasure, getting faster, as well as the occasional giggle and finally additional voices giggling and groaning. The music and sound effects then continue quietly under the first scene. Reviewer Sue Arnold wrote that Grove's production was 'gloriously atmospheric and shamelessly erotic'.[45] Jane Anderson stated that 'from the opening grunts' onwards, 'this is one of the sexiest productions of Shakespeare I've ever heard'.[46] Unlike earlier radio versions of the play, which shy away from its sexual context and content, Grove chooses to open with a direct evocation of it. By having the first scene's discussion about law and process carried out over the sound of behaviour the Duke later condemns as 'evil deeds' (1.3.38), the audience is left in no doubt as to what sort of deeds these might be.

Grove moves the setting out of Vienna; all references to it are changed to 'the city' or cut altogether (e.g. 1.1.44; 0:02:47; 2.1.177; 0:24:48; 5.1.275; 1:54:59). No specific new location is given, although the music, described by reviewers as 'enigmatic, sensual' and 'darkly brooding', suggests the eastern Mediterranean or Middle East.[47] The characters' accents do little to suggest a definite location either, although Arnold felt that Nadine Marshall, Jude Akuwudike and Adjoa Andoh had been cast in a specific way: 'Good and evil, black and white, the accent said it all.'[48] She goes on to add that

---

[43] *Measure for Measure*, BBC Radio 3, 1 February 2004, <https://learningonscreen.ac.uk/ondemand/index.php/prog/004C4B57?bcast=3247746> [accessed 2 July 2021].

[44] Bloom, p. 359.

[45] Sue Arnold, 'Review: Radio: He's Got Bats in the Belfry – or at Least in the Study', *The Observer*, 8 February 2004, p. 20.

[46] Jane Anderson, 'Measure for Measure', *Radio Times*, 29 January 2004, p. 118.

[47] Stephanie Billen, 'Radio: Sunday 1 February', *The Observer*, 1 February 2004, p. 42; Arnold, *The Observer*, 8 February 2004.

[48] Arnold, *The Observer*, 8 February 2004.

Claudio, Isabella and Mariana, 'the goodies or innocent victims', deliver 'their entreaties in seductively musical African-Caribbean while the bad guy, Angelo, was every inch the establishment smooth-talking Sir Humphrey'.[49] Arnold is largely correct in her assertions about the accents of Marshall and Akuwudike, and the same could also be said for the nun in act one, scene four, played by Claire Benedict: all three sound African. However, Andoh's Mariana does not. She speaks in an English voice with no discernible accent. Benedict uses a similar voice when playing Mistress Overdone. Chiwetel Ejiofor as the Duke also speaks with an English accent, not far removed from Anton Lesser's as Angelo; Arnold wrote that 'in wine-speak, his [Ejiofor's] voice was vintage posh with overtones of deep, sexy Mediterranean fruit'.[50] Grove's casting and use of voice is not as simplistic as Arnold suggests. Grove does not use accent to define character by race, but to show allegiances or to distinguish characters. The fact that Claudio, Isabella and the nun are all African suggests a common faith; other than the Friars Thomas and Peter (parts that are conflated in this production) they are the only characters who seem to genuinely hold such beliefs. The rulers – the Duke, Angelo and Escalus – all have middle-class English accents, the voice of authority. The comic parts, Pompey, Lucio and Elbow, are respectively played with Greek, Irish and Scottish accents, making them easy to differentiate. Grove wrote that 'skilful casting [. . .] can make characters more distinctive so that listeners will then find it easier to tell the voices apart'.[51] This seems to be at the heart of her use of accent, rather than making any race-related statement about good and evil.

Reviewers had mixed opinions on how the combination of sex and repression in the plot was presented by the leading actors. Anderson describes Marshall's Isabella as having a 'lush voice [. . .] laden with sexual promise'.[52] However, Moira Petty in *The Stage* felt Marshall 'withered in the glare of Lesser's bravura'.[53] Anderson suggests that Lesser's Angelo is 'a rigidly repressed man, barely keeping the lid on the force of his emotions', while Petty describes his performance as a 'grim, sanctimonious, cruel portrait'.[54] Both Lesser and Marshall

---

[49] Arnold, *The Observer*, 8 February 2004.
[50] Arnold, *The Observer*, 8 February 2004.
[51] Grove and Wyatt, pp. 27–8.
[52] Anderson, *Radio Times*, 29 January 2004.
[53] Moira Petty, 'Radio 3 Fails to Get the Measure of the Bard's "Problem Play"', *The Stage*, 19 February 2004, p. 29.
[54] Anderson, *Radio Times*, 29 January 2004; Petty, *The Stage*, 19 February 2004.

deliver low-key performances, but this is part of what makes radio drama different to other media. As McWhinnie writes: 'The fact that an actor does not project his voice, does not necessarily articulate clearly, does not overemphasize, does not strive after dramatic effects, all this does not mean that he is not acting; on the contrary.'[55] He goes on to note that the 'technique of radio acting is the ability to express all shades of meaning with, apparently, the minimum of vocal effort'.[56] Angelo's propositioning of Isabella in act two, scene four is an example of this. Neither actor shouts, even when their character is losing their temper or feels under threat. After Angelo says 'let me be bold' (2.4.130; 0:47:17), there is the sound of a thump and a gasp from Marshall, but she does not scream. Lesser then drops his voice, rather than raising it, increasing the sinister nature of what he is saying. When he says 'Believe me, on mine honour, / My words express my purpose' (2.4.144–5; 0:47:52), his voice is very low and urgent, suggesting he will not wait. Marshall almost hisses 'Seeming, seeming' with contained anger (2.4.147; 0:48:00), and when Lesser says 'And now I give my sensual race [pause] *the rein*' (emphasis in performance, 2.4.157; 0:48:31) there is such aggression in his voice, along with the sound effect of stumbling feet and a gasp from Marshall, that Isabella's situation seems desperate.

Throughout the scene, Marshall and Lesser give controlled and quiet performances, creating a highly tense, intimate and intimidating atmosphere. As such, they also reflect contemporary literary criticism. Petty states that she could not understand why Angelo would be 'drawn to risk all by seducing an Isabella intent on overdoing the nun act'.[57] But Marshall's performance seems to perfectly echo Jacqueline Rose's suggestion that the character's 'excessive propriety' has led to accusations that the woman who 'refuses to meet' the desire she provokes is 'unsettling'.[58] And Lesser's performance is in keeping with Bloom's description of a character whose 'sadomasochistic desire for the novice nun' is 'more palpable' 'virtually each time she speaks'.[59] Radio, with its more contained style of performance, particularly in the twenty-first century, brings out the underlying tensions in these characters.

[55] McWhinnie, p. 123.
[56] McWhinnie, p. 124.
[57] Petty, *The Stage*, 19 February 2004.
[58] Jacqueline Rose, 'Sexuality in the Reading of Shakespeare: *Hamlet* and *Measure for Measure*', in *Alternative Shakespeares*, ed. by John Drakakis, 2nd edn (London: Routledge, 2002), pp. 97–120 (p. 99, p. 106).
[59] Bloom, p. 365.

Leah Marcus states that in modern performances the Duke 'is often idealized as the wise exemplar of overarching authority', although 'almost as frequently [. . .] the duke comes closer to Lucio's description of the "fantastical Duke of darke corners"'.[60] Ejiofor's Duke does not sit easily in either of these definitions, perhaps prompting Petty's comment that he is 'non-descript'.[61] Ejiofor's interpretation is aloof and his is the only character not to exhibit high passion, either in public or in private. However, that does not mean there is not depth to his performance, described by Arnold as 'dispatched with panache'.[62] Ejiofor portrays the Duke as a man never less than in total command of everything in the city. After eavesdropping on Claudio and Isabella discussing Angelo's proposition, Ejiofor's approach to Marshall is extremely formal (3.1.153; 0:57:51). And later, when the Duke tells Isabella that her brother is dead, Ejiofor's voice remains steady and impassive, despite Marshall's anger and tears (4.3.110; 1:36:20). Ejiofor's Duke is unemotional and controlling.

This adds a level of complexity to a moment at the play's conclusion that has been the subject of much debate in the late twentieth and early twenty-first centuries: Isabella's silence at the Duke's proposal of marriage. Academics such as Bloom and Peter Lake suggest Isabella is broadly happy with the match.[63] However, two high-profile theatre productions of *Measure for Measure* in the same year as this radio production, both staged after this broadcast, were less convinced. Michael Billington's review of the National Theatre's production states that 'even his [the Duke's] final offer of marriage to Isabella becomes a demonstration of brutal authority'.[64] Shakespeare's Globe also staged the play, a production that was aired on the still relatively new television channel BBC Four. In this, the audience laughs heartily while Sophie Thompson's Isabella looks shocked and stunned.[65] Marshall's radio performance is close to Thompson's, giving a slight whimper at the first reference to marriage (5.1.496; 2:06:17) and a sigh at the second (5.1.537–40; 2:08:27). There is also cheering

---

[60] Leah Marcus, *Puzzling Shakespeare* (Oxford: University of California Press, 1988), p. 181.

[61] Petty, *The Stage*, 19 February 2004.

[62] Arnold, *The Observer*, 8 February 2004.

[63] Bloom, p. 380; Peter Lake, 'Ministers, Magistrates and the Production of "Order" in *Measure for Measure*', *Shakespeare Survey*, 54 (2001), 165–81 (180).

[64] Michael Billington, 'Measure for Measure [review]', *The Guardian*, 28 May 2004, <https://www.theguardian.com/stage/2004/may/28/theatre1> [accessed 2 July 2021].

[65] Measure for Measure *Live from the Globe*, BBC Four, 4 September 2004, <https://learningonscreen.ac.uk/ondemand/index.php/prog/004EDF0B?bcast=4201876> [accessed 2 July 2021], 2:45:25.

and applause, this time from the rest of the characters rather than a theatre audience but having much the same effect. However, Ejiofor's Duke is far from the bumbling lover portrayed by Mark Rylance at the Globe. His continual coolness does not suggest love for Isabella but control. Grove also adds the sound of thunder during his second entreaty, suggesting she did not see this as a happy ending.

Grove's production presents a complex and intense set of characters in a way that is specifically tailored to the medium. She does not shy away from what many twenty-first-century observers have seen as the difficult ending, nor does she definitively impose an opinion on what Isabella's reaction is or should be: listeners can interpret Marshall's performance as happy, sad or merely accepting, depending on their own views of the play. The complexity of Shakespeare's plays, particularly the later ones, seems to have attracted rather than deterred producers during this period. And the audience's likely lack of familiarity with the late romances especially appealed when tailoring a production to a regional setting in the 2006 version of *Cymbeline*.

Cymbeline (2006)[66]

In the early years of the BBC, the Cardiff station had a proud history of producing many of Shakespeare's plays on radio. Later, they moved into Welsh-language productions. But as the BBC became more unified, the role of Cardiff in producing Shakespeare became less prominent. However, in 2006, that tradition was revived with a production of *Cymbeline*. Producer Alison Hindell says she was drawn to the 'Celtic element' in the play: 'Most of my production career was in Wales and it was a case of "what hasn't been done" and "what could I do from a Welsh perspective and make a virtue of it being made in Wales".'[67] She goes on to explain that 'although not many of the characters are Welsh, a lot of the action is set in Wales, so I decided to do a kind of Celtic version. With some legitimacy because he [Cymbeline] was a Celtic king.'[68] Hindell's decision is plausible, with historians regarding ancient Britons as Celts and Wales as a modern Celtic nation.[69]

---

[66] *Cymbeline*, BBC Radio 3, 17 December 2006, <https://learningonscreen.ac.uk/onde mand/index.php/prog/005E09FE?bcast=23323945> [accessed 13 August 2021].
[67] Hindell, private Zoom conversation, 17 June 2021.
[68] Hindell, private Zoom conversation, 17 June 2021.
[69] Keith Branigan, 'Cunobelinus', in *The Oxford Companion to British History*, ed. by John Cannon and Robert Crowcroft, 2nd edn (Oxford: Oxford University Press,

However, it is in contrast to some contemporary literary criticism. Academics such as Jodi Mikalachki felt the play was more reflective of English nationalism in the early modern period.[70] Radio critics seemed oblivious to both, and while some did mention the fact the production was made in Wales, none seemed to see this as significant. This may be in part due to a lack of foreknowledge of the play, enabling Hindell to reframe it without critical dissent.

Hindell chooses an almost entirely Welsh cast; the only major character not to be played by a Welsh actor is Cymbeline himself, Bill Wallis, who is English. His accent wavers a little, sometimes more Irish, sometimes just English. His Queen is played by the Welsh but RP Siân Phillips. However, from the moment the play begins with the discussion between two gentlemen, the audience is greeted by strong Welsh accents and this is the case for the majority of the characters. The use of Welsh voices alone does not directly evoke a sense of Britain in the first century CE, though, and in fact there is little to suggest any specific era. The chief sound effect is birdsong, which indicates an outdoor setting but not a time period. Stephanie Billen felt Hindell mainly used it 'to reflect Shakespeare's bird imagery'.[71] Some of the play was recorded on location 'with a Neolithic burial mound serving as Belarius's cave', and while this may have aided the actors, creating an atmosphere for their performance, it adds little to the overall sound of the play.[72] There is also liberal use of music but, like the sound effects, it is not specifically ancient and hints more at the Jacobean. Written by Welsh composer John Hardy, it is sparse, often just a single string of a violin or a musical drone. Sometimes a hurdy-gurdy is used, an instrument which would have been common in Shakespeare's time, but generally the music is atmospheric rather than period specific.

Hindell's approach to cutting the text is to nibble away at scenes, removing lines here and there rather than large speeches. She also regularly disregards rhythm when cutting. Many lines in *Cymbeline* are enjambed, meaning that simply cutting a whole line or group of lines would make no sense. But cutting from mid-line to mid-line rarely means the original rhythm is retained. For example, 'So fair,

---

2015), p. 268; John Mackenzie, ed., 'Britons, Ancient', in *Cassell's Peoples, Nations and Cultures* (London: Weidenfeld & Nicolson, 2005), pp. 300–1.

[70] Jodi Mikalachki, 'The Masculine Romance of Roman Britain: Cymbeline and Early Modern English', *Shakespeare Quarterly*, 46.3 (1995), 301–22 (302).

[71] Stephanie Billen, 'Drama On 3: Cymbeline', *Observer TV and Radio*, 17 December 2006, p. 5.

[72] Billen, *Observer TV and Radio*, 17 December 2006.

and fastened to an empery / Would make the great'st king double, to be partner'd' (1.6.119–20) is reduced to 'So fair, to be partner'd' (0:28:36). Often it is subclauses which are cut, such as 'wherein you're happy—*which will make him know / If that his head have ear in music—doubtless / With joy his will embrace you,—*for he's honourable' (3.4.174–6; 1:14:28, cut in italics). However, perhaps because there is so much enjambment in the play and Shakespeare's own lines often deviate from strict iambic pentameter, in performance these slightly uneven rhythms are not particularly noticeable.

Hindell also cuts many of the asides, particularly those of the Second Lord which point up Cloten's stupidity (e.g. 2.1.33–4 and 44). Removing the Second Lord's solo speech beginning 'That such a crafty devil as is his mother / Should yield the world this ass!' (2.1.49–62) affects the portrayal of both Cloten and the Queen. The Queen's own first aside (1.1.103–6), which indicates she is plotting, is also removed. The song in act two, scene three, which is not ascribed to a particular character but is often performed by Cloten and used as another opportunity to make fun of him, is transferred from the main body of the play to the very beginning as opening music.[73] The combined effect of this is to make the Queen seem less evil and Cloten less of a fool, increasing his threat to Imogen.

Two scenes that are frequently referred to by literary critics as important are also highly visual: Iachimo emerging from a trunk in Imogen's bedroom in act two, scene two, and the appearance of Jupiter and the ghosts of the Leonati to Posthumus in prison in act five, scene four. In the case of the first, little is added in terms of sound to aid the listener and there is no additional text. Anyone unfamiliar with the play may not realise the slight sound of creaking before Iachimo's first line in this scene (0:35:53) represents the trunk being opened. Similarly, the lines 'Come off, come off— / As slippery as the Gordian knot was hard' (2.2.33–4; 0:37:23) are unlikely to alert listeners to the fact he is removing her bracelet, even with the addition of a slight metallic sound. However, although the visual plot points are difficult to interpret, the fact that the audience has only Iachimo's speech as a guide puts emphasis on his 'controlling male gaze', as everything is filtered through his description.[74]

---

[73] For examples of Cloten singing 'Hark, hark, the lark' (2.3.17–23), see the RSC's 2003 production and Cheek by Jowl's from 2007.

[74] Lawrence Danson, '"The catastrophe is a nuptial": The Space of Masculine Desire in *Othello*, *Cymbeline*, and *The Winter's Tale*', *Shakespeare Survey*, 46 (1993), 69–79 (76).

The scene in act five has the potential to be highly visual in the theatre as it includes the stage direction 'Jupiter descends in thunder and lightning, sitting upon an eagle. He throws a thunderbolt' (after 5.4.62). Literary critics were not enamoured of this sequence, with Bloom stating that 'I have reread this scene continually, trying to persuade myself that it is not bad, but it is awful, and I think deliberately so'.[75] And Wells suggests that its 'artificial mode and incantatory verbal style' has led many critics to find it 'distasteful' and even 'spurious', although he points out that 'it has obvious affinities with similar episodes preceding the resolutions of earlier plays'.[76] Rather than attempt to convey this scene through sound effects and music, or additions to the text, Hindell simply cuts the entire episode (5.3.30–92). Posthumus's sleep is merely indicated with mysterious-sounding music, and the text then resumes with his speech indicating what he has been dreaming about. This would not matter if it were not for the fact that there is nothing to indicate the presence of the 'deus ex machina of the oracle Posthumus finds on his bosom after dreaming of his family and lineage'.[77] Mikalachki suggests that this is essential for the 'resolution of the play's many riddles of identity'.[78] But while the lines remain, their context, without visuals, is missing, making it quite hard to understand what Posthumus is reading, where it has come from, and perhaps even that he is reading aloud at all. In both these scenes the visual is not well conveyed to the listening audience, especially one that is likely to be unfamiliar with the play. Like in earlier productions, there seems to be a reluctance from Hindell to add to the text, something that producers later in this period were more willing to do.

Unlike that of some of her contemporaries, Hindell's use of sound in this production is not extensive, and she does not alter or add to the text, creating a production that in many ways is similar to those of her predecessors. However, regional accents remained unusual in Shakespeare productions at this time, particularly those from the UK nations, and so to cast a largely Welsh body of actors did do something almost radical. Three months before this production aired, theatre company Kneehigh opened their adaptation of the play at the RSC's Swan theatre in Stratford-upon-Avon. Despite it being at a location renowned for Shakespeare, reviews suggest it was a radical

[75] Bloom, p. 633.

[76] Stanley Wells, *Shakespeare: A Life in Drama* (New York: Norton, 1995), pp. 357–8.

[77] Mikalachki, p. 320.

[78] Mikalachki, p. 320.

version that was 'neither complicated nor much like Shakespeare'.[79] Reviews of Hindell's production, on the other hand, describe it as 'something of an event' with 'powerful performances'.[80] As such, perhaps Hindell's production reflects a continued conservatism from critics about the performance of Shakespeare's plays, and provided her audience with something designed to please rather than challenge. However, the following year, Shakespeare on BBC radio would take something of a departure from convention, and from Europe, with a production of *The Two Gentlemen of Verona* that was retitled and relocated to India.

The Two Gentlemen of Valasna (2007)[81]

The period prior to the twenty-first century saw a marked lack of Shakespeare's less well-known plays on radio, but in the early 2000s they were reappearing. *The Two Gentlemen of Verona*, described by Jeffrey Masten as 'often ignored', is one of a number to be revived.[82] In the hands of independent director and producer Willi Richards and Roger Elsgood, the 2007 production of the play was transposed in time and place, from sixteenth-century Italy to nineteenth-century India, and renamed *The Two Gentlemen of Valasna*. It was also recorded on location in western India.

The pair had previously recorded *The Mrichhakatikaa* (2004) in Khandala for BBC Radio 3 and they returned to the hill station for *Valasna*. Richards explains:

> We recorded in ancient palatial houses, played croquet on a beautiful, manicured lawn, travelled to high remote reservoirs, raced semi-feral horses in dark forests, struggled to get on an ancient railway train, stood seemingly forever in crowded bazaars waiting for a distant auto-rickshaw to go away.[83]

---

[79] Sam Marlowe, 'Reviews First Night – Theatre, Cymbeline, Swan, Stratford', *The Times times2*, 25 September 2006, p. 18.

[80] Paul Donovan, 'Drama On 3: Cymbeline', *Sunday Times Culture*, 17 December 2006, p. 59; Billen, *Observer TV and Radio*, 17 December 2006.

[81] *The Two Gentlemen of Valasna*, BBC Radio 3, 29 July 2007, <https://learningon screen.ac.uk/ondemand/index.php/prog/006E66A2?bcast=26950075> [accessed 25 May 2021].

[82] Jeffrey Masten, 'The Two Gentlemen of Verona', in *Companion to Shakespeare's Works 3: The Comedies*, ed. by Richard Dutton and Jean E. Howard (Chichester: Blackwell, 2005), pp. 266–88 (p. 268).

[83] Richards, BBC Radio 3, 29 July 2007.

Their cast was drawn from the Indian film and television industries, as well as the English-speaking theatre tradition in the country.[84] Richards says it seemed 'essential' to him to record this way, 'in live environments, in the manner of making a movie – the process of filmic radio rather than theatrical radio'.[85] Only in the era of digital recording could such a project really be feasible, thanks to lighter-weight equipment and the ability to record hours of material, rather than just the fifteen minutes possible on one reel of a portable tape machine.

The concept behind the production was inspired by the year it was broadcast: 2007, the 150th anniversary of the Indian Mutiny. Elsgood says he was struck by the way Italy in the sixteenth century resembled India in the nineteenth: 'It's the same kind of politico, sociological, geographical, set-up.'[86] While it might seem a challenge to relocate an Italian play to India, William Carroll points out that although most of the action takes place in Milan, it 'is presented as a powerful but uncharacterized place in the play'.[87] The change of location led to many superficial alterations to the text, the most obvious of which are the characters' names. Valentine, Proteus, Julia and Silvia become Vishvadev, Parminder, Jumaana and Syoni – all retaining their first initial and their rhythm. Similar changes are made for the rest, with the only exception being the Duke, who is retitled the Maharaja. Place names also change: Verona becomes the 'imaginary Indian princely state' of Valasna.[88] Milan is Malpur. In addition, alongside Shakespeare's text, listeners can hear conversations in Hindi and Marathi, often in the background or at the start of scenes and sometimes indicating the tensions in India at the time the play is set. Pronoti Datta reported: 'As a cheeky inside joke, these allusions are made in Hindi so that Radio 3's predominantly English-speaking audience is left in the dark.'[89] She quotes Elsgood as telling her: 'We think that's a nice, little conceit [. . .] Because that was what was happening in India. [The British] didn't know what was going on behind their backs.'[90] Richards hoped this would 'lend a fresh

---

[84] Richards, BBC Radio 3, 29 July 2007.

[85] Richards, BBC Radio 3, 29 July 2007.

[86] Roger Elsgood, private phone conversation, 19 May 2021.

[87] William Carroll, 'Introduction', in William Shakespeare, *The Two Gentlemen of Verona* (London: Methuen Drama, 2004), pp. xix–130 (p. 78).

[88] Pronoti Datta, 'Air Play', *Time Out Mumbai*, 1997 [exact date unknown, copy from journalist's own archive].

[89] Datta, *Time Out Mumbai*, 1997.

[90] Datta, *Time Out Mumbai*, 1997.

perspective to Shakespeare's story'.[91] This was not the first time a radio Shakespeare production had consciously been transposed from its original setting, but it was the first time one had been moved to a specific time and location, making a political point in the process.

As well as the additions, the play is heavily cut. Despite it already being one of Shakespeare's shortest, around a third of the lines are removed, giving a running time of only just over ninety minutes. Elsgood was particularly aware of creating a pacy production: 'All Shakespeares are way too long anyway. For radio, you have to cut them down.'[92] However, the cuts also reduce the focus on male friendship in the play, not just between the main protagonists but also among the more minor parts: the lengthy comic exchange between Lance and Speed at the end of act three, scene one (3.1.256–363) is one of the many edits. However, there is less cutting of the female characters. Avantika Akerkar, who played Jumaana/Julia, told Datta that the play 'has a lot of issues we were trying to grapple with' and that the cast, director and producer 'would discuss it and try to present it in a manner that's modern'.[93] This may explain why Syoni/Silvia has a number of additional lines in the final scene, largely derived from other parts of the play (1:21:35; 1:28:11). Carroll notes the character's silence in Shakespeare's text after the 'attempted rape'.[94] And Masten suggests the character 'seemingly becom[es] a voiceless piece of particularly mobile property'.[95] By changing this dynamic, Richards and Elsgood alter what Datta suggests is the character's 'anachronistically subservient behaviour', no longer leaving Syoni/Silvia voiceless.[96]

Other cuts and changes are also made to help maintain the Indian setting. 'Villains' (4.1.5) are 'dacoits' (0:54:33) and 'breeches' (2.7.49) become 'churidar' (0:38:14). Elsgood and Richards also remove all the classical references, and the Christian references are changed: 'a beggar at Hallowmas' (2.1.23) becomes 'a beggar at Holi' (0:17:18); the 'abbey wall' (5.1.9) is the 'temple wall' (1:16:47); and 'Friar Laurence' (5.2.36) becomes 'a mendicant priest' (1:18:13). The original play's frequent uses of the words 'Sir' and 'Madam' are also changed: 'Sir' sometimes becomes 'Shri' or sometimes the suffix 'ji' is added to the end of names, such as 'Parminderji'. Both enable

[91] Richards, BBC Radio 3, 29 July 2007.
[92] Elsgood, private phone conversation, 19 May 2021.
[93] Datta, *Time Out Mumbai*, 1997.
[94] Carroll, p. 66.
[95] Masten, p. 275.
[96] Datta, *Time Out Mumbai*, 1997.

the maintenance of Shakespeare's rhythm in the verse sections. 'Madam' is frequently replaced with 'Sahiba'. All these changes firmly cement the reworked text in their new location and fit them to their Indian cast.

Richards told Datta that he was 'excited by the "very different accents and rhythm" he had to deal with. "Sometimes Shakespeare's convolution of thought for me was much better in my ear coming from these actors."'[97] Although Richards does not give examples of specific scenes, there are a number of occasions when the lines seem suited to the Indian voice and delivery. Kunaal Roy Kapoor as Sparsh/Speed makes 'No believing you, indeed, sir' (2.1.140; 0:20:20) sound completely natural. And Joy Sengupta gets all the humour out of his role as Lehk/Lance, in particular when he is talking about the bad behaviour of his dog (4.4.1–35; 1:05:39). This is a tricky scene for radio, as the audience is unable to see the relationship between the two and Sengupta has to make up for what Carroll describes as the 'comic richness' that stems from 'Crab's lack of interaction of any kind, beyond the occasional gaze at the audience'.[98] Sengupta conveys this entirely through his tone of voice, ably demonstrating Lehk's frustration and love, as well as his dog's lack of regard.

Richards's and Elsgood's commitment to 'filmic radio' did not stop at simple location recording; on occasion their actors were asked to perform scenes for real. They set act two, scene seven of the play, when Jumaana and Lavanya are discussing love, while Jumaana takes a bath, genuinely soaking Akerkar in the process (0:35:51). She recalled: 'I was trying not to scream because it was freezing cold water.'[99] Listening to the recording, there are at least a couple of genuine squeals during this scene, as she is drenched, apparently by the bucketful. Similarly, the final confrontation between Vishvadev and Parminder was recorded in a reservoir. As Datta explains: '[Nadir] Khan and [Arghya] Lahiri were required to kick and splash [. . .] As a result, Lahiri said, the two grazed themselves against rocks and had a lot of "mud up our noses".'[100] Elsgood states that he and Richards 'work in live environments' because '[i]f you do something in the real world it's great on a sound level but it's even better on an actor level'.[101] And he makes a direct comparison between recording on location and the majority of radio Shakespeare

[97] Datta, *Time Out Mumbai*, 1997.
[98] Carroll, p. 71.
[99] Datta, *Time Out Mumbai*, 1997.
[100] Datta, *Time Out Mumbai*, 1997.
[101] Elsgood, private phone conversation, 19 May 2021.

productions: 'What the real world does for actors is incredible. If you put an actor into that situation, you'll get a performance from them that you'll never, ever get from an actor in a dark, dead studio in the basement in Broadcasting House.'[102] This was commented on by a British blogger, although Stuart Ian Burns was not totally convinced by the production, stating that while 'the sounds of the landscape' had the effect of 'gifting much colonial atmosphere', he felt that 'something of the story was lost in the abbreviated text'.[103] Even in the twenty-first century, productions of Shakespeare's plays on radio continue to be judged on their Shakespeare content, rather than whether or not they work as radio.

Indian reviewers were happier, with H. P. Raimes in the *Times of India* stating that the play was 'beautifully spoken by beautiful voices [. . .] exuding such joy in the doing as to raise the spirits'.[104] Datta commented: 'Even though the practice of listening to radio plays vanished in India by the early 1990s, it takes little effort to sit through an hour and a half of Shakespeare.'[105] This suggests that the lack of familiarity with the conventions of presenting Shakespeare on radio enabled Indian listeners to enjoy the play for what it is, rather than comparing it to what they thought it should be.

By recording *The Two Gentlemen of Valasna* on location, and almost entirely outdoors, Elsgood and Richards broke with decades of traditional BBC radio production. In doing so they created a unique play that has yet to be emulated or surpassed for complexity of location setting and sound. However, other producers chose to achieve complex soundscapes purely from within Broadcasting House. This is especially true with Beeby's production of *Macbeth*.

Macbeth (2015)[106]

Thirty years before this production, Michael Goldman wrote: 'The experience of the play puts us inside Macbeth's head as he finds

[102] Elsgood, private phone conversation, 19 May 2021.
[103] Stuart Ian Burns, '*Macbeth* (Classic Radio Theatre)', The Hamlet Weblog, 16 May 2011, <http://thehamletweblog.blogspot.com/2011/05/macbeth-classic-radio-theatre.html> [accessed 25 May 2021].
[104] H. P. Raimes, quoted in '*The Two Gentlemen of Valasna*', Art and Adventure, <http://artandadventure.org/portfolio/the-two-gentlemen-of-valasna/> [accessed 25 May 2021].
[105] Datta, *Time Out Mumbai*, 1997.
[106] *Macbeth*, BBC Radio 3, 17 May 2015, <https://learningonscreen.ac.uk/ondemand/index.php/prog/09FD77AA?bcast=115660077> [accessed 9 July 2021].

himself wholly committed to deeds whose moral abhorrence he registers with the intensest sensitivity.'[107] With this production, radio does just that: putting the audience inside Macbeth's head. Beeby uses music and effects, as well as a variety of microphone techniques and sound mixing, coupled with the acting of Dudgeon as Macbeth, to create a version of the play that foregrounds the character's psychological state rather than telling a tale of good and evil.

This was not Dudgeon's first experience of Shakespeare on radio: ten years previously he had played Achilles for Beeby in *Troilus and Cressida* (2005). However, in the intervening period he had become a household name in the television drama *Midsomer Murders*. This did not escape the attention of reviewers, who felt compelled to mention it. Reynolds described him as 'taking a break' from the programme 'to play the villain'.[108] However, Andrew Male took a less simplistic view: 'Those listeners who appreciate the troubled northern English aspect that Neil Dudgeon brings to *Midsomer Murders* will delight in his nuanced turn as *Macbeth* in this deeply menacing new adaptation.'[109] Petty also comments on his performance, stating that he presents a Macbeth 'of discernible reason, puzzled rather than fired up by predictions of his elevation. He makes the tricky transition to a man emotionally charged by the lure of power, voice breaking, thoughts speeding, while the soundscape adds visceral punch and dark metaphor.'[110] Dudgeon's low-key portrayal of Macbeth makes the most of what Sandra Clark and Pamela Mason describe as 'a character whose commitment to evil causes him enormous suffering'.[111] Even when Dudgeon's Macbeth is in battle, there is an underlying hesitation which suggests a conflict in the mind.

During Macbeth's confrontation with Macduff, Dudgeon creates a character who is cautious with a sense of guilt, rather than fearful. When he says 'Of all men else I have avoided thee' (5.7.34; 1:53:09), there is remorse in his voice. As Macduff reveals that he was 'from his mother's womb / Untimely ripped' (5.7.45–6; 1:53:58), Beeby adds a booming single drumbeat. From this point on Dudgeon's

---

[107] Michael Goldman, *Acting and Action in Shakespearean Tragedy* (Princeton: Princeton University Press, 1985), p. 110.

[108] Gillian Reynolds, 'Radio: Pick of the Week', *Daily Telegraph*, 16 May 2015, pp. 50–1.

[109] Andrew Male, 'Pick of the Day: Sunday 17 May', *Sunday Times*, 17 May 2015, pp. 46–7.

[110] Moira Petty, 'Macbeth', *The Stage*, 13 May 2015.

[111] Sandra Clark and Pamela Mason, 'Introduction', in William Shakespeare, *Macbeth* (London: Bloomsbury Arden, 2015), pp. 1–124 (p. 2).

Macbeth sounds weary and unwilling. This is enhanced by Beeby's use of sound. He layers the noise of fighting going on around them, including the distant shouting of men and the clatter of metal, along with close focus sounds of the clanking of two swords and exertion from Dudgeon and Paul Hilton as Macduff. After Macbeth's last line 'Hold, enough' (5.7.64; 1:55:06) there is a final cry and a loud clank, with a long-held echo as the surrounding sounds quickly fade out. There is then one more echoey clank, which is also sustained, this time with no background sounds. After a brief pause, the sound of distant crows is faded in slowly before the final section of the scene takes place. Crook states: 'The general rule in sound production is that the more busy and over-populated soundtracks tend to generate a greater intensity of dramatic effect through silence.'[112] That is exactly what Beeby does here: by using silence rather than sound to represent Macbeth's death, it is more striking and more poignant. At all points in this production when a character might be expected to raise their voice, or sound effects and music might be expected to heighten emotion and atmosphere, Beeby chooses the alternative: low-key performances and low-level sounds.

The most extreme example of this is the opening of the play, which has no music or effects. This is a unique way to start *Macbeth* on BBC radio: all other productions open with one or both and frequently use the standard BBC sound effect of thunder. Instead, Beeby begins simply with the unadulterated voices of the witches, close to the microphone, with no other additions. Andrew Crisell suggests that silence 'can be a potent stimulus to the listener, providing a gap in the noise for his imagination to work'.[113] Beeby's use of silence, or at least removing all sound other than the actors' voices, may be doing just that. Just as silence at the death of Macbeth draws attention to one killing among so many, Beeby's choice to drop the familiar, perhaps over-familiar, sounds associated with the opening of the play in favour of silence allows the audience to create its own image of the witches. It might also suggest to listeners that the witches are not part of the world of the rest of the characters, which is richly populated with the sound of rain, horses' hooves and men talking at a distance (0:00:32). Beeby frequently returns to silence, or near silence, during the production. Immediately after Macbeth's 'Is this a dagger which I see before me' speech (2.1.33–64; 0:31:06), Beeby fades the sound down to almost nothing, with just the faintest rustle

---

[112] Tim Crook, *The Sound Handbook* (Abingdon: Routledge, 2012), p. vii.
[113] Andrew Crisell, *Understanding Radio* (London: Methuen & Co., 1986), p. 53.

of wind. Similarly, when Lady Macbeth, played by Emma Fielding, speaks the first line of the next scene, 'That which hath made them drunk hath made me bold' (2.2.1), there is almost no background noise. Rather than exaggerating these two speeches with music and effects, Beeby again chooses to underplay them with intimate delivery and no additional audio prompts.

Beeby does use music at times, though, and Timothy X. Atack's compositions are not dissimilar to those of Ilona Sekacz for the 1984 production. In both cases the music is sparse and uses unusual instruments. Atack says that Beeby asked him to come up with something where listeners might not be sure 'whether what they're hearing is score or sound effect', creating 'long, slowly shifting tonal atmospheres'.[114] He produced these 'from a combination of synths and treated field recordings' including the sounds of a 'series of gongs' created by artist Jaume Plensa: 'a noise that was equally beautiful, ghostly and ominous'.[115]

The music, and its lack of distinction from sound effects, is particularly effective in act three, scene four when Banquo's ghost appears. As Lennox says 'Here my good lord' (3.4.49; 1:02:10), there is the sound of a heavy breath, treated with echo, as well as a heavy drumbeat. Dudgeon whimpers slightly, and from here on the dialogue has two different sound qualities. The lords and Lady Macbeth sound distant and echoey, almost as if the listener's head is submerged in water. Macbeth's voice, however, remains clear. Added to this, Dudgeon stutters and pants his way through the next section of the scene, while the music/effects mainly consist of strange metallic noises and clicks. There are several additional heavy breaths before the exit of the ghost (3.4.74; 1:03:35), with the final one almost sounding like the word 'how' and clearly from the voice of Shaun Dooley, who plays Banquo. The effects and echo are then faded out to near silence, with just Dudgeon's heavy breathing, before the rest of the dialogue returns to normal. Beeby repeats this audio technique when the ghost reappears, later than in the text but when it is next referenced by Macbeth (3.4.95; 1:05:03). The sound effects and Dooley's laboured breathing make the ghost's presence very clearly felt while it remains apparent that the other characters are unaware of it. Furthermore, the treatment of the voices around Macbeth emphasises the internal conflict the character is suffering, placing the action inside his head. Petty writes that 'distinctive sound

---

[114] Timothy X. Atack, private email correspondence, 20 July 2021.
[115] Atack, private email, 20 July 2021.

design and clear lead performances take the listener into the heart of the human conscience'.[116] This scene in particular demonstrates that.

Beeby cuts little of the text and leaves all of Lady Macbeth's lines intact. However, by emphasising the play's focus on Macbeth and his perception of what is happening, Beeby risks reducing her to a minor character. Instead, Fielding brings a quiet strength and dignity to the role, creating what Petty describes as an 'in-step power double act' with Dudgeon.[117] This is clear from their first scene together. At Macbeth's arrival, the couple's voices are slightly muffled, as if they are hugging (0:18:45) and they even pant a little. Later, when she declares 'That which hath made them drunk hath made me bold' (2.2.1; 0:31:13), Fielding is very quietly spoken with a slight wobble in her voice suggesting she is not quite as bold as she claims. She is startled at the sound of an owl and when Macbeth reappears after murdering Duncan, she sounds as if she is almost in tears (2.2.9; 0:31:56). Throughout the scene, both seem equally nervous and afraid: Fielding is no bullying Lady Macbeth but her husband's equal and soulmate. Petty picks up on this in Dudgeon's performance in act five, scene five, stating that 'his "tomorrow and tomorrow and tomorrow" speech is deeply sorrowful' (5.5.19; 1:48:03).[118]

This production aired in May 2015, ahead of a film of the play which came out in the autumn. It starred Michael Fassbender, who said he believed that 'the murderous treachery of Macbeth would today be diagnosed as the result of post-traumatic stress disorder'.[119] Director Justin Kurzel also chose to open the film 'with Macbeth and Lady Macbeth [. . .] laying one of their children to rest'.[120] Beeby and Kurzel both put the couple's psychological state at the heart of the play, but while Kurzel uses visual imagery to suggest specific reasons for their behaviour, Beeby chooses to simply imply that they are damaged and distressed, rather than provide explanations for this.

Complex use of sound such as Beeby's has increasingly become the norm in more recent productions of Shakespeare's plays. However, gender- and colour-blind casting is still unusual: the only actor of colour in this production is Ayesha Antoine as one of the

---

[116] Petty, *The Stage*, 13 May 2015.

[117] Petty, *The Stage*, 13 May 2015.

[118] Petty, *The Stage*, 13 May 2015.

[119] Henry Barnes, 'Michael Fassbender: "Macbeth Suffered from PTSD"', *The Observer*, 4 June 2015, <https://www.theguardian.com/film/2015/may/23/michael-fassbender-macbeth-suffered-from-ptsd> [accessed 24 September 2024].

[120] Barnes, *The Observer*, 4 June 2015.

weird sisters, and there are no gender-flipped characters. However, in 2020, Harding embraced not only the complex use of sound but also diversity of casting for her production of *Othello*.

Othello (2020)[121]

This production brings together many of the main themes of this chapter. As well as Harding's decisions on sound and character, she set the play in a different era: again, something that remains rare. In addition, this production reflects the changes in broadcast technology that had taken place. The audience could listen live online, on DAB or FM. But they could also choose to download it via the BBC Sounds app, enabling them to start, stop and replay it wherever and whenever they liked. In addition, it was one of the first productions made available as a free podcast via the BBC Shakespeare Sessions website, giving listeners an opportunity to keep a copy of the play indefinitely.

Harding makes a distinctive casting choice with her lead role, choosing an actor of Arab heritage, Khalid Abdalla. The choice is well within the parameters of the text. Ferial J. Ghazoul states that Othello 'is a Moor and therefore an "Arab"', while Walter Cohen points out that in the Renaissance, the term could also refer to a Muslim.[122] These ideas were articulated immediately before the broadcast in a short introduction from Islam Issa: 'A Moor could have been any person with darker skin or who wasn't Christian, but it was a religiously loaded often derogatory term that usually referred to Mahometans.'[123] Issa goes on to suggest that Othello 'converted to Christianity' and 'adopts a militantly Christian tone to overcompensate for his otherness'.[124] Othello's possible Islamic background is suggested in this production during the drinking scene in act two, scene three. Lucy Popescu describes it as 'reminiscent of raucous male bonding down the pub; one knows it will end in trouble'.[125]

---

[121] *Othello*, BBC Radio 3, 19 April 2020, <https://learningonscreen.ac.uk/ondemand/index.php/prog/15E01903?bcast=131740325> [accessed 28 June 2021].
[122] Ferial J. Ghazoul, 'The Arabization of Othello', *Comparative Literature*, 50.1 (1998), 1–31 (1); Walter Cohen, '*Othello* [introduction]', in *The Norton Shakespeare*, 3rd edn, ed. by Stephen Greenblatt and others (London: W. W. Norton, 2016), pp. 2,073–9 (p. 2,073).
[123] Islam Issa, 'Introduction', in *Othello*, BBC Radio 3, 19 April 2020.
[124] Issa, 'Introduction', in *Othello*, BBC Radio 3, 19 April 2020.
[125] Lucy Popescu, 'Radio: Bold Bard without Stage Distraction', *Camden New Journal*, 16 April 2020, <http://camdennewjournal.com/article/radio-bold-bard-without-stage-distraction> [accessed 21 May 2021].

Instead of the two songs sung by Iago in Shakespeare's text, a single, modern song, sung by a rowdy group of men, is inserted:

> (*singing to the tune of 'My Old Man's a Dustman'*)
> Ali Khan's a Muslim
> He wears a Muslim's cap
> His father wears a burka (*singing continues, indistinct*)

0:37:59

Reviewer Maryam Philpott states that 'Harding was keen to explore how the play's concept of "otherness" [. . .] links to what may once have been a Muslim faith'.[126] By changing this scene, Harding suggests that not just Iago but the majority of Othello's soldiers do not respect him, increasing the 'otherness' already present as well as situating it in a twenty-first-century world many people will recognise.

Ian Smith suggests that 'notions of blackness saturate the play, turning a physiological fact into a racial idea expressing the collective cultural thinking'.[127] 'Black' or variants of it appear eleven times in Shakespeare's text but Harding cuts it to only four. It might be suggested she is substituting Islam for 'blackness', something particularly pertinent in a radio production where the colour of Othello's skin cannot be seen. Writing in 2016, Ayanna Thompson suggests that 'recently, black actors have expressed a belief that Othello is not actually about race'.[128] Harding's reinterpretation of the text along lines of religion rather than race fits with twenty-first-century ideas of reframing the play in other ways.

Harding also casts a woman of colour, Cassie Layton, as Desdemona. There is no reason for the audience to be aware of this, but the choice is an unusual one: directors in visual media tend to cast pale-skinned, often blonde women in the role, probably influenced by Shakespeare's repeated references to her being 'fair' and, notoriously, a 'white ewe' being tupped by a 'black ram' (1.1.86–7). However, Harding is more interested in Desdemona's character than her race. Ideas about Desdemona had shifted in the second half of the twentieth century; Thompson suggests that by 1964 the 'death

---

[126] Maryam Philpott, 'Othello – Drama on 3', *Cultural Capital*, 27 April 2020, <https://maryamphilpottblog.wordpress.com/tag/khalid-abdalla/> [accessed 21 May 2021].

[127] Ian Smith, 'Seeing Blackness: Reading Race in *Othello*', in *The Oxford Handbook of Shakespearean Tragedy*, ed. by Michael Neill and David Schalkwyk (Oxford: Oxford University Press, 2016), pp. 405–20 (p. 417).

[128] Ayanna Thompson, 'Introduction', in William Shakespeare, *Othello*, ed. by E. A. J. Honigmann (London: Arden Shakespeare, 2016), pp. 1–116 (p. 90).

of the ninny Desdemona had fully occurred'.[129] That does not mean there are not intrinsic issues. Reviewer Fiona Hughes suggests that 'boiled down' the play is 'a domestic-abuse horror show'.[130] She adds that 'it's hard for Desdemona [. . .] to come across as anything but a poor sap. Here, though, Cassie Layton gives her a strong voice.'[131] Popescu adds that 'Layton is delightfully feisty as Desdemona, outspoken, loyal and clear-headed to the end'.[132] Harding writes: 'I did consciously want to bring out the agency of the women in the play, especially in this 21st century setting. Desdemona is a woman who has chosen a husband counter to the prevailing prejudices of her society and rebelled against her father.'[133] She also wanted to suggest that the relationship between the couple was more equal than is often portrayed: 'It's also clear that Othello views her as his intellectual equal, and as a woman with a voice of her own.'[134]

Harding's determination to give Desdemona agency is evident in the brutal portrayal of her murder. Harding and Layton discussed this and 'agreed that we wanted Desdemona to fight back'.[135] Lasting almost a full minute without words, the scene includes sounds of her struggling, choking, gasping and slapping Othello (1:47:37). Abdalla also sounds exhausted and emotional at the end. Harding says that she 'wanted the murder to feel completely devastating' and to 'hear the full horror' of what was happening to Desdemona.[136] She says that to do this, she had 'one of the most upsetting studios' she had ever experienced:[137]

> We had Khalid and Cassie on the floor with pillows. I discussed how we were going to do it with the actors and they wanted to do it, kind of for real. We practised a way of doing it so that it wasn't really going to hurt her, he wasn't pressing very hard, and we recorded the sound through the pillow of that happening.[138]

Performance of this scene has come a long way since the 1939 production, where Desdemona's death is silent. Harding's choices

---

[129] Thompson, p. 96.
[130] Fiona Hughes, 'Pick of the Week', *Radio Times*, 14 April 2020, p. 111.
[131] Hughes, *Radio Times*, 14 April 2020.
[132] Popescu, *Camden New Journal*, 16 April 2020.
[133] Harding, private email correspondence, 26 August 2021.
[134] Harding, private email, 26 August 2021.
[135] Harding, private email, 26 August 2021.
[136] Harding, private Zoom conversation, 27 May 2021.
[137] Harding, private Zoom conversation, 27 May 2021.
[138] Harding, private Zoom conversation, 27 May 2021.

resonate with Jenkins's portrayal of violence, leaving the audience in no doubt of the horror of what has happened.

The presentation of Desdemona is not just in Layton's performance. Harding also makes textual cuts that affect the character; most significantly, she does not revive. Cohen states: 'Desdemona's last words may indicate a submissiveness bordering on suicide.'[139] But without them, this is reversed. Harding explains: 'Once he's smothered her so brutally, there's no coming back to speaking consciousness – and certainly not to take responsibility for her own murder!'[140] Othello's line 'For nought I did in hate, but all in honour' (5.2.288) is also removed, ensuring that Othello has no excuse for what he has done. Key lines are also cut from the other female characters. Emilia's line ''Tis proper I obey him' (5.2.191) is excised, negating the idea that a woman should only ever do what her husband dictates. Philpott comments that 'Bettrys Jones's Emilia is a more powerful force in the play than often seen, devoted to her mistress and proving her worth in the closing scene as she forcibly berates Othello'.[141] In the case of Bianca, she is cut entirely from act five, scene one, following the attack on Cassio by Roderigo. By doing this, Harding also removes Iago's branding of Bianca as a 'notable strumpet' and his claim that the incident is 'the fruits of whoring' (5.1.76, 114), as well as Emilia's similar accusation (5.1.119). This has the double impact of removing some of the misogynistic treatment of Bianca as well as avoiding the placing of the two female characters in conflict.

Harding also uses sound very effectively. Hughes writes that she 'brings the action into the near future, against a soundscape of whirring choppers and news broadcasts that puts one in mind of [TV series] *Homeland*'.[142] Philpott also acknowledges the skilful 'technical application of sound design', adding: 'there is considerable sophistication in the way audio effects are integrated into the production to prompt the audience's imagination.'[143] Harding says she felt the Cyprus location for the majority of the play was 'hugely important and rather overlooked. I was interested in using that a little bit more.'[144] She does this in a number of ways. The news broadcasts are not just in English. The music features artists singing

---

[139] Cohen, p. 2,076.
[140] Harding, private email, 26 August 2021.
[141] Philpott, *Cultural Capital*, 27 April 2020.
[142] Hughes, *Radio Times*, 14 April 2020.
[143] Philpott, *Cultural Capital*, 27 April 2020.
[144] Harding, private Zoom conversation, 27 May 2021.

in a language other than English, and often has a Middle Eastern feel. And the additional elements that are in English remind listeners that twenty-first-century Cyprus remains a disputed island. This is especially evident during the play's opening:

NEWSREADER 1	A spokesperson from the Ministry of Defence reported a recent escalation in the number of Turkish jets violating Greek airspace on a daily basis.
NEWSREADER 2	(*overlapping*) At a press conference earlier today the Turkish foreign minister reiterated his country's intention to buy the S600 missile system from Russia.

0:00:05

This continues with more specially written script, including 'actuality' of a Turkish minister and an EU official. Harding also restructures act two, scene two as a news broadcast, splitting the Herald's speech into an opening, delivered by a news anchor, then a reporter, and finally back to the news anchor for the end (0:33:18). By making greater use of Shakespeare's original setting, Harding brings the play into a world familiar to its audience.

Harding's highly effective use of sound extends into the soliloquies. While recording these 'close mic'd' is not unusual any more, Matthew Needham as Iago is extremely close and almost whispers his lines, giving the impression of an internal monologue. This was picked up by Philpott, who suggests it is 'as though Needham's hushed tones are poured directly into your ear in a bond of allegiance between you and him alone'.[145] This also suggests she was listening on headphones, something this production seems designed for, with its detailed soundscapes as well as the delivery of the soliloquies.

This production, more than any other, exemplifies the changes in radio production of Shakespeare's plays in the twenty-first century. While the other case studies in this chapter do make use of some of the same techniques, no other play to date combines quite the same level of diverse casting, complex sound mixing, nuanced radio performance and broadcast technology in the way this one does.

* * *

---

[145] Philpott, *Cultural Capital*, 27 April 2020.

Radio productions of Shakespeare's plays have developed greatly since the millennium. Producers are now using all the tools at their disposal, from location recording to complex mixing of multiple sounds. Actors seem more in tune with the best way to perform for audio, with fewer theatrical performances and much more subtlety. Low-key, quiet delivery of lines, especially when close mic'd, creates a sense of being inside a character's head, all the more palpable when listening on headphones, and enables listeners to feel even closer to and more intimately connected with the characters. There is also more boldness: sexier productions, using non-verbal sounds and effects to accentuate the texts; modernisation of settings, despite the complaints of reviewers; stronger portrayal of female characters. Simultaneously, technology has enabled improved accessibility and audio quality. In 2018, Maggs told an interviewer that twenty-five years previously he had begun to 'lose heart' over audio drama but that 'the advent of smartphones and podcasting has turned all that around. The internet has brought a complete reversal of fortune [. . .] I see a bright future for audio storytelling.'[146] The combination of technical skill and technology should ensure this is not only true for radio drama in general, but also specifically for Shakespeare.

---

[146] Dirk Maggs, quoted in Kevin Hilton, 'Dirk Maggs', *Resolution*, March 2018, pp. 32–6 (p. 36).

Conclusion: Radio Shakespeare Is Truly Immersive

On the face of it, I do not have a lot in common with those very first listeners to Shakespeare's plays on the BBC. Female university lecturers were a rarity in 1923 – the university I teach at did not even exist until the twenty-first century. I am writing this on a computer, rather than a typewriter (which would be much less forgiving of my clumsy typing). Technology is all around me – a click of the mouse and I can read journals from the 1800s or watch the latest hit drama on Netflix. And yet, when I put my headphones on to hear a Shakespeare play, I am doing exactly the same thing as those early wireless listeners. I am immersing myself in a world created by a man 400 years ago, realised by actors, producers and technicians, and I am travelling to fair Verona, the shores of Illyria, Elsinore or Bosworth Field.

This book has shown that radio productions of Shakespeare's plays are their own, unique genre: something far more than a simple reading aloud of the text. Audio Shakespeare is alone in terms of performance in that there are no visuals. While theatre can rely on beautiful sets and costumes to help tell a story, and film directors can take their casts to the real Verona, Elsinore or anywhere else of their choosing, radio has to conjure images purely in the minds of its audience. The demands of the medium mean that producers need to think carefully not only about how they convey moments of visual action crucial to the plot for which there is no text, but also about how they direct the performance of those involved more generally. While many actors, particularly in the BBC's early days, gave performances more in keeping with large auditoria, producers quickly recognised that the nature of radio meant that a more intimate delivery was often more effective. Although Shakespeare's plays were always intended for performance, their production on radio necessitates a change in style. Over the last century, radio professionals have repeatedly spoken about the need to think of the audience as a single person, not the thousands, or even millions, who are actually listening. As such, the actor is communicating on a one-to-one basis: a very different atmosphere to that of being in an auditorium, big or small.

The fact that radio forces the listener to use their imagination means they are not passively watching but actively participating in creating the production. Combining this with the fact that it is usually one-to-one communication and that, both at the start of the BBC's history and again now, many people listen on headphones, radio can put the listener in the heart of the action – something no other medium can do. Radio offers the opportunity for its audience to experience truly immersive productions of Shakespeare's plays. 'Immersive' has become a much-used word in the theatre, often indicating a promenade production where the audience is alongside the actors in a shared space. In radio, the audience is listening from a position inside the action, rather than watching from alongside or outside. In turn, this can lead to a greater connection to the characters. In radio performance, soliloquies and asides can take on a conspiratorial nature, with the listener becoming the character's confidant, rather than an observer. Actors are able to imbue their characters with a great level of psychological detail, such as in Neil Dudgeon's interpretation of Macbeth. This aspect of radio Shakespeare can also alter the way plays are perceived: Alec Guinness's performance as King Lear highlights the inherently domestic aspects of the text and the importance of the family relationships. Radio productions of Shakespeare's works increase the sense of intimacy already present in the texts, as well as highlighting the interiority of characters.

Not only are listeners generally alone or in very small groups, but radio actors too operate in a world with very few people around them. There is no audience for them to react to and interact with; even on a film or television set there will be many crew around during a take. However, with the possible exception of a spot effects SM, radio actors will be in the studio with only the other actors present in the scene – or even completely alone for a soliloquy. This may encourage them to deliver their lines in a more intimate style. It may also help forge rapport between actors, who usually only have a few days on a play. This speed of production can also lead to spontaneity, such as John Gielgud's suppressed giggle at Oswald in his *Hamlet* (1948), or ad-libbed lines between Launcelot and Jessica in

The Merchant of Venice (2018).[1] Actors may be reading from scripts but radio can still create Shakespearean performances that feel fresh and immediate.

Far from being the 'blind' medium that critics, and even advocates, often refer to, radio is highly visual, albeit the pictures are in the audience's heads. Producers including Creswell, Raikes and Branagh all had clear physical images in mind when they produced their plays and, through the use of sound, endeavoured to convey this to their respective audiences. And from the reactions of those at Savoy Hill for *Twelfth Night* (1923), who were convinced that sound alone gave the impression that a character was capering when he was actually standing still in front of a microphone, it seems listeners have always created their own visuals for these plays. What is more, each listener will have their own, unique visuals. No matter what the producer intends, every member of their audience will have created their own images and made their own connections to the characters and places portrayed. I can tell you exactly what I see when I listen to a Shakespeare play, but I know it will not be the same as you or as anyone involved in the production.

Radio presentation of Shakespeare also brings benefits to an audience that are not available in other media. As the listener has to create the visual elements of the text in their own imagination, they are not having these imposed upon them in the same way that they would by a visual medium. While an audio background will suggest a setting, this is not as definitive as a visual one. In the nineteenth and early twentieth centuries, some academics complained that on stage the visual interpretation of the plays got in the way, obscuring Shakespeare's text, and that the plays were better read than performed. Therefore, perhaps radio is the perfect medium for Shakespeare, just as Reith intimated a century ago. It is performance, but without the distraction of the visual. It is a way of engaging with the texts in one's head, rather than on the page or stage.

The fact that producers are not presenting their audience with a definitive visual *mise-en-scène* does not mean that they are not directly influencing the way listeners picture the production. Sound effects, music and acting performance can strongly suggest action and location. Producers such as Jenkins used these techniques to generate an almost visceral sensation in their audiences when creating scenes of violence, while Raikes used music as a major tool in creating two contrasting productions of *The Tempest*. Comparing

[1] Hatfull, pp. 11–12.

different productions of the same play – for example the case studies of *Macbeth* in this book – demonstrates that just like other forms of performance, radio can create a variety of productions from the same text through sound alone, and this in turn can convey the play differently to the audience.

Radio is by nature a word-driven medium, which means that there is more emphasis on Shakespeare's texts than in visual media. This offers an audience the opportunity to engage more with the language. It also requires a high level of skill in performance to make that language comprehensible and accessible. However, when this is successfully achieved, it enables listeners to form a greater understanding of the text. Radio also provides its audience with an opportunity to pay more attention to the sound of Shakespeare's words, not just their content. While the issue of how the text should be delivered has been one of constant debate, the medium brings that delivery to the fore, with the sound of an actor's voice playing an even more crucial role than in other forms of performance.

This book also shows that the evolving technology of radio has led to more creative performances. Early microphones allowed for little range in both volume and pitch of voice, necessarily restricting performance. Now, as microphones have become much more sensitive, actors can give more nuanced and varied performances without having to compensate for the inadequacies of the technology. Likewise, technology has enabled producers to be much more imaginative in their use of sound and sound effects, from the development of the Radiophonic Workshop through to digital editing and effects. The improvement in broadcast sound quality has also enabled producers to use sound more creatively: even if the recording equipment is better, there is little point in designing a complicated sound mix if the audience is unable to appreciate it. Now, through DAB and downloads, audiences can hear productions in virtually the same quality as the producer at the mixing desk.

The publication of this book does not mark the end of research into audio productions of Shakespeare's plays, but an entry point for further investigation. It is a field that has been largely overlooked despite its hundred-year history, and it is hoped others will now see the value in these productions for research. They provide a unique snapshot of both the BBC and Shakespeare production during the last century, as well as offering fresh insights into the texts. Any history of Shakespeare production in the UK is incomplete without the recognition that these plays were a significant part of it, reaching millions of listeners, many of whom will never have seen productions by companies such as the RSC, Shakespeare's Globe, the National Theatre or the Old Vic, all of which have garnered much greater academic attention to date. It is time radio grabbed a little bit of that limelight.

The BBC's corpus is ever-increasing, but it is not just new productions which offer opportunities for future examination of radio Shakespeare. This book has only tackled in depth a fraction of the extant productions held by the BBC, let alone those missing from the archive. It has acknowledged the many productions broadcast from the BBC's nations and regions, and while there is little audio available for scholars, there is documentary evidence on this work, with the Welsh productions of the 1920s in particular meriting further investigation, as do the later Welsh-language productions. There have also been scores of other productions across the UK that have never been acknowledged by academics until now. All these plays might yield interesting information about the reception and production of Shakespeare outside London. And this book does not cover the BBC's World Service and its predecessors, nor does it tackle audio Shakespeare beyond the UK. So far there is no comparable book on any other body of audio Shakespeare in English – let alone radio adaptations in other languages. In addition, this book specifically looks at radio productions within their own era, but perhaps they might have value to scholars working on the way Shakespeare's plays would have been received by their early modern audiences. The primacy radio places on rhetorical force and efficacy of Shakespeare's language might offer us an opportunity to recover the auditory experience of the original theatrical stagings. It is hoped that this book will inspire others to listen more closely to these productions and increase their academic audibility.

Radio Shakespeare is not just for researchers, however. It was created for the public and remains a source of entertainment for many. It can also be useful for those studying Shakespeare. Just as I sat on my own, trying to grasp the words and somewhat struggling until Samuel West and Damian Lewis came along to help me, others can benefit from these plays too. I recommend my students listen to radio productions to aid their comprehension of the works. Whether or not they follow along with the text as I used to – and as many early listeners did – these plays make Shakespeare accessible and great actors make them understandable. I often use clips in my teaching to help demonstrate the difference performance can make; no two Macbeths or Hamlets deliver the lines the same. I have even used extracts as a starting point for creative work; listening to and then discussing Forbes Masson's delivery of the Porter's scene in *Macbeth* (2022) led one writer to decide to try out stand-up comedy for the first time. There are also countless podcasts discussing Shakespeare and his work which can help those wanting to learn, or who just enjoy hearing more about the plays. But that is a whole new topic for another time.

The production of Shakespeare's plays on BBC radio has been an evolving practice across the last hundred years and is likely to continue to evolve in the future. As the previous century has shown, a number of factors influence this, and as these are constantly changing, so will the productions. Developing technology, an ever-changing audience, opinions on Shakespearean performance and academic thinking: all of these will continue to influence how these plays are broadcast. However, one thing is likely to remain that has been a constant throughout the century: these productions are immersive entertainment first and foremost. It is only the 'how' of achieving this that has changed.

Selected Bibliography

Below is a list of books and articles about or featuring radio Shakespeare and radio drama.

In addition, the BBC's Programme Index website contains listings of all its programmes throughout its history: <https://genome.ch.bbc.co.uk/>. Much of it is based on the content of the *Radio Times* and the website includes complete copies of the magazine up until the end of 1959, enabling access not only to the original printed listings but also to accompanying articles. Other useful sources include the BBC's *Handbooks* and *Year Books*, dating from the 1920s to the 1980s. Many of these are available via the World Radio History website: <https://www.worldradiohistory.com/>. The BBC's Written Archives Centre at Caversham Park holds many scripts on microfiche, while bound copies of scripts are available at the Library of Birmingham's Shakespeare Collection. Neither is a complete archive.

For those wanting to listen to Shakespeare's plays, the largest collection available online is housed by Learning on Screen's Box of Broadcasts website: <https://learningonscreen.ac.uk/bob-curated-playlists/bbc-radio-shakespeare/>. This requires an academic login and an institutional subscription to gain access. Some productions are available via the BBC Sounds app, the website Audible (personal subscription required) and via the BBC Shakespeare Sessions website: <https://www.bbc.co.uk/programmes/p0655br3/episodes/downloads>.

* * *

Allan, Elkan and Dorotheen, *Good Listening: A Survey of Broadcasting* (London: Hutchinson, 1951)
BBC Recording Training Manual (London: BBC, 1950)
BBC Variety Programmes Policy Guide for Writers and Producers 1948 (London: BBC, 1998)

Bebb, Richard, 'William Shakespeare – *Hamlet* [CD notes]', in William Shakespeare, *Hamlet*, read by John Gielgud and others (Naxos, NA341712D, 2006)

Beck, Alan, *Radio Acting* (London: A & C Black, 1997)

Black, Peter, *The Biggest Aspidistra in the World: A Personal Celebration of Fifty Years of the BBC* (London: BBC, 1972)

Briggs, Asa, *The History of Broadcasting in the United Kingdom: Volume I – The Birth of Broadcasting* (Oxford: Oxford University Press, 1995)

—— *The History of Broadcasting in the United Kingdom: Volume II – The Golden Age of Wireless* (Oxford: Oxford University Press, 1995)

—— *The History of Broadcasting in the United Kingdom: Volume III – The War of Words* (Oxford: Oxford University Press, 1995)

—— *The History of Broadcasting in the United Kingdom: Volume IV – Sound and Vision* (Oxford: Oxford University Press, 1995)

—— *The History of Broadcasting in the United Kingdom: Volume V – Competition* (Oxford: Oxford University Press, 1995)

Broadcasting in the Seventies (London: BBC, 1969)

Brooker, F. C., *Engineering Division Training Manual* (London: BBC, 1942)

Burrows, A. R., *The Story of Broadcasting* (London: Cassell, 1924)

Cain, John, *The BBC: 70 Years of Broadcasting* (London: BBC, 1992)

Carpenter, Humphrey, *The Envy of the World* (London: Weidenfeld & Nicolson, 1996)

Clare, Janet, 'Theatre of the Air: A Checklist of Radio Productions of Renaissance Drama 1922–86', *Renaissance Drama Newsletter*, Supplement Six, Summer 1986

Crisell, Andrew, *Understanding Radio* (London: Methuen & Co., 1986)

Crook, Tim, *Radio Drama: Theory and Practice* (London: Routledge, 1999)

—— *The Sound Handbook* (Abingdon: Routledge, 2012)

Davies, Anthony, 'Shakespeare and the Media of Film, Radio and Television: A Retrospect', *Shakespeare Survey*, 39 (1987), 1–11

Davies, John, *Broadcasting and the BBC in Wales* (Cardiff: University of Wales Press, 1994)

Dickson, Andrew, *The Rough Guide to Shakespeare* (London: Rough Guides, 2005)

Drakakis, John, *Alternative Shakespeares*, 2nd edn (London: Routledge, 2002)

—— ed., *British Radio Drama* (Cambridge: Cambridge University Press, 1981)

—— 'The Essence That's Not Seen: Radio Adaptations of Stage Plays', in *Radio Drama*, ed. by Peter Lewis (London and New York: Longman, 1981), pp. 111–33

Eckersley, P. P., *The Power Behind the Microphone* (London: Jonathan Cape, 1941)

Edwards, Norman, *Broadcasting for Everyone* (London: Herbert Jenkins, 1924)

Esslin, Martin, 'Drama and the Media in Britain', *Modern Drama*, 28.1 (1985), 99–109

—— 'The Electronic Media and British Drama', in *British Contemporary Theatre*, ed. by Theodore Shank (Basingstoke: Macmillan, 1994), pp. 169–80

—— 'Radio Drama Today', in *New Radio Drama*, ed. by anon. (London: BBC, 1966), pp. 7–11

Evans, Elwyn, *Radio: A Guide to Broadcasting Techniques* (London: Barrie & Jenkins, 1977)

Evans, Stuart, 'Shakespeare on Radio', *Shakespeare Survey*, 39 (1987), 113–22

Felton, Felix, *The Radio-Play: Its Technique and Possibilities* (London: Sylvan Press, 1949)

Gielgud, Val, *British Radio Drama 1922–1956* (London: George G. Harrap, 1957)

—— *Radio Theatre: Plays Specifically Written for Broadcasting* (London: Macdonald, 1946)

—— *The Right Way to Radio Playwriting* (Kingswood: Right Way Books, 1948)

—— *Years in a Mirror* (London: Bodley Head, 1965)

—— *Years of the Locust* (London: Nicholson & Watson, 1947)

Greenhalgh, Susanne, 'Listening to Shakespeare', in *Shakespeare on Film, Television and Radio: The Researcher's Guide*, ed. by Olwen Terris, Eve-Marie Oesterlen and Luke McKernan (London: British Universities Film and Video Council, 2009), pp. 74–93

—— 'Shakespeare and Radio', in *The Edinburgh Companion to Shakespeare and the Arts*, ed. by Mark Thornton Burnett and Adrian Streete (Edinburgh: Edinburgh University Press, 2011), pp. 541–57

—— 'Shakespeare Overheard: Performances, Adaptations, and Citations on Radio', in *The Cambridge Companion to Shakespeare and Popular Culture*, ed. by Robert Shaughnessy (Cambridge: Cambridge University Press, 2007), pp. 175–98

—— '"A Stage of the Mind": *Hamlet* on Post-War British Radio', *Shakespeare Survey*, 64 (2011), 133–44

Grove, Claire, and Stephen Wyatt, *So You Want to Write Radio Drama?* (London: Nick Hern Books, 2013)

Hand, Richard J., 'Radio Adaptation', in *The Oxford Handbook of Adaptation Studies*, ed. by Thomas Leitch (Oxford: Oxford University Press, 2017), pp. 340–55

—— and Mary Traynor, *The Radio Drama Handbook: Audio Drama in Context and Practice* (London: Continuum, 2011)

Hatfull, Ronan, 'Adapting *The Merchant of Venice* for Radio: An Interview with Emma Harding, Adapter and Director for BBC Radio Drama',

Shakespeare, 17.4 (2021), 1–15, <https://doi.org/10.1080/17450918.20 21.1960416> [accessed 6 October 2021]

Hendy, David, *The BBC: A People's History* (London: Profile Books, 2022)

—— *Life on Air: A History of Radio Four* (Oxford: Oxford University Press, 2007)

Hill, Christopher William, *Writing for Radio* (London: Bloomsbury Academic, 2015)

Hill, David Arthur, 'A Distrust of Tradition: The Study, Performance and Reception of Shakespeare in England in a Context of Social, Political and Technological Change, 1919–1939' (unpublished masters dissertation, Shakespeare Institute (University of Birmingham), 2011)

Hines, Mark, *The Story of Broadcasting House: Home of the BBC* (London: Merrell, 2008)

Horsfield, Margaret, 'Shakespeare on Radio' (unpublished masters dissertation, Shakespeare Institute (University of Birmingham), 1978)

Huwiler, Elke, 'Radio Drama Adaptations: Approach Towards an Analytical Methodology', *Journal of Adaptation in Film and Performance*, 3.2 (2010), 129–40

—— 'Storytelling by Sound: A Theoretical Frame for Radio Drama Analysis', *Radio Journal: International Studies in Broadcast & Audio Media*, 3.1 (2005), 45–59

'An International Database of Shakespeare on Film, Television and Radio', *British Universities Film and Video Council*, <http://www.bufvc.ac.uk/ shakespeare/> [accessed 7 October 2021]

Jackson, Russell, 'Two Radio Shakespeares: Staging and Text', *Actes des congrès de la Société française Shakespeare*, 12 (1994), 195–204

Jensen, Michael P., *The Battle of the Bard: Shakespeare on U.S. Radio in 1937* (Leeds: Arc Humanities Press, 2018)

—— 'Lend Me Your Ears: Sampling BBC Radio Shakespeare', *Shakespeare Survey*, 61 (2008), 170–80

—— '*The Noble Romans*: When *Julius Caesar* and *Antony and Cleopatra* Were Made Sequels', *Shakespeare Survey*, 69 (2016), 79–91

Kaplan, Milton A., 'The Radio Play as an Introduction to Drama', *The English Journal*, 39.1 (1950), 23–6

Lanier, Douglas, 'Shakespeare on the Record', in *A Companion to Shakespeare and Performance*, ed. by Barbara Hodgdon and W. B. Worthen (Oxford: Blackwell, 2005), pp. 415–36

—— 'Text, Performance, Screen: Shakespeare and Critical Media Literacy', *Cahiers Élisabéthains: A Journal of English Renaissance Studies*, 105.1 (2021), 117–27

—— 'WSHX: Shakespeare and American Radio', in *Shakespeare after Mass Media*, ed. by Richard Burt (Basingstoke: Palgrave, 2002), pp. 195–219

—— and Michael P. Jensen, 'Radio', in *Shakespeares after Shakespeare*, ed. by Richard Burt (Westport: Greenwood Press, 2007), pp. 506–84

Lea, Gordon, *Radio Drama and How to Write It* (London: George Allen & Unwin, 1926)

Lewis, C. A., *Broadcasting from Within* (London: George Newnes, 1924)

—— [as Cecil Lewis] *Never Look Back* (London: Hutchinson, 1974)

Lewis, Peter, 'Opening and Closing Doors: Radio Drama in the BBC', *Radio Journal: International Studies in Broadcast & Audio Media*, 1.3 (2004), 161–76

—— ed., *Radio Drama* (London and New York: Longman, 1981)

McMurtry, Leslie Grace, *Revolution in the Echo Chamber: Audio Drama's Past, Present and Future* (Bristol: Intellect Books, 2019)

McWhinnie, Donald, *The Art of Radio* (London: Faber, 1959)

Maine, Basil, *The BBC and its Audience* (London: Thomas Nelson & Sons, 1939)

Maschwitz, Eric, *No Chip on my Shoulder* (London: Herbert Jenkins, 1957)

Murphy, Kate, *Behind the Wireless: A History of Early Women at the BBC* (London: Palgrave Macmillan, 2016)

Niebur, Louis, *Special Sound* (New York: Oxford University Press, 2010)

Oesterlen, Eve-Marie, 'Lend Me Your 84 Million Ears: Exploring a Special Radio Event Shakespeare's *King Lear* on BBC World Service Radio', *Radio Journal: International Studies in Broadcast & Audio Media*, 6.1 (2009), 33–44

Owen, Roger, '"Y Brenin Llŷr": W. J. Gruffydd's Adaptation of Shakespeare's "King Lear" (1949)' (unpublished paper, Translating Theatre Symposium, October 2016)

Pepler, Christina S. L., 'Discovering the Art of Wireless: A Critical History of Radio Drama at the BBC, 1922–1928' (unpublished doctoral thesis, University of Bristol, 1988)

Peters, Lloyd Hamilton, 'Media Practice and New Approaches to Mise-En-Scène and "Auteur" Theory in Broadcast Radio' (unpublished doctoral thesis, University of Salford, 2014)

Pratt, Carroll C., 'The Design of Music', *The Journal of Aesthetics and Art Criticism*, 12.3 (1954), 289–300

Radio Year Book 1935 (London: George Newnes Ltd, 1935)

Reith, J. C. W., *Broadcast over Britain* (London: Hodder & Stoughton, 1924)

Rixon, Paul, 'Questions of Intermediality: An Analysis of Radio Listings and Radio Highlights in British Newspapers 1920–1960', *TMG Journal for Media History*, 22.4 (2019), 24–42

—— 'Radio and Popular Journalism in Britain: Early Radio Critics and Radio Criticism', *Radio Journal: International Studies in Broadcast & Audio Media*, 13.1–2 (2015), 23–36

Rodero, Emma, 'See It on a Radio Story: Sound Effects and Shots to Evoked Imagery and Attention on Audio Fiction', *Communication Research*, 39.4 (2012), 458–79

—— 'Stimulating the Imagination in a Radio Story: The Role of Presentation Structure and the Degree of Involvement of the Listener', *Journal of Radio and Audio Media*, 19.1 (2012), 45–60

Rodger, Ian, *Radio Drama* (London and Basingstoke: Macmillan Press, 1982)

Roginska, Agnieszka, and Paul Geluso, eds, *Immersive Sound: The Art and Science of Binaural and Multi-Channel Audio* (Abingdon: Routledge, 2018)

Sackville-West, Edward, *The Rescue* (London: Martin Secker & Warburg, 1945)

Sawyer, Robert, 'Broadcasting the Bard: Orson Welles, Shakespeare and War', in *Broadcast your Shakespeare*, ed. by Stephen O'Neill (London: Bloomsbury Arden Shakespeare, 2018), pp. 47–65

Scannell, Paddy, and David Cardiff, *A Social History of British Broadcasting: Volume One, 1922–1939 – Serving the Nation* (Oxford: Basil Blackwell, 1991)

Shacklady, Norman, and Martin Ellen, *On Air: A History of BBC Transmission* (Orpington: Wavechange Books, 2003)

Shingler, Martin, 'Some Recurring Features of European Avant-Garde Radio', *Journal of Radio Studies*, 7.1 (2000), 196–212

Steadman, Mairé Jean, 'The Presentation of Shakespeare's Plays on BBC Radio' (unpublished doctoral thesis, Shakespeare Institute (University of Birmingham), 1997)

Terris, Olwen, 'An International Database of Shakespeare on Film, Television and Radio', *Shakespeare Survey*, 64 (2011), 52–8

——, Eve-Marie Oesterlen and Luke McKernan, eds, *Shakespeare on Film, Television and Radio: The Researcher's Guide* (London: British Universities Film and Video Council, 2009)

Tydeman, John, 'The Producer and Radio Drama: A Personal View', in *Radio Drama*, ed. by Peter Lewis (London and New York: Longman, 1981), pp. 12–27

Tyson, Raymond, 'Acting for Radio', *Quarterly Journal of Speech*, 25.4 (1939), 634–40

Verma, Neil, *Theater of the Mind: Imagination, Aesthetics, and American Radio Drama* (Chicago: University of Chicago Press, 2012)

Wade, David, 'Popular Radio Drama', in *Radio Drama*, ed. by Peter Lewis (London and New York: Longman, 1981), pp. 91–110

Wander, Tim, *2MT Writtle – The Birth of British Broadcasting* (Stowmarket: Capella Publications, 1988)

Wood, Roger, 'Radio Drama at the Crossroads: The History and Contemporary Context of Radio Drama at the BBC' (unpublished doctoral thesis, De Montfort University, 2008)

Index

Abdalla, Khalid, 159, 183, 185
accent, 36–7, 69, 77, 115–17, 165,
  166–7, 173
  African-Caribbean, 166–7
  Caribbean, 133
  cockney, 36, 47, 69, 86
  English, 113, 167, 159
  Greek, 167
  Indian, 177
  Irish, 113, 159, 167
  northern English, 138
  Scottish, 113, 130n, 167
  Welsh, 74, 113, 159, 171
  yokel, 36
  Yorkshire, 159
  see also Received Pronunciation (RP)
Ackland, Joss, 88, 90, 148, 150
adaptation (adaptor), 2–4, 5, 8–16, 30,
  40, 43, 47, 49, 58, 79, 86
Aebischer, Pascale, 125
Ainley, Henry, 52, 53–4, 55, 59, 111,
  121
Akerkar, Avantika, 176, 177
Akuwudike, Jude, 166–7
Aldridge, Michael, 113
Allam, Roger, 162
Allan, Elkan and Dorotheen, 9
Allen, Mary Hope, 57, 59
All's Well That Ends Well, 6
Anderson, Jane, 166, 167
Andoh, Adjoa, 133, 166
Andrew, Nigel, 129, 136, 138
anti-Jewish stereotype, 115–16
Antoine, Ayesha, 182
Antony and Cleopatra, 6, 11, 67, 71,
  97, 132, 162
  1954 production, 80–3

cast, large, 67
editing, 38
music, use of, 66
Noble Romans, 163
voices, 36, 121
Arden of Faversham, 62, 158; *see also*
  Shakespeare Apocrypha
Arkangel Shakespeare, 134
Armatrading, Tony, 134
Arne, Thomas, 59
Arnold, Sue, 166–7, 169
Arnold-Forster, Val, 107–8, 114, 115,
  116, 117–18, 120, 125n, 129n
Arthos, John, 84, 85
As You Like It, 22n, 27, 39, 55, 132
  1944 production, 56–60
  1978 production, 99–101
  accent, 36
  British Empire Shakespeare Society,
    31
  cross-gender disguise in voice, 14–15
  non-verbal noises, 75
  quadraphony, 99–100
  strong female characters, 157
Ashcroft, Peggy, 68, 80, 81–2, 97
Atack, Timothy X., 181
Atkins, Eileen, 108
Atkins, Robert, 1
Audible (audiobook and podcast
  service), 4
audience figures, 72; *see also* RAJAR
Avens, Sally, 135, 150, 151–4, 157

Badel, Alan, 114, 115–16, 117
Badel, Sarah, 15, 108–9, 114
Baetens, Jan, 3
Barber, C. L., 87n

EU representative:
Easy Access System Europe
Mustamäe tee 50, 10621 Tallinn, Estonia
Gpsr.requests@easproject.com

www.ingramcontent.com/pod-product-compliance
Lightning Source LLC
Chambersburg PA
CBHW060047100426
42742CB00014B/2727